W9-CED-774

Contents

Frommer's®

P O R T A B L E

Cayman Islands

1st Edition

by Darwin Porter & Danforth Prince

Here's what critics say about Frommer's:

"Amazingly easy to use. Very portable, very complete."

—*Booklist*

"Detailed, accurate, and easy-to-read information for all price ranges."

—*Glamour Magazine*

"Hotel information is close to encyclopedic."
—*Des Moines Sunday Register*

"Frommer's Guides have a way of giving you a real feel for a place."
—*Knight Ridder Newspapers*

Wiley Publishing, Inc.

Published by:

WILEY PUBLISHING, INC.
111 River St.
Hoboken, NJ 07030

ISBN 0-7645-3913-2
ISSN 1544-3337

Editor: Elizabeth Albertson
Production Editor: Donna Wright
Photo Editor: Richard Fox
Cartographer: Elizabeth Puhl
Production by Wiley Indianapolis Composition Services

For information on our other products and services or to obtain technical support, please contact our Customer Care Department within the U.S. at 800-762-2974, outside the U.S. at 317-572-3993 or fax 317-572-4002.

Wiley also publishes its books in a variety of electronic formats. Some content that appears in print may not be available in electronic formats.

Manufactured in the United States of America

5   4   3

List of Maps

About the Authors

A native of North Carolina, **Darwin Porter** was a bureau chief for the *Miami Herald* when he was 21, and later worked in television advertising. A veteran travel writer, he is the author of numerous best-selling Frommer's guides, including those to the Bahamas, Bermuda, and Caribbean. He is assisted by **Danforth Prince,** formerly of the Paris Bureau of the *New York Times*. They are frequent travelers to the Cayman Islands.

An Invitation to the Reader

In researching this book, we discovered many wonderful places—hotels, restaurants, shops, and more. We're sure you'll find others. Please tell us about them, so we can share the information with your fellow travelers in upcoming editions. If you were disappointed with a recommendation, we'd love to know that, too. Please write to:

Frommer's Portable Cayman Islands, 1st Edition
Wiley Publishing, Inc. • 111 River St. • Hoboken, NJ 07030

An Additional Note

Please be advised that travel information is subject to change at any time—and this is especially true of prices. We therefore suggest that you write or call ahead for confirmation when making your travel plans. The authors, editors, and publisher cannot be held responsible for the experiences of readers while traveling. Your safety is important to us, however, so we encourage you to stay alert and be aware of your surroundings. Keep a close eye on cameras, purses, and wallets, all favorite targets of thieves and pickpockets.

FROMMER'S STAR RATINGS, ICONS & ABBREVIATIONS

Every hotel, restaurant, and attraction listing in this guide has been ranked for quality, value, service, amenities, and special features using a **star-rating system.** In country, state, and regional guides, we also rate towns and regions to help you narrow down your choices and budget your time accordingly. Hotels and restaurants are rated on a scale of zero (recommended) to three stars (exceptional). Attractions, shopping, nightlife, towns, and regions are rated according to the following scale: zero stars (recommended), one star (highly recommended), two stars (very highly recommended), and three stars (must-see).

In addition to the star-rating system, we also use **seven feature icons** that point you to the great deals, in-the-know advice, and unique experiences that separate travelers from tourists. Throughout the book, look for:

Finds	Special finds—those places only insiders know about
Fun Fact	Fun facts—details that make travelers more informed and their trips more fun
Kids	Best bets for kids—advice for the whole family
Moments	Special moments—those experiences that memories are made of
Overrated	Places or experiences not worth your time or money
Tips	Insider tips—some great ways to save time and money
Value	Great values—where to get the best deals

The following **abbreviations** are used for credit cards:

AE	American Express	DISC	Discover	V	Visa
DC	Diners Club	MC	MasterCard		

FROMMERS.COM

Now that you have the guidebook to a great trip, visit our website at **www.frommers.com** for travel information on more than 3,000 destinations. With features updated regularly, we give you instant access to the most current trip-planning information available. At Frommers.com, you'll also find the best prices on airfares, accommodations, and car rentals—and you can even book travel online through our travel booking partners. At Frommers.com, you'll also find the following:

- Online updates to our most popular guidebooks
- Vacation sweepstakes and contest giveaways
- Newsletter highlighting the hottest travel trends
- Online travel message boards with featured travel discussions

The Best of the Cayman Islands

In the Cayman Islands, you can hike through untouched woodland, pay a visit to colorful reefs and fish on a scuba diving or snorkeling trip, or plunk yourself down on the white sands with a frosted drink in hand. You can rent a little, isolated West Indian cottage, or stay in a luxurious resort. You can chow down on fresh fried fish at a waterside shack, or indulge in a world-class five-course meal. No matter what your tastes and budget are, in this chapter we'll guide you to the best that the Cayman Islands have to offer.

1 Frommer's Favorite Cayman Experiences

- **"Petting" the Stingrays:** Called the "world's best 4m (12-ft.) dive site," Stingray City lies in Grand Cayman's North Sound. Snorkelers and divers can swim among, pet, and feed 30 to 50 graceful, "tame" Atlantic Southern stingrays. See "Scuba Diving & Snorkeling" in chapter 5.
- **Diving in the Cayman Islands:** Rainbow-hued marine life and an incredible variety of dive sites, including shipwrecks and dramatic "wall dives," combine to make the Cayman Islands perhaps the single most popular spot for scuba diving in the Western Hemisphere. Many sites lie offshore of Grand Cayman, but the archipelago's smaller islands, Little Cayman and Cayman Brac, are also filled with pristine reefs and dramatic drop-offs, including Little Cayman's Bloody Bay Wall, hailed as the most sensational wall dive in the Caribbean. See "Scuba Diving & Snorkeling" in chapter 5, "Diving" in chapter 9, and "Diving & Other Outdoor Pursuits" in chapter 10.
- **Exploring Deep into the Wild Interior:** On Grand Cayman, you can walk back in time on the 3.2km (2-mile) Mastic Trail, which runs through the Caribbean's best example of a dry subtropical forest. A wide variety of plants and animals unique to the Cayman Islands live in this area, where the woodland has evolved undisturbed for 2 million years. See p. 128.

- **Escaping to Little Cayman:** As much as we like to visit Grand Cayman, we also like to escape from it sometimes. If you want a place where the only footprints in the sand will be yours, head for Little Cayman, a tiny, cigar-shaped island only 16km (10 miles) long. Once here, you'll discover deserted, pearl-white sandy beaches; spectacular bonefishing; barbecue cook-outs under the stars; and some of the best scuba diving and snorkeling in the world. See chapter 10, "Little Cayman."

- **Boating Over to Owen Island for a Picnic:** Our favorite picnic spot in all of the Caribbean is Owen Island, lying 180m (200 yards) off the shore of Little Cayman. Easily accessible by a rowboat, this is 4.4 hectares (11 acres) of pure bliss, with a pearl-white sandy beach and a blue lagoon. See p. 196.

- **Down into the Deep in a Submarine:** Atlantis Adventures and its competitor, *Nautilus,* will take you under the sea to explore the vivid, colorful life of one of the most incredible marine habitats on the planet. The companies cover the full spectrum of submarine experiences, from trips to the teeming shallow reefs and shipwrecks of George Town Harbour, to voyages to coral canyons at 30m (100 ft.). There is even a trip to the Cayman Wall at 300m (1,000 ft.). See p. 119.

- **Spending the Day on Seven Mile Beach:** This strip of golden sand, running the length of the western side of Grand Cayman, is what makes this island a year-round destination. Soft white sands, roped-off swimming sections, and casuarina shade trees make for a Caribbean cliché of beachfront charm. For jogging, sunning, swimming, windsurfing, kayaking, water-skiing, parasailing, snorkeling, scuba diving, or just plain walking, this is one of the greatest beachfronts in the Western Hemisphere, complemented by a string of hotels, restaurants, and shops that lines the entire length of the beach. See p. 112.

- **Visiting the World's Only Green-Sea-Turtle Farm:** The Cayman Turtle Farm was created to provide a safe habitat for the endangered green sea turtle. Thousands of these magnificent creatures are hatched and raised here. See p. 124.

- **Going Fishin':** This is the "national sport" of the Cayman Islands—a tremendously popular pastime for locals and visitors alike. The catches (which can turn up as close as .4km/a quarter of a mile offshore on all three islands) include such prizes as blue marlin, wahoo, dolphin (mahimahi), tuna, and other species. Bonefishermen will be lured to the flats off Little Cayman. See p. 122 for fishing off Grand Cayman,

p. 194 for Little Cayman fishing, and p. 178 for Cayman Brac fishing.

- **Snorkeling in an Underwater Paradise:** Great snorkeling, which can be fun for the entire family, is found close to shore on all three islands. From encounters with the rays of Stingray City to explorations of wrecks, there are underwater thrills galore awaiting you here. See "The Best Snorkeling Sites" later in this chapter for our favorite sites, and see chapters 5, 9, and 10 for more information on great snorkeling beaches and outfitters for each island.

2 The Best Beaches

- **The Best Beaches on Grand Cayman:** Caribbean beaches don't get much better than **Seven Mile Beach.** The powdery white sands here are litter-free and souvenir hawker–free, and are set against a backdrop of resorts, beach bars, restaurants, and shops. This is the Miami Beach of the Caribbean. See p. 112.

  Rum Point is a secluded beach of white sands lying 40km (25 miles) north of George Town. Although it can't compare to the spectacular Seven Mile Beach, this excellent tree-shaded beach has tranquil, gin-clear waters that teem with rainbow-hued fish, making it a great spot for snorkeling. See p. 113

- **The Best Beach on Little Cayman: Point of Sand,** at the southeastern tip of Little Cayman, is the best beach on the island, with a strip of luminescent pink sand. This spot is also ideal for snorkeling. On many weekdays, you'll have much of the beach to yourself. See p. 195.

- **The Best Beaches on Cayman Brac:** There are a series of nearly deserted white sand beaches on Cayman Brac, centered mainly on the southwest coast. These are small and relatively undiscovered beaches that remind many visitors of the Caribbean "the way it used to be." Book into the Brac Reef Beach Resort or Divi Tiara Beach Resort, and you'll be able to walk straight from your room to the sands. See chapter 9.

3 The Best Scuba Diving Sites

- **Eden Rock Dive Center:** One of the Grand Cayman's most popular dive sites, this area offers two alluring reefs, Eden Rock and Devil's Grotto, that are located close to shore at a depth of 14m (45 ft.). You'll find caves, grottos, and a mini-wall, plus tunnels that rise up 12m (40 ft.) from the sand. Divers and snorkelers are treated to an array of colorful fish, sea fans, and sponges, along with an "in-residence" family of tarpon.

- **The Maze:** Located in Grand Cayman's South Channel, close to the famous Wreck of the Ten Sails, this is a honeycomb of deep, narrow coral ravines that evoke a maze. Sponges and soft corals greet you at every turn, along with such creatures as Caribbean reef sharks, green turtles, and spotted eagle rays. The depth is from 17m to 30m (55 ft.–100 ft.).

- **Snapper Hole:** A favorite with beginners and one of the top dive sites in the islands, this is a network of chutes, tunnels, and caverns at a depth of 20m (65 ft.) located off Grand Cayman, southeast of Morritt's Tortuga Club. Tarpon occupy many of the caverns and tunnels, and schools of snapper swim by, sharing the water with nurse or blacktip sharks, eagle rays, and other denizens of the deep. Visibility is in excess of 24m (80 ft).

- **Tarpon Alley:** Near Stingray City, this Grand Cayman wall is at a depth of 15m to 24m (50 ft.–80 ft.). It's named for the many (at least 100) tarpon who find food and refuge in the reef. Many of these "silver kings" are 1m (3 ft.) long, and some can reach a length of 1.2m (4 ft.). Hawksbill turtles also inhabit the site, as do barracuda, stingrays, yellowtail snapper, and other creatures. Because of its drop-offs and canyons, Tarpon Alley is a favorite with underwater photographers.

- **Julie's Wall:** Opposite the town of Old Man Bay on Grand Cayman, this is an exposed and rather windy intermediate-level dive site, but it has excellent underwater visibility at depths ranging from 20m to 30m (65 ft.–100 ft.). The wall here is home to stunning black coral formations. Rays and other marine life are often found here.

- **Grand Canyon** (also called White Stroke Canyon and 3-Bs Wall): Along the North Wall, off Grand Cayman, this is an undersea canyon at a depth of 15m to 30m (50 ft.–100 ft.). Two mammoth coral buttresses form a wide recess here, which is filled with a variety of sponges and soft corals. Visibility is usually some 30m (100 ft.). Bermuda chub, purple Creole wrasse, spotted eagle rays, and green sea turtles inhabit the site.

- **Japanese Gardens:** This site is located inside Grand Cayman's South Wall drop-off, with depths of 9m to 15m (30 ft.–50 ft.). It has a maze of passageways and is known for its schools of

Bermuda chub and the tiny, bright blue "juvenile fish" that hide in its dramatic strands of elkhorn coral.

- **The *Keith Tibbetts* Wreck:** A 5- to 20-minute boat ride from most resorts on Cayman Brac, this is one of the most famous wreck dives in the Caribbean. A Russian frigate sent over from Cuba was deliberately sunk in 1996 on the north side of Cayman Brac at a depth ranging from 12m to 30m (40 ft.–100 ft.). The wreck is home to many creatures, including barracudas, green moray eels, big groupers, scorpion fish, and an array of other tropical species. The coral formations, including beautiful yellow tube sponges, are stunning.

- **Bloody Bay Marine Park:** This dive site, located off Little Cayman, is one of the best in the Caribbean. It roughly covers the area between Jackson Point in the east and Spot Bay to the west. There are two separate walls here: Jackson Wall to the east and Bloody Bay Wall to the west, both combining to form Bloody Bay Marine Park. This area encompasses 22 of the little island's dive sites. Many of the dives here are deep, as the reef plummets to 1,800m (6,000 ft.). However, the reef starts at 6m (20 ft.), so more shallow dives are possible. Grouper, horse-eye jacks, triggerfish, and many small tropical fish call this area home.

4 The Best Snorkeling Sites

- **The Wreck of the *Cali*:** Don't think wreck sites are just for scuba divers. Just a short swim from George Town's shores lies the wreck of the *Cali*, sitting in shallow water and an easy snorkeling adventure. The wreck lies in 6m (20 ft.) of calm waters about 30m (100 ft.) offshore. Built in 1944, the *Cali* was a 66m (220-ft.) masted schooner that was labeled as a shipping hazard in 1957. She was blown up by the British Corp of Army Engineers and has been a popular snorkeling site since then.

- **Stingray City:** There's no experience in the Caribbean that's quite like this Grand Cayman adventure of feeding, petting, and swimming among majestic stingrays. See "Frommer's Favorite Cayman Experiences," earlier in this chapter, and p. 117.

- **Seven Mile Beach & Cemetery Beach:** Many snorkelers staying on Grand Cayman snorkel off Seven Mile Beach because it's so convenient to many of the resorts and rented villas and condos, and it offers colorful reefs right offshore. The snorkeling right offshore at the Marriott and Westin resorts is especially excellent. To the north, Cemetery Reef and the public beach are good spots for an underwater probe. Cemetery Beach is at the southern tier of Boggy Sand Road and is reached by following the cemetery that's located opposite the fire station on West Bay Road. At Cemetery Reef, we've seen shoals of parrotfish and sergeant major fish, and even the elusive reef shark.

- **Devil's Grotto:** Just south of Eden Rock, this popular Grand Cayman snorkeling site lies 45m (150 ft.) off Parrot's Landing Rock. You can wind through a series of long and intricate tunnels here. The fun begins at a depth of 3m (10 ft.). Tarpon are often seen at rest during daylight hours.
- **The *Keith Tibbetts* Wreck:** Cayman Brac's celebrated diving site, a Russian frigate wreck, can also be enjoyed by snorkelers. It lies just a short swim from the shore. For more details, see "The Best Scuba Diving Sites," above.
- **Bloody Bay Wall:** Little Cayman's fantastic diving attraction boasts some excellent spots for snorkelers as well, who frequent many of the island's shallower dive sites. The best snorkel site is Jackson Point. Other interesting sites include the amusingly named Nancy's Cup of Tea, lying just west of Jackson Point. For more details, see "The Best Scuba Diving Sites," above, and p. 193.

5 The Best Accommodations

All prices in this section are given in US dollars.

- **The Best Accommodations for Honeymoons & Weddings:** With its landscaped grounds and romantic suites, **Westin Casuarina Resort,** Grand Cayman (✆ **800/WESTIN-1**), on Seven Mile Beach, offers one of the best honeymoon packages on Grand Cayman. The deal is for a 4-night minimum stay and includes a bottle of champagne, a 1-day Jeep rental, a couples massage, and a sunset cruise on a ferry to Rum Point. In winter, this package costs from $2,368 to $2,617 per couple, lowered to $1,763 to $2,065 off-season. See p. 61.

    Treasure Island Resort, Grand Cayman (✆ **800/203-0775**), is closer to George Town than the other resorts (in case your spouse is an inveterate shopper). The resort's Romantic Escape Honeymoon Package, with a 3-night minimum, is a great deal. Extras include a rum cake, a snorkel trip to Stingray

City, a sunset cruise, a bottle of champagne, daily breakfast, and a romantic dinner. Packages start as low as $955 in the high season, lowered to $730 off-season. See p. 67.

Holiday Inn, Grand Cayman (© **800/HOLIDAY**), is located on the northern edge of Seven Mile Beach. It offers a Honeymoon Package requiring a minimum stay of 5 nights. Newlyweds are given an oceanview room, a daily buffet breakfast, champagne, flowers, a sailing excursion on a catamaran, and a snorkel trip to Stingray City. Packages in winter range from $1,750 to $2,100, lowered to just $1,100 off-season. See p. 64.

The **Marriott Resort Grand Cayman,** Grand Cayman (© **800/333-3333**), with its enviable location on Seven Mile Beach, doesn't offer honeymoon packages, but it caters to a lot of honeymooners nonetheless. The hotel can make all wedding arrangements for you if given sufficient notice. The price depends on your requirements. See p. 66.

Hyatt Regency Grand Cayman, Grand Cayman (© **800/ 233-1234**) is the place to go if you're looking to spend your honeymoon in the most posh, luxurious hotel on Grand Cayman (complete with a first-rate golf course). The honeymoon suite here is the island's best, costing $765 daily in winter, lowered to $515 off-season. The hotel staff is also experienced at making wedding plans. See p. 61.

The Best Places to Get Away from It All: Located on a tranquil point, **Retreat at Rum Point,** Grand Cayman (© **866/ 947-9135**), opens onto a white sandy beach. Although this condo complex is only a 35-minute drive away from the bustle of George Town, it seems worlds away. See p. 75.

Morritt's Tortuga Club & Resort, Grand Cayman (© **800/ 447-0309**), is located on 3.2 beach-bordering hectares (8 acres) at the eastern end of the island. The area around the condos offers some of Grand Cayman's very best diving, but you don't have to be a diver to enjoy this secluded, tranquil spot. See p. 78.

The Reef Resort, Grand Cayman (© **800/232-0541**), a time-share/condo complex, lies in the remote East End, a 32km (20-mile) drive from the airport and a 45-minute trip from George Town. The large, luxurious beachfront units, each boasting a balcony, overlook serene Colliers Bay. This is an idyllic getaway for those seeking peace and quiet. See p. 78.

Walton's Mango Manor, Cayman Brac (© **345/948-0518**), located within a lush garden on 1.2 hectares (3 acres) of land on Cayman Brac's remote north shore, is an excellent B&B. See p. 169.

Almond Beach Hideaways, Cayman Brac (© **866/222-8528**), features two-bedroom villas that open onto a beachfront of white sand and coconut palms, guaranteeing tranquility and privacy. See p. 169.

Little Cayman Cottage, Little Cayman (© **345/945-4144**), a little two-bedroom cottage set on a white sandy beach, is the perfect hideaway. You'll have an instant home here, with room enough for six, plus a fully equipped kitchen. The only sound you'll hear is the pounding surf. See p. 189.

The Best Luxury Hotels: Hyatt Regency Grand Cayman, Grand Cayman (© **800/233-1234**), reigns supreme on the island, at least until the Ritz-Carlton opens. A luxurious and stylish retreat, it opens onto one of the most beautiful stretches of Seven Mile Beach, 3km (2 miles) north of George Town. The resort offers the most complete watersports program of all the hotels on Grand Cayman. For golfers, the excellent golf course makes this the obvious lodging choice. See p. 61.

Westin Casuarina Resort, Grand Cayman (© **800/WESTIN-1**), also opens onto the sands of Seven Mile Beach and is set on its own luxurious grounds. This resort is so complete that some visitors virtually never leave the complex until it's time to catch their plane back home. Featuring excellent watersports, golf, diving, and dining, it is among the top three best resorts in the entire Cayman archipelago. See p. 61.

Caribbean Club, Grand Cayman (© **345/945-4099**), located at a midpoint along Seven Mile Beach, is a low-key and exclusive series of well-furnished, elegant villas serviced by one of the most helpful staffs on the island. Built around a two-story club center, this is an oasis of charm and grace with some of the finest dining on Grand Cayman. See p. 76.

Southern Star, Cayman Brac (© **345/948-1577**), is a complex of five townhouses, offering some of the most elegant and gracious living on this remote island. It stands near a reef-protected lagoon and a private sandy beach with shade trees. Furnishings are stylishly Caribbean, and the space is generous. See p. 172.

The Club at Little Cayman, Little Cayman (© 345/948-1033), stands on lush grounds and offers the most luxurious living on this sparsely populated island. The private villas here open onto a beach, and the complex features the finest pool on the island. See p. 186.

The Best Resort for Divers: Cobalt Coast Resort, Grand Cayman (© 800/622-9626), is the best resort for divers on Grand Cayman (it's great for nondivers as well). Opening onto Boatswains Bay, in the residential community of West Bay, it is a charming self-contained community that houses its guests in a series of well-furnished accommodations that include oceanfront suites. See p. 68.

6 The Best Restaurants

- **Cecil's Restaurant/Kaibo Beach Bar & Grill,** Grand Cayman (© 345/947-9975), serves superb international cuisine, often focusing on recipes from Louisiana. The fun, exciting Kaibo Beach Bar has a Polynesian setting that features flaming torches and multilevel terraces. Cecil's, located upstairs, is the gem here for dining and evokes a cross between a pagan temple and a treehouse. See p. 84.
- **Grand Old House,** Grand Cayman (© 345/949-9333), is set in a converted plantation house south of George Town. The restaurant combines American, Caribbean, and Pacific Rim cuisine. Each dish is prepared exceedingly well, especially the fresh seafood and lobster. See p. 87.
- **Ottmar's Restaurant and Lounge,** Grand Cayman (© 345/945-5879), is one of the island's most outstanding dining choices, serving finely honed international, French, and Caribbean cuisine. See p. 89.
- **Hemingway's,** Grand Cayman (© 345/949-1234), features one of the most imaginative menus on Grand Cayman. This place is known for serving the finest seafood on island, along with first-rate international cuisine. Don't miss the catch of the day here. See p. 87.
- **The Reef Grill,** Grand Cayman (© 345/945-6358), is nestled in the Royal Palms, at the heart of Seven Mile Beach. From the memorable seafood chowder to the lobster-filled ravioli, the seafood offerings here are prepared with fresh, top-quality ingredients and plenty of skill. See p. 91.

- **Captain's Table,** Cayman Brac (© **345/948-1418**), at the Brac Caribbean Beach Village, offers the finest American cuisine on the island, prepared with deftly handled quality produce. Enjoy your conch fritters and catch of the day outside by the pool. See p. 173.
- **Pirates Point Resort Restaurant,** Little Cayman (© **345/ 948-1010**), serves international cuisine created by the restaurant's owner and manager, Gladys Howard, a graduate of Cordon Bleu in Paris. Try the smoked salmon cheesecake; you won't regret it. See p. 192.

2

Planning Your Trip to the Cayman Islands

First things first—just what are the Cayman Islands? A British Overseas Territory, the three islands that compose the Cayman archipelago are part of the geographic entity known as the Cayman Ridge, which extends westward from Cuba. Lying off the west coast of Florida, on the way to Mexico, they consist of Grand Cayman, the largest island, followed by Cayman Brac and Little Cayman, two smaller islands. The Cayman Trench, the deepest part of the Caribbean Sea, which measures in at a depth of just over 6.4km (4 miles), separates this trio of small islands from Jamaica, which lies 290km (180 miles) to the southeast.

Columbus found the Cayman Islands by accident when he was blown off course while en route from Panama to Hispaniola in 1503. A backwater for years, the Cayman Islands emerged as a tourist destination in the 1970s. Since then, their growth has been astoundingly rapid.

Today, Grand Cayman is the condo capital of the Caribbean and a major center of the offshore financial industry. With its fabled Seven Mile Beach, it is also one of the fastest-growing beach havens in the Caribbean and one of the world's best and most popular destinations for scuba diving and snorkeling.

The weather here is perfectly reliable. Chances are that you'll have ideal tanning conditions under sunny skies, with warm temperatures relieved by the cooling, ever-present trade winds. From November to April, the height of the winter tourist season, there is little rainfall. The so-called "rainy season," which stretches from May to October, brings showers, but they are often brief (though intense), with the sun breaking through the clouds shortly thereafter. Of course, there are hurricanes here, but you are likely to be warned way in advance.

A beach buff? You're in luck. For the most part, the sand on the Cayman Islands is sugary white, the surf is warm and gentle, and the

colors are primarily aqua and turquoise. Grand Cayman is celebrated for its magnificent stretch of white sands, known as Seven Mile
Beach, which is lined with hotels and condos. Crowding is rarely a
problem on the beach, even when there are heavy cruise-ship arrivals.
For the Robinson Crusoe in you, there are many hidden coves, beautiful sheltered bays, and expanses of coastline where you can flee from
the crowds at Seven Mile Beach to find your own little piece of paradise. The other Cayman Islands, Cayman Brac and Little Cayman,
also have hidden beaches and coves.

When you tire of the beach—if that's possible—you'll find some of
the world's best scuba diving and snorkeling, from the sheer plunge at
Bloody Bay Wall to the calm waters and gentle stingrays at Stingray
City. The variety of dive sites, the abundant marine life and clear
waters, and some of the best scuba diving and snorkeling outfitters in
the world make the Caymans a top diving and snorkeling destination.

In addition to little divers' inns, Grand Cayman boasts some of
the grandest resort hotels in the Caribbean, along with dozens of
beachfront condos and timeshares along Seven Mile Beach. The
downside is that there are few modest budget inns, as the Caymans,
for the most part, remain an upmarket destination, doing little to
attract the frugal traveler in the way that such Caribbean countries
as the Dominican Republic do.

The Caymans offer excellent dining. The restaurants on the
island are diverse and inventive, and they often boast outstanding
European- or American-trained chefs. In addition to the upscale
venues here, there are plenty of relatively affordable restaurants serving standard Cayman fare.

Once the sun sets, there's not a lot of entertainment, although the
nightlife scene has improved vastly in recent years. Sipping tropical
punch in a bar remains the preferred form of after-dark activity. If
you are a casino devotee, know that gambling is not allowed in the
Cayman Islands and hustle yourself off to somewhere like Puerto
Rico or Aruba.

The islands have one of the highest standards of living in the
Caribbean. Most of its residents are hospitable and courteous, and
there is little instance of panhandling or aggressive souvenir hawking. If safety is a factor in your choice of Caribbean vacation, you can
rest assured that the low crime rate in the Cayman Islands is the envy
of many small nations in the Caribbean.

The downside? Although the Cayman Islands do have splashes of
floral and faunal color, along with rows of royal palms and tall pines

swaying in the trade winds, there are far prettier and more geo-graphically dramatic islands in the Caribbean. While some of Grand Cayman's beaches, found primarily on the west and northern coasts, rank among the most beautiful in the Caribbean, there are no spectacular land vistas.

Most people come to the Cayman Islands to get away from it all in a secluded, safe haven, and many visitors come back after sampling the Caymans for the first time, including honeymooners who often return to celebrate their anniversaries.

1 The Islands in Brief

GRAND CAYMAN   The largest of the three islands and a real diving mecca, Grand Cayman has become one of the hottest tourist destinations in the Caribbean in recent years. With more than 500 banks, its capital, George Town, is the offshore banking center of the Caribbean (no problems finding an ATM here!). Retirees are drawn to the peace and tranquility of this British crown colony, site of a major condominium development. Almost all of the Cayman Islands' 38,000-strong population live on Grand Cayman. The civil manners of the locals reflect their British heritage.

CAYMAN BRAC   Short on sandy beaches and devoid of the clichéd Caribbean attractions, Cayman Brac may appear to be a poor sibling of Grand Cayman. However, this island has its devotees, mainly adventure seekers and scuba divers who are drawn to its 30 excellent dive sites, its snorkeling, its bone- and deep-sea fishing, and its bird-watching. The island lies 143km (89 miles) northeast of Grand Cayman and 7.4km (4.6 miles) from Little Cayman, and is 19km (12 miles) long, with an average width of 3.5km (2.2 miles). In all, its land mass is a total of only 39 sq. km (15 sq. miles), with its highest point being the Bluff at 42m (140 ft.) above sea level. The island's population is under 2,000.

LITTLE CAYMAN   The smallest island of the archipelago, the aptly named Little Cayman, 109km (68 miles) northeast of Grand Cayman, is only 16km (10 miles) long with an average width of 1.6km (1 mile). Relatively flat, it comprises a total land mass of only 16 sq. km (10 sq. miles), with its highest point at 12m (40 ft.) above sea level. About 125 people reside on the island full time, sharing living space with some 20,000 red-footed boobies. Most of Little Cayman's residents aren't Caymanian at all, but include long-term residents from the United States and elsewhere, including Great

Britain and Canada. Who comes here and why? Little Cayman is hailed as one of the three best scuba-diving areas in the world and is a haven for nature lovers, photographers, and tranquility seekers in search of peace and quiet.

2 Visitor Information

Before you go, check out the **Cayman Islands Department of Tourism** (www.caymanislands.ky), which offers an extensive search engine designed to help you find information about accommodations, dining, shopping, watersports, and other travel services. You can also sign up for printed or e-mail brochures, and book vacations directly on this site. If you don't have Internet access, you can write to the Cayman Department of Tourism at P.O. Box 67, George Town, Grand Cayman, B.W.I., or call the Cayman Department of Tourism at ℂ **345/949-0623.**

Once you land in George Town on Grand Cayman, you can visit the **Department of Tourism,** located in the Pavilion Building on Cricket Square (ℂ **345/949-0623**). Hours are Monday to Friday from 8:30am to 5pm.

In the United States, the **Cayman Islands Department of Tourism** has the following offices in the United States: 8300 NW 53 St., Miami, FL 33166 (ℂ **305/599-9033;** fax 305/599-3766); 18 W. 140 Butterfield Rd., Suite 920, Oakbrook Terrace, IL 60181 (ℂ **630/705-0650;** fax 630/705-1383); Two Memorial City Plaza, 820 Gessner, Suite 1335, Houston, TX 77024 (ℂ **713/461-1317;** fax 713/461-7409); and 3 Park Ave., 39th Floor, New York, NY 10016 (ℂ **212/889-9009;** fax 212/889-9125).

In Canada, contact Earl B. Smith, **Traveling Marketing Consultants,** 234 Eglinton Ave. E., Suite 306, Toronto, ON M4P 1K5 (ℂ **416/485-1550;** fax 416/485-7578).

In the United Kingdom, contact **Cayman Islands,** 6 Arlington St., London SW1 1RE (ℂ **0207/491-7771;** fax 0207/409-7773).

The **Cayman Islands Government** (www.gov.ky) website is full of important tourist and travel information, reports current local news, and features a community and sports calendar. **Destination Cayman Islands** (www.destination.ky) is another great information source that features a Cayman business directory in addition to a visitor center with travel news and local forecasts, annual events, photographs, and much more. **Changes In L'Attitudes** (www. cayman-islands.com) gives general information about the Caymans, including information about getting married here, as well as last-minute Cayman Island vacation deals.

TRAVEL AGENTS   Travel agents can save you time and money by uncovering the best package deals, airfare, and rental car rates. Most are professional, but the occasional unscrupulous agent may push deals that bag the juiciest commissions, so shop around and ask hard questions. Arm yourself with the information in this book, and don't let anyone pressure you.

If you enlist a travel agent, use one who's a member of the **American Society of Travel Agents (ASTA),** 1101 King St., Suite 200, Alexandria, VA 22314 (© **703/739-2782;** www.astanet.com). Call ASTA or visit their website for a list of members in your area.

3 Entry Requirements & Customs

ENTRY/EXIT REQUIREMENTS   U.S., British, or Canadian citizens traveling as tourists or attending meetings can enter the Cayman Islands with a valid passport, a naturalization certificate, or an original, certified birth certificate and photo identification. Customs no longer allows a voter registration card as acceptable identification. Citizens of other countries need a valid passport. All visitors, including those from U.S. and Commonwealth countries, must have a valid return or ongoing ticket. There is a departure tax of CI$10 (US$13) for all persons 12 years of age and older. Tax is included in the airfare.

For information on how to get a passport, go to the "Fast Facts" section of this chapter—the websites listed provide downloadable passport applications as well as the current fees for processing passport applications. For an up-to-date country-by-country listing of passport requirements around the world, go the "Foreign Entry Requirement" Web page of the U.S. State Department at **http://travel.state.gov/foreignentryreqs.html**.

CUSTOMS
WHAT YOU CAN BRING INTO THE CAYMAN ISLANDS
Cayman Islands Customs authorities enforce strict regulations concerning temporary importation into or export from the Cayman Islands of firearms of any kind, spear guns, pole spears, Hawaiian slings, live plants, and plant cuttings. Raw fruits and vegetables are also restricted. Visitors age 18 and over are allowed to bring in—duty-free—4 liters of wine or one case of beer; 1 liter of alcohol; and 200 cigarettes, 25 cigars, or 250 grams of tobacco.

Tips U.S. Ban on Sea Turtle Products

Visitors from the U.S. should be aware that products made from farmed green sea turtles at the Cayman Turtle Farm are only offered for local consumption. The importation of genuine sea turtle products is strictly prohibited by any countries which have signed the convention on International Trade in Endangered Species, including the United States. In addition, U.S. Customs prohibits the shipment of turtle products through the U.S. Any products discovered will be confiscated. It is advisable to contact the Collector of Customs (© 345/ 949-2473) for specific information regarding Customs requirements.

WHAT YOU CAN TAKE HOME FROM THE CAYMAN ISLANDS   Returning **U.S. citizens** who have been away for at least 48 hours are allowed to bring back, once every 30 days, $800 worth of merchandise duty-free. You'll be charged a flat rate of 4% duty on the next $1,000 worth of purchases. Be sure to have your receipts handy. On mailed gifts, the duty-free limit is $200. With some exceptions, you cannot bring fresh fruits and vegetables into the United States. For specifics on what you can bring back, download the invaluable free pamphlet *Know Before You Go* online at **www.customs.gov**. (Click on "Travel" and then click on "Know Before You Go!") Or contact the **U.S. Customs Service,** 1300 Pennsylvania Ave., NW, Washington, DC 20229 (© **877/287-8867**) and request the pamphlet.

For a clear summary of **Canadian** rules, write for the booklet *I Declare,* issued by the **Canada Customs and Revenue Agency** (© **800/461-9999** in Canada, or 204/983-3500; www.ccra-adrc. gc.ca). Canada allows its citizens a C$750 exemption, and you're allowed to bring back duty-free one carton of cigarettes, one can of tobacco, 40 imperial ounces of liquor, and 50 cigars if you meet the minimum age requirements set by the province or territory where you enter Canada. In addition, you're allowed to mail gifts to Canada valued at less than C$60 each day, provided they're unsolicited and don't contain alcohol or tobacco (write on the package "Unsolicited gift, under $60 value"). All valuables should be declared on the Y-38 form before departure from Canada, including serial numbers of valuables you already own, such as expensive foreign cameras. *Note:* The C$750 exemption can only be used once a year and only after an absence of 7 days.

U.K. citizens returning from **a non-EU country** have a customs allowance of 200 cigarettes; 50 cigars; 250 grams of smoking tobacco; 2 liters of still table wine; 1 liter of spirits or strong liqueurs (over 22% volume); 2 liters of fortified wine, sparkling wine, or other liqueurs; 60cc (ml) of perfume; 250cc (ml) of toilet water; and £145 worth of all other goods, including gifts and souvenirs. People under 17 cannot have the tobacco or alcohol allowance. For more information, contact HM Customs & Excise at (*(*)) **0845/010-9000** (from outside the U.K., 020/8929-0152), or consult their website at www.hmce.gov.uk.

The duty-free allowance in **Australia** is A$400 or, for those under 18, A$200. Citizens over age 18 can bring in 250 cigarettes or 250 grams of loose tobacco, and 1,125 milliliters of alcohol. If you're returning with valuables you already own, such as foreign-made cameras, you should file form B263. A helpful brochure available from Australian consulates or Customs offices is *Know Before You Go.* For more information, call the **Australian Customs Service** at (*(*)) **1300/363-263,** or log on to www.customs.gov.au.

The duty-free allowance for **New Zealand** is NZ$700. Citizens over 17 can bring in 200 cigarettes, 50 cigars, or 250 grams of tobacco (or a mixture of all three if their combined weight doesn't exceed 250g); plus 4.5 liters of wine and beer, or 1.125 liters of liquor. New Zealand currency does not carry import or export restrictions. Fill out a certificate of export, listing the valuables you are taking out of the country; that way, you can bring them back without paying duty. Most questions are answered in a free pamphlet available at New Zealand consulates and Customs offices: *New Zealand Customs Guide for Travellers, Notice no. 4.* For more information, contact **New Zealand Customs,** The Customhouse, 17–21 Whitmore St., Box 2218, Wellington ((*(*)) **04/473-6099** or 0800/428-786; www.customs.govt.nz).

4 Money

The Cayman Islands is one of the most upmarket destinations in the Caribbean, although it doesn't charge the sky-high prices that the French island of St. Barts or the British-affiliated island of Anguilla do. Nevertheless, it is not the best choice for a frugal traveler, who will do better in such countries as Puerto Rico or the Dominican

Republic. It is estimated that the cost of living is about 20% higher in the Cayman Islands than it is in the United States.

Brace yourself for the high prices that resorts charge. There is almost nothing in the budget category. To give you an idea of the price structure, an "inexpensive" room in Grand Cayman is often one charging under US$150 a night for a double, a price that might buy you a first-class hotel in many parts of America.

Most of the big hotels along Seven Mile Beach don't offer meal plans, such as MAP (the Modified American Plan, which includes breakfast and dinner). You'll often have to pay for your food a la carte. Food prices are high since most everything is imported, but they are not nearly as lofty as the hotel prices; $20 to $30 will get you a main course at a typical restaurant. "Budget" would be any restaurant offering main courses for $15 and under.

Although ATMs are hard to come by on Cayman Brac and Little Cayman, there are banks galore in George Town, the capital of Grand Cayman, each with ATMs dispensing money. You can usually request U.S. dollars or Cayman dollars at most banks and ATMs.

CURRENCY   Legal tender is the Cayman Islands dollar (CI$), which is permanently fixed at US$1.25. Stated differently, CI 80¢ equals US$1. It's helpful to know that U.S. dollars are usually readily accepted across the Cayman Islands. As it related to the British pound, one Cayman Islands dollar equals approximately 80 pence. Stated differently, one pound equals approximately CI$1.25. And as it relates to the Canadian dollar, one Cayman Islands dollar equals approximately 2 Canadian dollars. Stated differently, one Canadian dollar equals approximately CI50¢.

Though the rate between the CI$ and the US$ is permanently fixed as part of an international banking agreement, the ratios between the CI$, the British pound, and the Canadian dollar fluctuate slightly, based on a complicated series of frequently changing financial and political factors. *Warning:* Be alert about which currency is being quoted at any given time. Hotels tend to quote their rates in U.S. dollars, while most restaurants and virtually all nightclubs and gift shops quote their rates in Cayman Island dollars. Misunderstanding the currency being quoted for any given transaction can be embarrassing and expensive.

ATMs   The easiest and best way to get cash away from home is from an ATM (automated teller machine). The **Cirrus** (✆ **800/ 424-7787;** www.mastercard.com) and **PLUS** (✆ **800/843-7587;**

The Cayman Islands Dollar, the U.S. Dollar, the British Pound & the Canadian Dollar

CI$	U.S.$	U.K.£	C$	CI$	U.S.$	U.K.£	C$
1	1.25	0.80	2.00	75	93.75	60.00	150.00
2	2.50	1.60	4.00	100	125.00	80.00	200.00
3	3.75	2.40	6.00	125	156.25	100.00	250.00
4	5.00	3.20	8.00	150	187.50	120.00	300.00
5	6.25	4.00	10.00	175	218.75	140.00	350.00
6	7.50	4.80	12.00	200	250.00	160.00	400.00
7	8.75	5.60	14.00	225	281.25	180.00	450.00
8	10.00	6.40	16.00	250	312.50	200.00	500.00
9	11.25	7.20	18.00	275	343.75	220.00	550.00
10	12.50	8.00	20.00	300	375.00	240.00	600.00
15	18.75	12.00	30.00	350	437.50	280.00	700.00
20	25.00	16.00	40.00	400	500.00	320.00	800.00
25	31.25	20.00	50.00	500	625.00	400.00	1,000.00
50	62.50	40.00	100.00	1,000	1,250.00	800.00	2,000.00

www.visa.com) networks span the globe; look at the back of your bank card to see which network you're on, then call or check online for ATM locations at your destination. Be sure you know your personal identification number (PIN) before you leave home and be sure to find out your daily withdrawal limit before you depart. Also keep in mind that many banks impose a fee every time a card is used at a different bank's ATM, and that fee can be higher for international transactions (up to $5 or more) than for domestic ones (where they're rarely more than $1.50). On top of this, the bank from which you withdraw cash may charge its own fee. To compare banks' ATM fees within the U.S., use www.bankrate.com. For international withdrawal fees, ask your bank.

You can also get cash advances on your credit card at an ATM. Keep in mind that credit card companies try to protect themselves from theft by limiting the funds someone can withdraw outside their home country, so call your credit card company before you leave home.

TRAVELER'S CHECKS If you want to avoid ATM service charges, if you're staying in a remote place, or if you just want the

What Things Cost in Grand Cayman	CI$	U.S.$	U.K.£	C$
Taxi from airport to Seven Mile Beach	9.60	12	7.68	19.20
Average Bus Fare	1.52	1.90	1.85	3.04
Local Telephone Call	.16	.20	.13	.32
Lunch for one at the Brasserie (moderate)	16	20	12.80	32
Lunch for one at Chicken, Chicken (inexpensive)	6.24	7.80	5	12.48
Dinner for one, without wine, at Grand Old House (expensive)	36	45	28.80	72
Dinner for one, without wine, at La Bodega (moderate)	27.20	34	21.75	54.40
Dinner for one, without wine, at Al la Kebab (inexpensive)	9.60	12	7.68	19.20
Double room at the Beachcomber (very expensive)	356	445	284.80	712
Double room at Comfort Suites (moderate)	136	170	108.80	272
Double room at Adam's Guest House (inexpensive)	68	85	54.40	136
Half a liter of beer	2.80	3.50	2.25	5.60
Coca-Cola in a Restaurant	2	2.50	1.60	4
Cup of coffee	1.20	1.50	.96	2.40
Glass of wine	4.80	6	3.84	9.60
Roll of film (36 exposures)	5.60	7	4.48	11.20
Movie Ticket	6.40	8	5.12	12.80

security of knowing you can get a refund in the event that your wallet is stolen, you may want to purchase traveler's checks—provided that you don't mind showing identification every time you want to cash one.

You can get traveler's checks at almost any bank. **American Express** offers checks that usually incur a service charge ranging from 1% to 4%. You can buy American Express traveler's checks over the phone by calling ℂ **800/221-7282.** American Express gold or platinum cardholders can avoid paying the 1% service fee by ordering over the telephone. **American Automobile Association** members can obtain checks fee-free at most AAA offices.

Visa offers traveler's checks at Citibank locations nationwide, as well as at several other banks. The service charge ranges between 1.5% and 2%; checks come in denominations of $20, $50, $100, $500, and $1,000. Call ℂ **800/732-1322** for information. **Master-Card** also offers traveler's checks. Call ℂ **800/223-9920** for a location near you.

If you carry traveler's checks, be sure to keep a record of their serial numbers (separately from the checks, of course), so you're ensured a refund in case they're lost or stolen.

CREDIT CARDS   Credit cards are a safe way to carry money, they provide a convenient record of all your expenses, and they generally offer good exchange rates. You can also withdraw cash advances from your credit cards at banks or ATMs, provided you know your PIN. If you've forgotten yours, or didn't even know you had one, call the number on the back of your credit card and ask the bank to send it to you. It usually takes 5 to 7 business days, though some banks will provide the number over the phone if you tell them your mother's maiden name or some other personal information.

Tips **Show Me the Cash (& Small Change)**

When you change money, ask for some small bills or loose change. It's always a good idea to carry around some cash and change for small expenses like cab rides, or for that rare occasion when a restaurant or small shop doesn't take plastic, which can happen if you're dining at a neighborhood joint or buying from a small vendor. A supply of US$100 (CI$80) in cash (with plenty of small change, which is useful for public transportation and tipping) should see you through. Consider keeping the change separate from your larger bills, so that it's readily accessible and you'll be less of a target for a pickpocket. Remember that U.S. dollars are accepted almost everywhere on the islands.

Tips **Dear Visa: I'm Off to the Cayman Islands!**

Some credit card companies recommend that you notify them of any impending trip abroad so that they don't become suspicious when the card is used numerous times in a foreign destination and your charges are blocked. Even if you don't call your credit card company in advance, you can always call the card's toll-free emergency number (see "Fast Facts," later in this chapter) if a charge is refused—a good reason to carry the phone number with you. But perhaps the most important lesson here is to carry more than one card with you on your trip; a card might not work for any number of reasons, so having a backup is the smart way to go.

Your credit card company will likely charge a commission (1% or 2%) on every foreign purchase you make, but don't sweat this small stuff; for most purchases, you'll still get the best deal with credit cards when you factor in things like ATM fees and higher traveler's check exchange rates.

5 When to Go

THE HIGH SEASON & THE OFF-SEASON

Hotels charge their highest prices during the peak winter period, from mid-December to mid-April. You'll have to make your reservations well in advance for winter travel. If you want to travel over Christmas or in the depths of February, especially around U.S. President's Day weekend, you should make your reservations months in advance.

The off-season in the Cayman Islands—roughly from mid-April to mid-December (although this varies from hotel to hotel)—is one big summer sale, though summer has become more popular in recent years. In most cases, hotels, inns, and condos slash 20% to 50% off their winter rates. Dollar for dollar, you'll spend less money by renting a summer house or self-sufficient unit in the Cayman Islands than you would on Cape Cod, Fire Island, or Laguna Beach. You just have to be able to tolerate strong sun if you're considering coming in the summer.

Off-season, the beaches are less crowded and you can get good deals, but restaurants are often closed, and hotels offer fewer facilities. Some hotels also use the off-season for construction—so make sure to ask if any work is going on and make sure your room is far away from the noise. If you're single and going off-season, ask for the hotel's occupancy rate. You want crowds!

Because there's such a drastic difference in high-season and low-season rates at most hotels, we've included both on every property we review. You'll see the incredible savings you can enjoy if your schedule allows you to wait a couple of months for your fun in the sun.

WEATHER

High season in all three Cayman Islands is from mid-December to mid-April. The weather at this time is perfect for hanging out on the beach—it's usually dry and the cooling trade winds that blow in from the northeast moderate high temperatures. Sometimes a few days will be windy and cloudy, but these periods of inclement weather usually come and go quickly.

In some ways, April is the most idyllic month in the Cayman Islands, boasting perfect warm weather before the heat of summer comes in May. In spite of the heat, many Europeans prefer a summer visit. As one visitor on the beach who hails from Yorkshire told us, "After a cold winter in the north of England, I've come just for the heat."

Rainy season is from late May until late November. That doesn't mean, however, that it rains every day. Often the showers are short bursts that are followed by clear skies and plenty of sun.

Even though the Cayman Islands are one of the world's leading scuba-diving destinations, divers often avoid the islands in August and September, when tropical storms can churn the waters. However, because the islands have so many dive sites, you can nearly always find places to dive, even in August and September.

If you want to know how to pack just before you go, check the Weather Channel's online 5-day forecast at **www.weather.com** for the latest information, or call the nearest branch of the **National Weather Service,** listed in your phone directory under the "U.S. Department of Commerce."

Tips **A Mighty Wind: Hurricanes on the Cayman Islands**

The curse of Cayman weather—the hurricane season—lasts officially from June 1 to November 30. But there's no cause for panic: Satellite forecasts give enough warning that precautions can be taken.

Average Temperature & Rainfall in Grand Cayman

	Jan	Feb	Mar	Apr	May	June	July	Aug	Sept	Oct	Nov	Dec
Temp. (°F)	77	77	79	81	82	84	84	84	83	82	81	78
Temp. (°C)	25	25	26	27	28	29	29	29	28	28	27	26
Rainfall (in.)	2.3	1.7	1.2	1.9	5.1	7.2	7.0	6.7	8.3	9.3	4.7	2.3

HOLIDAYS

Caymanians observe New Year's Day (Jan 1), Ash Wednesday (Feb or Mar), National Heroes' Day (Jan 27), Good Friday (Mar or Apr), Easter (Mar or Apr), Discovery Day (third week in May), Whitsun (May or June), the Queen's Birthday (June 16), Constitution Day (July 7), Remembrance Day (second Mon in Nov), Christmas Day (Dec 25), and Boxing Day (Dec 26).

CAYMAN ISLANDS CALENDAR OF EVENTS

January

International Scuba-Diving Hall of Fame   Some of the leading scuba divers in the world show up for this annual ceremony at the Harquail Theatre on Grand Cayman. Entertainment at the event includes audiovisual presentations of scuba-diving feats, live music by local bands, and a food-and-cocktail reception. Tickets cost from US$37 and are available at the tourist office. The contact is Shomari Scott at ✆ **345/244-1263.** Third week of January.

Art@Government House   This excellent annual event, featuring displays of various art forms by local and resident artists, takes place on the front lawn of Government House. The day is full of entertainment, food, and local art and crafts. Children can create their own unique works of art in the Kids Corner. Contact the National Gallery at ✆ **345/945-8111.** January 25.

February

The Cayman Islands Orchid Show   This annual orchid show takes place at the Queen Elizabeth II Botanic Park from 9am to 5pm. Stop by the park to view the exquisite displays of orchids in bloom, or to buy your favorite one. The Orchid Society hosts a special orchid talk and demonstration. Contact Queen Elizabeth II Botanic Park at ✆ **345/947-3558** or the Quincentennial Celebrations Office at ✆ **345/946-9992,** or visit www.cayman500.ky. February 14 to 16.

March

Little Cayman Mardi Gras Festival   Everybody on this small island turns out for this festive event. Parade participants show up from Grand Cayman and Cayman Brac. The parade begins in the morning at Head O' Bay and continues to the airport. Contact Gladys Howard at © **345/948-1010.** Shrove Tuesday each year.

April

Cayfest (The National Festival of the Arts)   This 2-week event celebrates and showcases the art and culture of the Cayman Islands. The expo opens at Seven Mile Beach with a re-enactment of a traditional boat launch. In George Town, you'll find open-air events featuring local bands, arts and crafts, native cooking, and other demonstrations of local talent, such as culinary and song competitions. For more information, contact Michele Mogg at © **345/949-5477.** April 17 to 30.

Cayman Islands Million Dollar Run   Launched in 2003 and taking place on Grand Cayman, this is a show of power and speed on the water, attracting powerboat aficionados and fun seekers from around the world. The hottest, fastest, and most exotic boats gather for this race, with captains competing for US$10,000 in cash and prizes. For more information, call © **345/949-VIBE.** Third week of April.

Round the Island Regatta   The Cayman Islands Sailing Club sponsors this annual event off Grand Cayman. The race attracts many boaters, who show up in catamarans ranging from 6m to 24m (20 ft.–80 ft.). Highlights include a race to the Banks, a dinghy regatta, and a sail around the island to North Sound. Call © **345/947-7913** for dates and more specific information. Staged right before Easter.

May

Annual Batabano Carnival   This Mardi Gras–like event in George Town features popular carnival music and live soca (a type of calypso music with elements of soul that often features lyrics on topical or humorous subjects), and calypso bands. The event is enhanced by concession stands offering Caymanian and Caribbean cuisine and delicacies. Contact Donna Myrie at © **345/945-5982** for more information. Held a short time after Ash Wednesday (call for exact dates).

June

Cayman Island International Aviation Week   This annual air show, off Grand Cayman, includes aerial feats, displays, safety seminars, and a "fly-in" to Cayman Brac. It's sponsored by Cayman Caravan (© **850/872-2495;** www.caymancaravan.com) in Panama City, FL. Third week of June.

Queen's Birthday   To honor the British heritage of the Cayman Islands, the Queen's birthday is celebrated every year in George Town on Grand Cayman. The streets of the capital are filled with a full military dress parade, there is a 21-gun salute, and you can attend an open house and garden reception at Government House. Dates vary, and the event is not always on the queen's actual birthday. Contact the Cayman Islands Tourism Associations at ℂ 345/949-8522 for dates and details.

July

Taste of Cayman   This event, taking place on Grand Cayman, is the "eatfest" of the islands, showcasing a sampling of different cuisines from more than 40 restaurants. Live entertainment, games for kids, and tasty cooking competitions are also part of the fun. Contact the Cayman Islands Tourism Association at ℂ 345/949-8522. First weekend in July.

October

Cayman Islands Pirates' Week   This is a national festival in which cutlass-bearing pirates and sassy wenches storm George Town, capture the governor, throng the streets, and stage a costume parade. The celebration, which is held throughout the Caymans, pays tribute to the nation's past and its cultural heritage. For the exact dates, contact the **Pirates Week Festival Administration** (ℂ 345/949-5078). Late October and early November.

November

Also see Cayman Islands Pirates' Week, above.

CITA Wet Fest   This is Grand Cayman's annual festival of watersports, including snorkeling, parasailing, and kayaking. Kiosks sell island food, there is entertainment by live bands, and wave-runner rides are offered. Contact the Cayman Islands Tourism Association at ℂ 345/949-8522 for more details and the exact date. One day during the second week of November.

Remembrance Day   This is the Cayman Islands' national day of mourning and remembrance for the military heroes lost during World Wars I and II, and for all sailors and mariners lost at sea during the long maritime history of the Cayman Islands. The event is defined as a national holiday when all schools, banks, and businesses are closed. In a public ceremony, wreaths are laid on two war monuments near the corner of Fort Street and North Church Street in downtown George Town, on Grand Cayman. Solemn music is broadcast on the radio and churches hold special ceremonies and masses. The second Monday in November.

December

Reliving the Birth of Democracy   This is a period re-enactment of the historic meeting at Pedro St. James on December 5, 1831, when the decision was made to form an elected assembly. Participants will include descendants of those who took part in the original meeting. Contact Quincentennial Celebrations Office at ℂ **345/946-9992;** www.cayman500.ky. December 5, 2003.

6 Travel Insurance

Check your existing insurance policies and credit card coverage before you buy travel insurance. You may already be covered for lost luggage, cancelled tickets, or medical expenses. The cost of travel insurance varies widely, depending on the cost and length of your trip, your age and health, and the type of trip you're taking.

TRIP-CANCELLATION INSURANCE   Trip-cancellation insurance helps you get your money back if you have to back out of a trip, if you have to go home early, or if your travel supplier goes bankrupt. Allowed reasons for cancellation can range from sickness to natural disasters to the State Department declaring your destination unsafe for travel. (Insurers usually won't cover vague fears, though, as many travelers discovered who tried to cancel their trips in October 2001 because they were wary of flying.) Insurance policy details vary, so read the fine print—and especially make sure that your airline or cruise line is on the list of carriers covered in case of bankruptcy. For information, contact one of the following insurers: **Access America** (ℂ 866/807-3982; www.accessamerica.com); **Travel Guard International** (ℂ 800/826-4919; www.travelguard.com); **Travel Insured International** (ℂ 800/243-3174; www.travelinsured.com); and **Travelex Insurance Services** (ℂ 888/457-4602; www.travelex-insurance.com).

MEDICAL INSURANCE   Most health insurance policies cover you if you get sick away from home—but check, particularly if you're insured by an HMO. With the exception of certain HMOs and Medicare/Medicaid, your medical insurance should cover medical treatment—even hospital care—overseas. However, most out-of-country hospitals make you pay your bills upfront, and send you a refund after you've returned home and filed the necessary paperwork. And in a worst-case scenario, there's the high cost of emergency evacuation. If you require additional medical insurance, try **MEDEX International** (ℂ **800/527-0218** or 410/453-6300;

www.medexassist.com) or **Travel Assistance International** (© 800/
821-2828; www.travelassistance.com; for general information on
services, call the company's Worldwide Assistance Services, Inc., at
© 800/777-8710).

LOST-LUGGAGE INSURANCE   On domestic flights, checked
baggage is covered up to $2,500 per ticketed passenger. On inter-
national flights (including U.S. portions of international trips),
baggage is limited to approximately $9.07 per pound, up to approx-
imately $635 per checked bag. If you plan to check items more valu-
able than the standard liability, see if your valuables are covered by
your homeowner's policy, get baggage insurance as part of your
comprehensive travel-insurance package, or buy Travel Guard's
"BagTrak" product. Don't buy insurance at the airport, as it's usually
overpriced. Be sure to take any valuables or irreplaceable items with
you in your carry-on luggage, as many valuables (including books,
money, and electronics) aren't covered by airline policies.

If your luggage is lost, immediately file a lost-luggage claim at the
airport, detailing the luggage contents. For most airlines, you must
report delayed, damaged, or lost baggage within 4 hours of arrival.
The airlines are required to deliver luggage, once found, directly to
your house or destination free of charge.

7 Health & Safety

STAYING HEALTHY
GENERAL AVAILABILITY OF HEALTH CARE
There are no particular health concerns in the Cayman Islands. It is
one of the safest destinations in the Caribbean, with some of the
best medical facilities found on Grand Cayman.

While medical facilities are fully developed on Grand Cayman,
only adequate clinics are available on Little Cayman or Cayman
Brac. If a visitor develops a serious illness while vacationing on the
two smaller sibling islands, he or she is quickly airlifted to George
Town. On Grand Cayman, it's easy to get over-the-counter medicine
if necessary, less so on Cayman Brac or Little Cayman. If you're visiting these smaller islands, stock up on whatever medication you
think you'll need. For details on medical facilities and pharmacies
on Grand Cayman, refer to "Fast Facts" at the end of chapter. For
details on medical facilities on Little Cayman and Cayman Brac,
refer to p. 185 and p. 165, respectively.

Pack prescription medications in your carry-on luggage. Carry
written prescriptions in generic, not brand-name, form, and dispense

all prescription medications from their original labeled vials. Many people try to slip drugs such as cocaine into the Cayman Islands (or pick them up there). Drugs are often placed into a container for prescription medication after the legal medications have been removed. Customs officials are well aware of this type of smuggling and often check medications if they suspect a passenger is bringing illegal drugs into or out of a country.

COMMON AILMENTS

DIETARY RED FLAGS   See "Water" under "Fast Facts" at the end of this chapter.

SUN EXPOSURE   The Cayman sun can be brutal. Wear sunglasses and a hat, and use sunscreen liberally. Limit your time on the beach the first day. If you do overexpose yourself, stay out of the sun until you recover. If fever, chills, a headache, nausea, or dizziness follows your overexposure to the sun, see a doctor.

BUGS & BITES   One of the biggest menaces is the "no-see-ums," which appear mainly in the early evening. You can't see these gnats, but you sure can "feel-um." Mosquitoes are also a nuisance. Window screens don't keep these critters out, so carry bug repellent.

WHAT TO DO IF YOU GET SICK AWAY FROM HOME

Finding a good doctor in the Cayman Islands is not a problem, and all of them speak English. See the "Fast Facts" section at the end of this chapter and in chapters 9 and 10 for hospitals and clinics to call.

If you worry about getting sick away from home, you might want to consider medical travel insurance (see the section on travel insurance above). In most cases, however, your existing health plan will provide all the coverage you need. Be sure to carry your identification card in your wallet.

If you suffer from a chronic illness, consult your doctor before your departure. For conditions such as epilepsy, diabetes, or heart problems, wear a **Medic Alert** identification tag (© **800/825-3785;** www.medicalert.org), which will immediately alert doctors to your condition and give them access to your records through Medic Alert's 24-hour hot line.

Contact the **International Association for Medical Assistance to Travelers (IAMAT)** (© **716/754-4883** in the U.S. or 519/ 836-0102 in Canada; www.iamat.org) for tips on travel and health concerns in the countries you'll be visiting, plus lists of local English-speaking doctors.

Safety & Security for Scuba Divers

On average, one American citizen per month drowns or suffers cardiac arrest while snorkeling or scuba diving in the Cayman Islands. These deaths may be attributed to tourists attempting to do more than they are trained to do or may be due to poor physical fitness or pre-existing medical conditions that are exacerbated when snorkeling or diving. Inexperienced or first-time divers should obtain proper training, and may wish to undergo a physical examination before diving. **Divers Alert Network (© 800/ 446-2671** or 919/684-8111; www.diversalertnetwork.org) insures scuba divers.

STAYING SAFE

Violent crime is rare in the Cayman Islands, but petty thefts, pick-pocketing, and purse snatchings occasionally occur. There have been incidents of sexual assault, some reportedly involving the use of so-called "date rape" drugs, such as Rohypnol. To avoid becoming a victim of a crime, visitors should exercise common sense and take basic precautions, including being aware of one's surroundings, not walking alone after dark or in remote areas, and using reasonable caution when offered food or beverages from strangers.

The loss or theft abroad of a passport should be reported immediately to the local police and the nearest embassy or consulate. U.S. citizens may refer to the Department of State's pamphlet, *A Safe Trip Abroad,* for ways to experience a trouble-free journey. The pamphlet is available by mail from the Superintendent of Documents, U.S. Government Printing Office, Washington, DC 20402; via the Internet at www.gpoaccess.gov; or via the Bureau of Consular Affairs home page at travel.state.gov.

DEALING WITH DISCRIMINATION

See the discussion on the Cayman Islands' negative attitude towards gays and lesbians under "Gay & Lesbian Travelers" within "Specialized Travel Resources."

8 Specialized Travel Resources

TRAVELERS WITH DISABILITIES

Like most islands of the Caribbean, the Cayman Islands should do more to welcome vacationers with disabilities. If you're traveling with a disability, we'd recommend that you confine your visit to Grand Cayman and not the remote "adventure" islands of Cayman Brac or Little Cayman. Your best bet is to check into one of the major resorts along Seven Mile Beach, which are far more accessible than the smaller lodgings on the island. It is always advisable to call the hotel of your choice and personally discuss your needs before booking a vacation.

Many travel agencies offer customized tours and itineraries for travelers with disabilities. **Flying Wheels Travel** (© 507/451-5005; www.flyingwheelstravel.com) offers escorted tours and cruises that emphasize sports and private tours in minivans with lifts. **Accessible Journeys** (© 800/846-4537 or 610/521-0339; www.disability travel.com) caters specifically to slow walkers, wheelchair travelers, and their families and friends.

Organizations that offer assistance to disabled travelers include the **Moss Rehab Hospital** (www.mossresourcenet.org), which provides a library of accessible-travel resources online; the **Society for Accessible Travel and Hospitality** (© 212/447-7284; www.sath. org; annual membership fees: $45 adults, $30 seniors and students), which offers a wealth of travel resources for all types of disabilities and informed recommendations on destinations, access guides, travel agents, tour operators, vehicle rentals, and companion services; and the **American Foundation for the Blind** (© 800/232-5463; www.afb.org), which provides information on traveling with Seeing Eye dogs.

For more information specifically targeted to travelers with disabilities, the community website **iCan** (www.icanonline.net/channels/travel/index.cfm) has destination guides and several regular columns on accessible travel. Also check out the quarterly magazine **Emerging Horizons** ($14.95 per year, $19.95 outside the U.S.; www.emerginghorizons.com); **Twin Peaks Press** (© 360/694-2462; http://disabilitybookshop.virtualave.net/blist84.htm), which offers travel-related books for travelers with special needs; and *Open World Magazine*, published by the Society for Accessible Travel and Hospitality (see above; subscription: $18 per year, $35 outside the U.S.).

FOR BRITISH TRAVELERS   The **Royal Association for Disability and Rehabilitation (RADAR),** Unit 12, City Forum, 250 City Rd., London, EC1V 8AF (**© 020/7250-3222;** fax 020/7250-0212; www.radar.org.uk), publishes holiday "Fact Packs," three in all, which sell for £2 each or all three for £5. The first one provides general information, including planning and booking a holiday, insurance, finances, and useful organization and holiday providers. The second outlines transportation available when going abroad and equipment for rent. The third deals with specialized accommodations.

GAY & LESBIAN TRAVELERS

Most of the gay and lesbian community regards the Cayman Islands as gay hostile as opposed to gay friendly. No island in the Caribbean is completely gay friendly, even the more liberal destinations like Puerto Rico and St. Croix. But the government of the Cayman Islands has been particularly vocal in expressing its anti-gay attitudes with no apologies for its mindless prejudices.

In 1998 the Cayman Islands government turned away Norwegian Cruise Lines *Leeward,* which was carrying 900 gay passengers. The tourism directors at George Town stated at the time: "We cannot count on this group to uphold the standards of appropriate behavior expected of visitors to the Cayman Islands." The decision drew massive protest in America, with many groups, even travel agents, discouraging travel to the Cayman Islands or calling for a complete boycott on the Cayman Islands.

Although the government officially sanctioned the ban of the *Leeward,* such intolerance is often not endorsed by individual hotel owners, who told us privately that they welcome gay and lesbian patronage. Nonetheless, the official attitude doesn't make for a happy vacation, and displays of same-sex affection are severely frowned upon in the Cayman Islands.

As a gay or lesbian traveler, you have to make a personal choice of whether you want to spend your hard-earned vacation dollars in the Cayman Islands, or if you would prefer to vacation in friendlier and more tolerant climes.

The **International Gay & Lesbian Travel Association (IGLTA)** (**© 800/448-8550** or 954/776-2626; www.iglta.org) is the trade association for the gay and lesbian travel industry, and offers an online directory of gay- and lesbian-friendly travel businesses; go to their website and click on "Members."

Many agencies offer tours and travel itineraries specifically for gay and lesbian travelers. **Above and Beyond Tours** (© 800/397-2681; www.abovebeyondtours.com) is the exclusive gay and lesbian tour operator for United Airlines. **Now, Voyager** (© 800/255-6951; www.nowvoyager.com) is a well-known San Francisco–based gay-owned and -operated travel service. **Olivia Cruises & Resorts** (© 800/631-6277 or 510/655-0364; www.olivia.com) charters entire resorts and ships for exclusive lesbian vacations and offers smaller group experiences for both gay and lesbian travelers.

FOR SENIORS

Mention the fact that you're a senior citizen when you make your travel reservations. Although all of the major U.S. airlines except America West have cancelled their senior discount and coupon book programs, many hotels still offer discounts for seniors. Plus, people over the age of 60 often qualify for reduced admission to theaters, museums, and other attractions, as well as discounted fares on public transportation. Don't be shy about asking for discounts, but always carry some kind of ID, such as a driver's license, especially if you've kept your youthful glow.

Members of **AARP** (formerly known as the American Association of Retired Persons), 601 E St. NW, Washington, DC 20049 (© 800/424-3410 or 202/434-2277; www.aarp.org), get discounts on hotels, airfares, and car rentals. AARP offers members a wide range of benefits, including *AARP The Magazine* and a monthly newsletter. Anyone over 50 can join.

Many reliable agencies and organizations target the 50-plus market. **Elderhostel** (© 877/426-8056; www.elderhostel.org) arranges study programs for those aged 55 and over (and a spouse or companion of any age) in the U.S. and in more than 80 countries around the world. Most courses last 5 to 7 days in the U.S. (2–4 weeks abroad), and many include airfare, accommodations in university dormitories or modest inns, meals, and tuition. **ElderTreks** (© 800/741-7956; www.eldertreks.com) offers small-group tours to off-the-beaten-path or adventure-travel locations, restricted to travelers 50 and older.

Recommended publications offering travel resources and discounts for seniors include: the quarterly magazine *Travel 50 & Beyond* (www.travel50andbeyond.com); *Travel Unlimited: Uncommon Adventures for the Mature Traveler* (Avalon); *101 Tips for Mature Travelers,* available from Grand Circle Travel

(© **800/221-2610** or 617/350-7500; www.gct.com); *The 50+ Traveler's Guidebook* (St. Martin's Press); and *Unbelievably Good Deals and Great Adventures That You Absolutely Can't Get Unless You're Over 50* (McGraw-Hill).

FAMILY TRAVEL

Check out p. 69 for family-friendly lodging and p. 93 for family-friendly restaurants.

Familyhostel (© **800/733-9753**; www.learn.unh.edu/family hostel) takes the whole family, including kids ages 8 to 15, on moderately priced domestic and international learning vacations. Lectures, fields trips, and sightseeing are guided by a team of academics.

You can find good family-oriented vacation advice on the Internet from sites like the **Family Travel Network** (www.familytravel network.com); **Traveling Internationally with Your Kids** (www.travelwithyourkids.com), a comprehensive site offering sound advice for long-distance and international travel with children; and **Family Travel Files** (www.thefamilytravelfiles.com), which offers an online magazine and a directory of off-the-beaten-path tours and tour operators for families.

9 Getting Married in the Cayman Islands

See "The Best Accommodations for Honeymoons & Weddings" in chapter 1 for information on specific resorts that offer wedding and honeymoon packages.

If you want to take the plunge and get married on these sun-dappled islands, there's some red tape. Visitors have to call ahead and arrange for an authorized person to marry them. The name of the "marriage officer," as the person is called, has to appear on the application for a marriage license. The application for a special marriage license costs US$200 and can be obtained from the **Deputy Secretary's Office,** Third Floor, Government Administration Building, George Town (© **345/949-7900**). There is no waiting period. Present a birth certificate, the embarkation/disembarkation cards issued by the island's immigration authorities, and, if applicable, divorce decrees or proof of a spouse's death.

A brochure, *Getting Married in the Cayman Islands,* is available from **Government Information Services,** Broadcasting House, Grand Cayman (© **345/949-8092;** fax 345/949-5936).

The Cayman Islands are one of the few Caribbean destinations that allows U.S. citizens to marry the same day they arrive, instead of requiring a minimum on-island stay before the wedding.

The Cayman Islands is a wedding-friendly destination, where it is easy to make wedding and honeymoon arrangements. The host hotel or a wedding service handles all ground arrangements. Wedding service companies perform all the necessary functions related to the ceremony, providing musicians, catering, flowers, and photography, as well as the marriage application with the civil registrar or marriage officer.

Celebrations, P.O. Box 10599 APO (℗ **345/949-2044;** fax 345/949-6947; www.celebrationsltd.com), is an excellent wedding planner, offering packages ranging from US$660 to US$2,800. Bridal packages include everything from prerecorded wedding music to a personal wedding coordinator on the day of the grand event.

Competitor **Cayman Weddings,** P.O. Box 678 GT (℗ **345/949-8677;** fax 345/949-8237; www.caymanweddings.com.ky), is another good choice, with packages starting at US$600 and going up into the stratosphere for deluxe weddings. You get such thoughtful extras as 36 candid photographs, two crystal memento glasses, and a two-tier wedding cake.

After arrival, rest, and perhaps a rehearsal dinner, guests usually convene the following day for a sumptuous island-style wedding. Choose from many romantic, tropical locations: a hotel, chapel, or church; the Caymanian-style Bride House; a beach at sunset; an oceanfront gazebo; a waterside restaurant; or perhaps the depths of the ocean (underwater weddings are extremely popular with divers).

10 Planning Your Trip Online

SURFING FOR AIRFARES

The "big three" online travel agencies, **Expedia, Travelocity,** and **Orbitz,** sell most of the air tickets bought on the Internet. (Canadian travelers should try Expedia.ca and Travelocity.ca; U.K. residents can go for Expedia.co.uk and Opodo.co.uk.) Each has different business deals with the airlines and may offer different fares on the same flights, so it's wise to shop around. Expedia and Travelocity will also send you **e-mail notification** when a cheap fare becomes available to your favorite destination. Of the smaller travel agency websites, **SideStep** (www.sidestep.com) has gotten the best reviews from Frommer's authors. It's a browser add-on that purports to "search 140 sites at once," but in reality only beats competitors' fares as often as other sites do.

Also remember to check **airline websites,** especially those for low-fare carriers such as Southwest, JetBlue, AirTran, WestJet, or

Frommers.com: The Complete Travel Resource

For an excellent travel-planning resource, we highly recommend **Frommers.com** (www.frommers.com). We're a little biased, of course, but we guarantee that you'll find the travel tips, reviews, monthly vacation giveaways, and online-booking capabilities thoroughly indispensable.

Ryanair, whose fares are often misreported or simply missing from travel agency websites. Even with major airlines, you can often shave a few bucks from a fare by booking directly through the airline and avoiding a travel agency's transaction fee. But you'll get these discounts only by **booking online:** Most airlines now offer online-only fares that even their phone agents know nothing about. For the websites of airlines that fly to and from your destination, go to "Getting There," later in this chapter.

Great **last-minute deals** are available through free weekly e-mail services provided directly by the airlines. Most of these are announced on Tuesday or Wednesday and must be purchased online. Most are only valid for travel that weekend, but some (such as Southwest's) can be booked weeks or months in advance. Sign up for weekly e-mail alerts at airline websites or check mega-sites that compile comprehensive lists of last-minute specials, such as **Smarter Living** (smarterliving.com). For last-minute trips, **site59.com** in the U.S. and **lastminute.com** in Europe often have better deals than the major-label sites.

If you're willing to give up some control over your flight details, use an **opaque fare service** like **Priceline** (www.priceline.com; www.priceline.co.uk for Europeans) or **Hotwire** (www.hotwire.com). Both offer rock-bottom prices in exchange for travel on a "mystery airline" at a mysterious time of day, often with a mysterious change of planes en route. The mystery airlines are all major, well-known carriers—and the possibility of being sent from Philadelphia to Chicago via Tampa is remote; the airlines' routing computers have gotten a lot better than they used to be. But your chances of getting a 6am or 11pm flight are pretty high. Hotwire tells you flight prices before you buy; Priceline usually has better deals than Hotwire, but you have to play their "name our price" game. If you're new at this, the helpful folks at **BiddingForTravel** (www.biddingfortravel.com) do a good job of demystifying Priceline's prices. Priceline and Hotwire are great for flights within North America and between the U.S. and Europe. But for flights to other parts of the world, consolidators will almost always beat their fares.

For much more about airfares and savvy air-travel tips and advice, pick up a copy of *Frommer's Fly Safe, Fly Smart* (Wiley Publishing, Inc.).

SURFING FOR HOTELS

Of the "big three" sites, **Expedia** may be the best choice, thanks to its long list of special deals. **Travelocity** runs a close second. Hotel specialist sites **hotels.com** and **hoteldiscounts.com** are also reliable. An excellent free program, **TravelAxe** (www.travelaxe.net), can help you search multiple hotel sites at once, even ones you may never have heard of.

Priceline and Hotwire are even better for hotels than for airfares; with both, you're allowed to pick the neighborhood and quality level of your hotel before offering up your money. Priceline is much better at getting five-star lodging for three-star prices than at finding anything at the bottom of the scale. *Note:* Hotwire overrates its hotels by one star—what Hotwire calls a four-star is a three-star anywhere else.

SURFING FOR RENTAL CARS

For booking rental cars online, the best deals are usually found at rental-car company websites, although all the major online travel agencies also offer rental-car reservations services. Priceline and Hotwire work well for rental cars, too; the only "mystery" is which major rental company you get, and for most travelers the difference between Hertz, Avis, and Budget is negligible.

11 The 21st-Century Traveler

INTERNET ACCESS AWAY FROM HOME
WITHOUT YOUR OWN COMPUTER

Although there's no definitive directory for cybercafes—these are independent businesses, after all—three places to start looking are at **www.cybercaptive.com**, **www.netcafeguide.com**, and **www.cyber cafe.com**. For information on cable and wireless services in the Caymans, go to **www.candw.ky**.

You can access the Internet at **Café del Sol/the Cyberloft,** a brightly painted cafe that serves up a tempting variety of specialty coffees, pastries, and baguette sandwiches along with its computer terminals. Computer use is CI$3.75 (US$4.70) per half-hour, and CI$6 (US$7.50) per hour. It's in the Marquee Shopping Centre, Harquail Bypass near West Bay Road on Grand Cayman (© **345/946-2233**). Hours are Monday to Thursday 7am to 10pm, Friday and Saturday 7am to 11pm, and Sunday 8am to 8pm.

To retrieve your e-mail, ask your **Internet Service Provider (ISP)** if it has a Web-based interface tied to your existing e-mail account. If your ISP doesn't have such an interface, you can use the free **mail2web** service (www.mail2web.com) to view (but not reply to) your home e-mail. For more flexibility, you may want to open a free, Web-based e-mail account with **Yahoo! Mail** (http://mail.yahoo.com). (Microsoft's Hotmail is another popular option, but Hotmail has severe spam problems.) Your home ISP may be able to forward your e-mail to the Web-based account automatically.

If you need to access files on your office computer, look into a service called **GoToMyPC** (www.gotomypc.com). The service provides a Web-based interface for you to access and manipulate a distant PC from anywhere—even a cybercafe—provided your "target" PC is on and has an always-on connection to the Internet (such as with Road Runner cable). The service offers top-quality security, but if you're worried about hackers, use your own laptop rather than a cybercafe to access the GoToMyPC system.

WITH YOUR OWN COMPUTER

Major Internet Service Providers (ISPs) have **local access numbers** around the world, allowing you to go online by simply placing a local call. Check your ISP's website or call its toll-free number and ask how you can use your current account away from home, and how much it will cost.

If you're traveling outside the reach of your ISP, the **iPass** network has dial-up numbers in most of the world's countries. You'll have to sign up with an iPass provider, who will then tell you how to set up your computer for your destination(s). For a list of iPass providers, go to www.ipass.com and click on "Reseller Locator." Under "Select a Country" pick the country that you're coming from, and under "Who is this service for?" pick "Individual." One solid provider is **i2roam** (www.i2roam.com; © **866/811-6209** or 920/235-0475).

Wherever you go, bring a **connection kit** of the right power and phone adapters, a spare phone cord, and a spare Ethernet network cable. See "Fast Facts," at the end of this chapter, for information on electrical currents in the Cayman Islands.

USING A CELLPHONE

The three letters that define much of the world's **wireless capabilities** are GSM (Global System for Mobiles), a big, seamless network that makes for easy cross-border cellphone use throughout Europe and dozens of other countries worldwide. In the U.S., T-Mobile, AT&T Wireless, and Cingular use this quasi-universal system; in Canada, Microcell and some Rogers customers are GSM, and all Europeans and most Australians use GSM.

If your cellphone is on a GSM system, and you have a world-capable phone such as many (but not all) Sony Ericsson, Motorola, or Samsung models, you can make and receive calls across civilized areas on much of the globe, from Andorra to Uganda. Just call your wireless operator and ask for international roaming to be activated on your account. Unfortunately, per-minute charges can be high—usually $1 to $1.50 in Western Europe and up to $5 in places like Russia and Indonesia.

World-phone owners can bring down their per-minute charges with a bit of trickery. Call up your cellular operator and say you'll be going abroad for several months and want to "unlock" your phone to use it with a local provider. Usually, they'll oblige. Then, in your destination country, pick up a cheap, prepaid phone chip at a mobile phone store and clip it into your phone. (Show your phone to the salesperson, as not all phones work on all networks.) You'll get a local phone number in your destination country—and much, much lower calling rates.

Otherwise, **renting** a phone is a good idea. While you sometimes can rent a phone from overseas sites, including kiosks at airports and at car-rental agencies, we highly suggest renting the phone before you leave home. That way you can give loved ones your new number, make sure the phone works, and take the phone wherever you go—as opposed to renting overseas, where phone-rental agencies bill in local currency and may not let you take the phone to another country. Phone rental isn't cheap. You'll usually pay $40 to $50 per week, plus airtime fees of at least a dollar a minute. Shop around.

Two good wireless rental companies are **InTouch USA** (© 800/872-7626; www.intouchglobal.com) and **RoadPost** (© 888/290-1606 or 905/272-5665; www.roadpost.com). Give them your itinerary, and they'll tell you what wireless products you need. InTouch will also, for free, advise you on whether your existing phone will work overseas; simply call © **703/222-7161** between 9am and 4pm EST, or go to http://intouchglobal.com/travel.htm.

12 Getting There

BY PLANE

Flights to Grand Cayman Island land at **Owen Roberts Airport** (© 345/949-5252). The airport lies just east of George Town, the capital, and is only a short taxi ride from most of the hotels along Seven Mile Beach. Customs can be aggressive at times, and you'll need to show a firmly booked hotel reservation and an ongoing or return ticket.

The Department of Tourism operates an information bureau (© 345/949-2635) right at the airport, which is open daily from 11am to 9pm. You'll find many conveniences in the airport. A restaurant, the **Hungry Horse** (© 345/949-8056), is open daily from 6:15am to 6:30pm, accepting MasterCard and Visa. You can order soft drinks, burgers, sandwiches, snacks, and full meals here. You'll also find ATMs in the airport, which can give money in either Cayman Island or U.S. dollars.

There is a gift shop, plus some duty-free stores selling the famous rum cake of the Cayman Islands, plus jewelry, perfume, and souvenirs. Alcohol can also be purchased here.

Many car rental companies operate kiosks in the airport. It's best to reserve before flying to Grand Cayman. For specifics, see "Getting Around Grand Cayman," later in this chapter.

FROM THE UNITED STATES   The Cayman Islands are easily accessible. Flying time from Miami is 1 hour 20 minutes; from Houston, 2 hours 45 minutes; from Tampa, 1 hour 40 minutes; and from Atlanta, 1 hour 30 minutes. Only a handful of nonstop flights are available from the U.S. Midwest, so most visitors use Miami as their gateway.

Cayman Airways (© 800/422-9626 in the U.S. and Canada, or 345/949-2311; www.caymanairways.com) offers the most frequent service to Grand Cayman, with three daily flights from Miami, five flights a week from Tampa, and three nonstop flights a week from Houston. Service from Fort Lauderdale is Thursday to Tuesday.

Many visitors also fly to Grand Cayman on **American Airlines** (© 800/433-7300; www.aa.com), which, as of this writing, offers direct non-stop flights from Detroit to Grand Cayman from January 3 to April 24 (Sat only) and offers flights from Detroit via Memphis to Grand Cayman from December 18 to April 30 (daily). **Northwest Airlines** (© 800/447-4747; www.nwa.com) flies to Grand Cayman from Detroit and Memphis. **US Airways** (© 800/428-4322; www.usairways.com) offers daily nonstop flights from

Charlotte, N.C. On Saturday and Sunday, they also fly to George Town from Philadelphia. **Delta** (© **800/221-1212;** www.delta. com) flies daily into Grand Cayman from its hub in Atlanta. **Continental Airlines** (© **800/231-0856;** www.continental.com) offers service between its Houston hub and Grand Cayman on Wednesday, Friday, Saturday, and Sunday. It also flies from Newark, N.J., on Saturday, Sunday, Tuesday, and Thursday.

FROM CANADA Air Canada (© **888/247-2262;** www.air canada.ca) flies nonstop from Toronto to George Town twice weekly, on Wednesday and Sunday. The flight takes 4 hours.

FROM THE U.K. British Airways (© **800/AIRWAYS** in the U.S. or 0845/77-333-77 in the U.K.; www.britishairways.com), has direct flights from London's Heathrow to Grand Cayman on Tuesday, Wednesday, Friday, and Saturday, with returning flights on the same day. The plane touches down briefly at Nassau in the Bahamas (or perhaps San Juan). Total flight time is 10 hours. BA also flies twice a day seven days a week from Heathrow to Miami, where continuing flights can be booked on Cayman Airways into George Town. Trip time to Miami is 8½ hours.

GETTING INTO TOWN FROM THE AIRPORT

Flights to Grand Cayman Island land at **Owen Roberts Airport** (© **345/949-5252**). Plenty of taxis meet all arriving planes. A taxi rank is found outside the arrivals gate, and cabs are allocated on a first-come, first-served basis. The government sets taxi fares, which apply for one to three passengers sharing a ride. Typical prices are as

---

Tips Travel in the Age of Bankruptcy

At press time, several major U.S. airlines were struggling in bankruptcy court and most of the rest weren't doing very well, either. To protect yourself, **buy your tickets with a credit card,** as the Fair Credit Billing Act guarantees that you can get your money back from the credit card company if a travel supplier goes under (and if you request the refund within 60 days of the bankruptcy). **Travel insurance** can also help, but make sure it covers against "carrier default" for your specific travel provider. And be aware that if a U.S. airline goes bust midtrip, a 2001 federal law requires other carriers to take you to your destination (albeit on a space-available basis) for a fee of no more than $25, provided you rebook within 60 days of the cancellation.

follows: US$12 from the airport to the southern end of Seven Mile Beach; US$25 from the airport to the northern end of Seven Mile Beach; US$60 from the airport to the East End; and US$60 from the airport to Rum Point on the north shore. Each additional person (additional to a group of three) pays 25% of the fares stated.

To protect taxi drivers and their livelihood, the government doesn't allow buses to run back and forth between town and the airport.

TIPS ON FINDING THE BEST AIRFARE

Before you do anything else, read the section on "Package Deals," below. But if a package isn't for you, and you need to book your airfare on your own, keep in mind these money-saving tips:

- If you fly in **spring, summer,** and **fall,** you're guaranteed substantial reductions on airfares to the Cayman Islands.

- Passengers who can book their ticket **long in advance,** who can **stay over Saturday night,** or who **fly midweek** or **at less-trafficked hours** will pay a fraction of the full fare. If your schedule is flexible, say so, and ask if you can secure a cheaper fare by changing your flight plans.

- You can also save on airfares by keeping an eye out in local newspapers for **promotional specials** or **fare wars,** when airlines lower prices on their most popular routes.

- Search **the Internet** for cheap fares (see "Planning Your Trip Online," earlier in the chapter).

- **Consolidators,** also known as bucket shops, are great sources for international tickets, although they usually can't beat the Internet on fares within North America. Start by looking in Sunday newspaper travel sections; U.S. travelers should focus on the *New York Times, Los Angeles Times,* and *Miami Herald. Beware:* Bucket shop tickets are usually nonrefundable or rigged with stiff cancellation penalties, often as high as 50% to 75% of the ticket price, and some put you on charter airlines with questionable safety records.

  Several reliable consolidators are worldwide and available on the Net. **STA Travel** is now the world's leader in student travel, thanks to their purchase of Council Travel. It also offers good fares for travelers of all ages. **Flights.com** (© 800/TRAV-800; www.flights.com) started in Europe and has excellent fares worldwide, but particularly to that continent. It also has "local" websites in 12 countries. **FlyCheap** (© 800/FLY-CHEAP; www.1800flycheap.com) is owned by package-holiday megalith MyTravel and so has especially good access to fares for

sunny destinations. **Air Tickets Direct** (© **800/778-3447;**
www.airticketsdirect.com) is based in Montreal and leverages
the currently weak Canadian dollar for low fares; it'll also book
trips to places that U.S. travel agents won't touch, such as
Cuba.

- Join **frequent-flier clubs.** Accrue enough miles, and you'll be
  rewarded with free flights and elite status. You don't need to fly
  to build frequent-flier miles—**frequent flier credit cards** can
  provide thousands of miles for doing your everyday shopping.
- For many more tips about air travel, including a rundown
  of the major frequent-flier credit cards, pick up a copy of
  Frommer's Fly Safe, Fly Smart (Wiley Publishing, Inc.).

BY CRUISE SHIP

Here's a brief rundown of some of the major cruise lines that serve
the Caribbean. For more detailed information, pick up a copy of
Frommer's Caribbean Cruises & Ports of Call.

BOOKING A CRUISE

If you've developed a relationship with a favorite travel agency, then
by all means, leave the details to the tried-and-true specialists. Many
agents will propose a package deal that includes airfare to your port
of embarkation. It's possible to purchase your air ticket on your own
and book your cruise ticket separately, but in most cases you'll save
big bucks by combining the fares into a package deal.

You're also likely to save money—sometimes *lots* of money—by
contacting a specialist who focuses on cruise bookings. He or she
will be able to match you with a cruise line whose style suits you,
and can also steer you toward any special sales or promotions.

Here are some travel agencies to consider: **Cruises, Inc.** (© 800/
854-0500 or 954/958-3700), **Cruise Masters** (© 800/242-9000 or
310/555-2925), **the Cruise Company** (© 800/289-5505 or 402/
339-6800), **Kelly Cruises** (© 800/837-7447 or 630/990-1111),
Hartford Holidays Travel (© 800/828-4813 or 516/746-6670), and
Mann Travel and Cruises (© 800/849-2301 or 704/556-8311).
Cruise lines don't profit if their megaships don't fill up near peak
capacity, so price wars pop up all the time. These companies listed
above are tuned into last-minute sales resulting from the price wars.

You're likely to sail to the Cayman Islands from Miami, which has
become the cruise capital of the world. Other departure ports in
Florida include Port Everglades (at Fort Lauderdale), Port Canaveral,
and Tampa.

CRUISE LINES

- **Carnival Cruise Lines** (© 800/327-9501 or 305/599-2200; www.carnival.com): Offering affordable vacations on some of the biggest and most vividly decorated ships afloat, Carnival is the brashest and most successful mass-market cruise line in the world. More than 17 of its vessels depart for the Caribbean from Miami, Tampa, New Orleans, Port Canaveral, and San Juan (including *Paradise,* one of the very few totally nonsmoking ships in the world), and five of them specialize in 7-day or longer tours that feature stopovers at selected ports throughout the eastern, western, and southern Caribbean, including Grand Cayman; one 4-day cruise also calls at Grand Cayman. The cruises offer good value and feature nonstop activities, plus lots of brightly colored drinks. Passengers tend to be young at heart, ready to party, and keyed up for nonstop, round-the-clock fun. While it's one of the best lines to choose if you're single, Carnival's ships certainly aren't overrun by singles—families (who appreciate the well-run children's programs) and couples are definitely in the majority. The average onboard age is a relatively youthful 42. Note that cruisers under age 21 cannot sail unless accompanied by an adult over 25.

- **Celebrity Cruises** (© 800/327-6700 or 305/539-6000; www.celebritycruises.com): Celebrity maintains nine newly built, stylish, medium to large ships offering cruises that last between 7 and 14 nights and visit ports such as Key West, San Juan, Grand Cayman, St. Thomas, Ocho Rios, Antigua, and Cozumel, Mexico, to name a few (three ships will visit Grand Cayman in 2004). The ships themselves are works of art—gorgeously designed, and featuring clean lines and modern materials—and the onboard atmosphere is classy without being at all stuffy. Accommodations are roomy and well equipped, cuisine is the most refined of any of its competitors, and service is impeccable. The ships also feature beautiful spas. Plus, cruises are competitively priced (though you should watch out for the pricey extras). Clients choose Celebrity because it offers a well-balanced cruise, with lots of activities and a glamorous, exciting atmosphere that's both refined (think champagne and cozy lounges) and fun (think "dress your husband up in women's clothes" contests). Most passengers are couples in their mid-30s and up (the average age in 2002 was 49), with decent numbers of honeymooners and couples celebrating anniversaries, as well as families with children in summer and during the holidays.

- **Costa Cruise Lines** (© **800/462-6782** or 305/358-7325; www.costacruises.com): Costa sails the 2,112-passenger *CostaAtlantica* and the 1,928-passenger *CostaVictoria* on western and eastern Caribbean cruises on alternate weeks, departing from Fort Lauderdale. Ports of call during the eastern Caribbean itineraries include stopovers in San Juan, St. Thomas, and Nassau. Itineraries through the western Caribbean include stopovers at Grand Cayman, Ocho Rios or Montego Bay (Jamaica), Key West, and Cozumel. There's an Italian flavor and lots of Italian design on board here, and an atmosphere of relaxed indulgence. The food is mediocre. Costa attracts passengers of all ages who want lots of action and who deliberately avoid all-American megaships like those of Carnival. Italian-Americans are heavily represented aboard every Caribbean cruise, and in general passengers like to participate and have a good time. In the Caribbean, Costa appeals to retirees and young couples alike, although there are more passengers over 50 than under. Typically you won't see more than 40 or 50 kids on any one cruise except during holidays such as Christmas and spring break. While about 80% to 90% of passengers are from North America, there's usually a healthy percentage from Europe and South America as well.
- **Holland America Line–Westours** (© **800/426-0327** or 206/281-3535; www.hollandamerica.com): Holland America offers the most old-world-style cruise experience of the mainstream lines, aboard a fleet of respectably hefty and good-looking ships. The cruise line offers solid value, with few jolts or surprises, and attracts a solid, well-grounded clientele of primarily older travelers (so late-night revelers and serious partiers might want to book cruises on other lines, such as Carnival). Seven- and 10- to 14-day cruises stop at deep-water mainstream ports throughout the Caribbean, including Key West, Grand Cayman, St. Martin, St. Lucia, Curaçao, Barbados, and St. Thomas (10 cruises will visit Grand Cayman in 2004). Although younger faces are starting to pepper the mix, most HAL passengers still tend to be low-key, fairly sedentary 55-plus North American couples. Only about 30 or 40 people per cruise will be traveling solo.

GETTING INTO TOWN FROM THE CRUISE-SHIP TERMINAL

Cruise ships anchor off George Town and then ferry passengers to the terminals along Harbour Drive, which is in the heart of the shopping and sightseeing attractions. The waters are often choppy here, so anticipate a rough ride. The Grand Cayman tourist office dispenses information from a little kiosk at the pier when cruise ships arrive. Taxis line up to meet arriving passengers. If you need to call home, there's a phone center accepting credit cards right nearby along Shedden Road.

13 Package Deals

Before you start your search for the lowest airfare, you may want to consider booking your flight as part of a travel package. Package tours are not the same thing as escorted tours. Package tours are simply a way to buy the airfare, accommodations, and other elements of your trip (such as car rentals, airport transfers, and sometimes even activities) at the same time and often at discounted prices—kind of like one-stop shopping. In most cases, a package to the Cayman Islands will include airfare, hotel, and transportation to and from the airport—and it'll cost you less than just the hotel alone if you booked it yourself. Packages are sold in bulk to tour operators—who resell them to the public at a cost that usually undercuts standard rates. A package deal might not be for you if you want to stay in a more intimate inn or guesthouse, but if you like resorts, read on.

Many land-and-sea packages include meals, and you might find yourself locked into eating in your hotel dining room every night if your meals are prepaid. If you're seeking a more varied dining experience, avoid **AP (American Plan),** which means full board, and opt for **MAP (Modified American Plan),** meaning breakfast and either lunch or dinner at your hotel.

One good source of package deals is the airlines themselves. Most major airlines offer air/land packages, including **American Airlines Vacations** (℃ 800/321-2121; www.aavacations.com), **Delta Vacations** (℃ 800/221-6666; www.deltavacations.com), **Continental Airlines Vacations** (℃ 800/301-3800; www.coolvacations.com), and **United Vacations** (℃ 888/854-3899; www.unitedvacations. com). Several big **online travel agencies**—Expedia, Travelocity, Orbitz, Site59, and Lastminute.com—also do a brisk business in packages. If you're unsure about the pedigree of a smaller packager, check with the Better Business Bureau in the city where the company is based, or go online at www.bbb.org. If a packager won't tell you where it's based, don't fly with them.

Just-A-Vacation Inc. (✆ **301/559-0510;** www.justavacation. net) and Travelocity also specialize in good deals for resorts in the Cayman Islands.

Travel packages are also listed in the travel section of your local Sunday newspaper. Or check ads in the national travel magazines such as *Arthur Frommer's Budget Travel Magazine, Travel & Leisure, National Geographic Traveler,* and *Condé Nast Traveler.*

The biggest hotel chains and resorts also offer package deals. If you already know where you want to stay, call the resort itself and ask if it offers land/air packages.

To save time comparing the prices and value of all the package tours out there, contact **TourScan Inc.** (✆ **800/962-2080** or 203/655-8091; www.tourscan.com). Every season, the company computerizes the contents of travel brochures that contain about 10,000 different vacations at 1,600 hotels in the Caribbean. TourScan selects the best-value vacation at each hotel and condo. Two catalogs are printed each year, which list a choice of hotels. The price of a catalog ($4) is credited toward any TourScan vacation.

Package tours can vary by leaps and bounds. Some offer a better class of hotels than others. Some offer the same hotels for lower prices. Some offer flights on scheduled airlines, while others book charters. Some limit your choice of accommodations and travel days. You are often required to make a large payment up front. On the plus side, packages can save you money, offering group prices but allowing for independent travel. Some even let you to add on a few guided excursions or escorted day trips (also at prices lower than if you booked them yourself) without booking an entirely escorted tour.

Before you invest in a package tour, get some answers. Ask about the **accommodations choices** and prices for each. Then look up the hotels' reviews in a Frommer's guide and check their rates for your specific dates of travel online. You'll also want to find out what **type of room** you get. If you need a certain type of room, ask for it; don't take whatever is thrown your way. Request a nonsmoking room, a quiet room, a room with a view, or whatever you fancy.

Finally, look for **hidden expenses.** Ask whether airport departure fees and taxes, for example, are included in the total cost.

Tips **Close Encounter of the Bird Kind**

Focus On Nature Package Tours, Inc., P.O. Box 9021, Wilmington, DE 19809 (© **800/721-9986** or 302/529-1876; www.focusonnature.com) arranges bird-watching and nature tours in the Cayman Islands for those who want close encounters with such birds as the West Indian whistling duck and the rose-throated parrot.

---

14 Getting Around Grand Cayman

This section includes information on getting around Grand Cayman, the largest island in the Grand Cayman Islands. For information on getting around on Little Cayman and Cayman Brac, see p. 184 and p. 164, respectively.

BY RENTAL CAR

Is it necessary to rent a car on Grand Cayman? It depends. If you want to explore the island, you can do so on a far less expensive organized tour. Many visitors prefer to settle into their hotels at Seven Mile Beach for the duration of their visit, perhaps taking one tour or venturing into George Town for a shopping expedition. If you fall into this category, you can easily depend on buses or taxis and save yourself the hassle and expense of a renting a car. However, if you wish to explore the island and don't want to depend on taxis, a rental car is an excellent idea.

The British tradition of *driving on the left* is followed in the Cayman Islands. It is mandatory to have a driving permit if you rent a car. All car-rental companies are required by law to issue this permit and collect the fee of US$7.50. Permits, which are valid for 6 months, are also issued at the George Town Police Station on Elgin Avenue (© **345/949-4222**).

The speed limit is 48kmph (30 mph) in built-up areas such as George Town and along Seven Mile Beach, or 64kmph (40 mph) on most other island roads. The highest speed limit on the island is in the East End, where posted speeds go up to 81kmph (50 mph).

Prices of car rentals depend on the season, with the highest rates charged from mid-December to mid-April. In the off-season, prices are often reduced by around 35%. Collision insurance in the Cayman Islands ranges from US$14.95 to US$16.95 per day, depending on the make of the car. Zero deductible will be another US$5

> **Tips   Renting a Car 101**
>
> All the major car-rental companies maintain kiosks within walking distance of the airport, although some visitors find it easier to take a taxi to their hotel and arrange for their car to be delivered to the hotel.
>
> All major companies suggest that car rentals be reserved while you're still on the mainland—at least 6 to 36 hours in advance. In midwinter, you should reserve days in advance because of heavy demand.
>
> There is definite age "discrimination" in the Cayman Islands. Always check the age requirement with the rental agency before cementing a deal. At Avis you can be 21 years old, but at Hertz, for example, you must be 25. Budget also requires that you be 25 years old and—get this—definitely not beyond 70 years of age.

per day. Most car-rental companies will quote you a reduced rate if you keep the car for a week or more.

Cayman Auto Rental, 135 N. Church St. in George Town (© **345/949-1013**), is one of the best rental companies. A good offer here is a Jeep Wrangler from US$70 per day. Another good is choice is **Budget Rent-a-Car** (© **345/949-5605**), which lies right across the street from the airport. A typical rental here is a Jeep Suzuki from US$40 a day. Another reliable firm is **Cico Avis Rent-a-Car** (© **345/949-2468**), also found at the airport, with Jeep Wranglers costing from US$75 per day and subcompact vehicles going from US$36 a day. **Coconut Car Rentals** (© **345/949-4377**) has four locations: at the airport; at the Dittman Building on Fort Street in George Town; at 480 Crewe Rd.; and at Coconut Place at Seven Mile Beach. It rents a variety of cars and jeeps, with Suzuki Altos starting at US$38 per day and Nissan Sentras starting at US$49 a day. **Economy Car Rental,** with a location on Airport Road and also at the Falls, West Bay Road (© **345/959-9550**), offers a fleet of cars, including Hyundais, costing from US$40 per day. **Sunshine Car Rentals,** Seven Mile Shops, Seven Mile Beach (© **345/949-3858**), charges from US$45 for an economy car.

BY TAXI

Cabs, with drivers who are generally informative and friendly, are plentiful at the airport and in front of the cruise-ship terminals in

George Town. You'll also find them parked in front of the major resorts along Seven Mile Beach. For the most part, drivers are among the most honest you are likely to find in the Caribbean. Shirtless, wet, or damp passengers are frowned upon, and may not be taken at all. If you're going out at night, a member of the staff at your resort will often call a taxi for you.

Many cabs can be hired for an independent tour of the island (p. 140).

The government sets cab prices and regulates the cabbies, so every driver should have the official government rate sheet. Inform the driver where you're heading and agree on the fare before getting into the cab. You may want to ask to see the official rate sheet. If you're paying in U.S. dollars, don't expect the driver to accept denominations larger than $20. Tipping cabbies between 15% and 20% is the local custom.

Holiday Service (© 345/945-4491) and **Websters** (© 345/ 947-1718) are the most convenient taxi companies, since they operate 7 days a week, 24 hours a day. The island's major taxi companies include **Burtons Taxi Service** (© 345/947-1173) and **A.A. Transportation** (© 345/949-7222). If you're going to be out late, you'll have to make advance arrangements with either of these companies for pickup. Contact the companies from Monday to Friday from 7am to 11pm or Saturday from 7am to 6pm, to arrange late-night pickup times. Limited service is offered by **River Tours & Taxi** (© 345/ 916-1855), which has cabs running daily from 7am to 6pm.

BY BUS

Buses are mainly used by islanders going to and from work, although visitors who have endless patience and plenty of time to get around also take advantage of them. Bus service was first launched in 1998, with a new terminal installed adjacent to the Public Library on Edward Street in the center of George Town. This terminal serves as the dispatch point for buses to all districts. In all, 38 minibuses serve eight routes. There is daily service from 6am to midnight, with most fares costing CI$1.50 to CI$2 (US$1.89–US$2.50).

Buses serve all the main points on the island, including Seven Mile Beach, West Bay, Bodden Town, East End, and North Side. There is no central number to call, since most of these buses are independently operated. However, for complaints and feedback, you can call © 345/945-5100, although you'll often hear only a recording.

BY FERRY

Rum Pointer, a ferry (© **345/947-9203**), traverses North Sound between the Hyatt Regency dock on the east side of Seven Mile Beach and Rum Point in the far northwestern corridor. This is an open-sided, two-deck boat carrying 150 passengers. The trip takes 45 minutes. Be warned that this is not a luxury cruise: There are no toilets, no drinks sold, and no shade. It's advised that you carry a bottle of water onboard on a hot day. Fares are US$8 each way and US$15 round-trip, with children 6 to 11 paying half fares and children 5 and under traveling free. Tickets are on sale at the Hyatt dock. Ferry schedules change depending on the season. The ferry usually departs from the Hyatt Regency Canal dock at 10am, noon, and 4pm Monday through Thursday, and 10am, noon, and 6pm Friday through Sunday. The return times from Rum Point are 11am, 3pm, and 6:30pm Monday through Thursday, and 11am, 3:30pm, and 9:15pm Friday and weekends.

BY BIKE OR SCOOTER

Grand Cayman is one of the best islands in the Caribbean for biking, as its main arteries are relatively flat, decently paved, rather wide, and properly signposted. If you stick to the coastal route, you'll experience few difficulties except for unexpected downpours. Side roads, however, can be difficult, especially if you're attempting to venture a bit into the interior. You should avoid the morning and evening rush hours at George Town and along Seven Mile Beach if possible.

In spite of Grand Cayman's reputation for safety, bicycle theft is a problem. If you're going to leave your bike unguarded, perhaps while going for a swim on a beach, make sure that it's secured, just as you would in any urban area.

The most reliable independent outfitter for bike and scooter rentals is **Cayman Cycle Rentals,** Coconut Place, West Bay Road (© **345/945-4021**), which is open daily from 9am to 5pm, offering a fleet of scooters, 10-speed bikes, and mountain bikes. They also provide locks and maps. Some of the bike rentals have baskets. Bikes cost US$15 per day, and scooters are US$30 a day. There is no reduction by the week. A US$100 deposit is required for bikes and a US$200 deposit is required for a scooter. If you don't have a credit card, a cash deposit of US$500 is required for both bikes and scooters. Insurance (which is optional) costs another US$26 per day.

Before arranging a bike rental at Cayman Cycle Rentals, check with your hotel to see if they rent bikes—many of them do.

Cayman law requires that all scooter riders wear a helmet.

15 Tips on Accommodations

WATCH OUT FOR THOSE EXTRAS!

The government of the Cayman Islands imposes a 10% surcharge on all hotel room rentals, which is included in the price.

Hotels also charge a room tax. Sometimes the room tax depends on the quality of the hotel—it might be relatively low for a guest-house but steeper for a first-class resort. When booking a room, make sure you understand whether the price you've been quoted includes the room tax (which is different from the 10% hotel room surcharge), so that you avoid an unpleasant surprise when it comes time to pay the bill.

Furthermore, most hotels routinely add 10% to 12% for "service," even if you didn't see much evidence of it. That means that with tax and service, some bills are 17% or even 25% higher than the price that was originally quoted to you! Naturally, you need to determine just how much the hotel, guesthouse, or inn plans to add to your bill at the end of your stay, and whether it's included in the initial price.

That's not all. Some hotels slip in little hidden extras that mount quickly. For example, it's common for many places to quote rates that include a continental breakfast. Should you prefer ham and eggs, however, you will pay extra charges. If you request special privileges, like extra towels for the beach, beach chairs, or laundry done in a hurry, surcharges may mount. It pays to watch those extras and to ask questions before you commit.

TYPES OF ACCOMMODATIONS

HOTELS & RESORTS   Many budget travelers assume they can't afford the big hotels and resorts. But there are so many packages out there and such frequent sales that even in winter you might be pleasantly surprised.

The rates given in this book are "rack rates"—that is, the officially posted rate that you'd be given if you just walked in off the street. Almost everyone ends up paying less than the rack rate through packages, bargaining, and discounts. Think of the rates in this book as guidelines to help you comparison shop.

Some hotels are often quite flexible about their rates, and many offer discounts and upgrades whenever they have a big block of rooms to fill and few reservations. The smaller hotels and inns are not as likely to be generous with discounts, much less upgrades. A good travel agent may know which hotels have reduced their rates and can help you save serious money.

CONDOS, VILLAS & COTTAGES   Particularly if you're traveling with your family or a group of friends, a "housekeeping holiday"
can be one of the least expensive ways to vacation in the Caymans.
And if you like privacy and independence, it's a good way to go.
Accommodations with kitchens are available on all the islands.
Some are individual cottages, others are condo complexes with swimming pools, and some are private homes that owners rent out while
they're away. Many (though not all) places include maid service and
fresh linens as well.

In the simpler rentals, you will need to do your own cooking and
laundry and, in a few cases, your own housekeeping. This may not
be your idea of a good time in the sun, but it saves money— a lot of
money. The savings, especially for a family of three to six people, or
two or three couples, can range from 50% to 60% of what a hotel
would cost. Groceries are sometimes priced 35% to 60% higher
than on the U.S. mainland, as nearly all foodstuffs have to be
imported, but even so, preparing your own food will be a lot
cheaper than taking all your meals at restaurants.

Most villas, condos, and cottages have a staff, or at least a maid
who comes in a few days a week, and they also provide the essen-
tials, including linens and housewares. Condos usually come with a
reception desk and are often comparable to a suite in a big resort
hotel. Nearly all condo and villa complexes have pools (some more
than one). Like condos, villas range widely in price and may begin
at $700 per week for a modest one and go over $50,000 a week for
a luxurious one.

There are many lavish private homes for rent. You'll spend a lot
of money, but you'll be staying in the lap of luxury in a prime beachfront setting, usually with maid service (though you may need to
arrange this in advance).

You'll have to approach all these rental properties with a certain
sense of independence. There may or may not be a front desk to
answer your questions, and you will most likely have to plan your
own watersports. Always ask when you book.

Tips Keep Those Hotel Bills Down

True budget travelers will rent an apartment or condo
(shared with friends or families), so they can cut costs by
cooking their own meals. Divers will want to find hotels or
small resorts that include a half day's dive in their tariffs.

Make your reservations well in advance. We've listed a few agencies that rent condos, villas, and private homes throughout the Caymans. You can ask each island's tourist office for suggestions on additional rental agencies.

- **Cayman Villas,** 177 Owen Roberts Dr., Grand Cayman (*€* 800/235-5888 in the U.S., or 345/945-1444; www.cayman villas.com), is a booking agency that specializes in renting more than 100 private beachfront homes and condos on all three islands. The properties range from cozy studio cottages to large villas that have as many as five to seven bedrooms. Some properties have the added luxury of a private pool or a maid, and sometimes even a cook. Most of the rentals have kitchenettes, Internet access, a washer and dryer, and kitchenware. The range is from budget to deluxe, so most pocketbooks can be accommodated. Rentals range from $100 to $2,000 per night.
- **Villas of Distinction** (*€* 800/289-0900 in the U.S., or 914/273-3331;www.villasofdistinction.com) offers upscale private villas with one to six bedrooms and a pool. Accommodations offered range from townhouses to beachfront villas, and all are beautifully furnished.
- **Hideaways International** (*€* 888/843-4433 in the U.S., or 603/430-4433; fax 603/430-4444; www.hideaways.com) publishes *Hideaways Guide,* a pictorial directory of home rentals throughout the world, including the Cayman Islands. Rentals range from cottages to staffed villas. Hideaways International can also help you charter yachts, and arrange cruises, flights, car rentals, and hotel reservations. Annual membership is $145.

 FAST FACTS: The Cayman Islands

American Express You can find an American Express office at **Cayman Travel Services,** Shedden Road, Elizabethan Square, George Town (*€* **345/949-8755**).

Area Codes The area code for all of the Cayman Islands is **345.**

Business Hours Normally, banks are open Monday through Thursday from 9am to 2:30pm, and Friday from 9am to 1pm and 2:30 to 4:30pm. Most shops are open Monday to Saturday from 9am to 5pm, but hours can vary greatly.

Car Rentals See "Getting Around Grand Cayman," earlier in this chapter.

Currency See "Money" on p. 17.

Driving Rules See "Getting Around Grand Cayman," earlier in this chapter.

Drugstores If you're flying on to Little Cayman or Cayman Brac, don't depend on local outlets there to have the drugs or medication you need. Stock up before you go. On Grand Cayman, the most convenient pharmacies are **Strand Pharmacy,** the Strand Shopping Centre on West Bay Road, Seven Mile Beach (© **345/945-7759**), open Monday to Saturday 7am to 10pm and Sunday 9am to 6pm; **Cayman Drug,** Kirk Freeport Centre, George Town (© **345/949-2597**), open Monday to Friday 8:30am to 5:30pm and Saturday 8:30am to 4:30pm; and **Island Pharmacy,** West Shore Centre, West Bay Road, Seven Mile Beach (© **345/949-8987**), open Monday to Saturday 9am to 7pm and Sunday 10am to 6pm.

Electricity Electricity on the Cayman Islands is 110-volt AC (60 cycles), so U.S. and Canadian appliances will not need adapters or transformers, but appliances from Europe, Australia, or New Zealand will require adapters and transformers.

Embassies & Consulates No nations maintain an embassy or consulate in the Cayman Islands.

Emergencies On Grand Cayman, dial © **555** for an ambulance; © **345/949-0241** for an Air Ambulance; and © **911** for police, fire, or medical emergency. See p. 165 for emergency numbers on Cayman Brac, and p. 185 for emergency numbers on Little Cayman.

Etiquette & Customs You should pay attention to dress codes in the Cayman Islands, as it still remains a "proper" British crown colony, and its residents are often conservative in dress and manners. Avoid wearing bathing suits or scanty beach wear outside a beach area or cruise ship. Cover up in public areas, especially when walking and sightseeing on the streets of George Town. There are no nude beaches, and public nudity, including topless bathing, is strictly prohibited by law. Visitors will want to wear smart casual tropical resort wear at most restaurants. When attending church, "Sunday dress" is appropriate—that is, no shorts and T-shirts. Men don't have to wear ties, however. There are no special language issues except the avoidance of profanity in public, which is extremely frowned upon.

Hospitals On Grand Cayman, **George Town Hospital** (© 345/949-8600) lies south of George Town on Hospital Road (south of Smith Road). For hospitals and clinics on Cayman Brac and Little Cayman, see p. 165 and p. 185, respectively.

Internet Access Most large resorts and hotels have Internet access. You can also access the Internet at **Café del Sol/the Cyberloft** (p. 37).

Language English is the official language of the islands.

Liquor Laws Beer, wine, and liquor are sold at most grocery and convenience stores Monday to Saturday. It is legal to have an open container on the beach.

Lost & Found Be sure to tell all of your credit card companies the minute you discover your wallet has been lost or stolen and file a report at the nearest police precinct. Your credit card company or insurer may require a police report number or record of the loss. Most credit card companies have an emergency toll-free number to call if your card is lost or stolen; they may be able to wire you a cash advance immediately or deliver an emergency credit card in a day or two. Visa's emergency number is © **800/847-2911** or 410/581-9994. American Express cardholders and traveler's check holders should call © **800/221-7282.** MasterCard holders should call © **800/307-7309** or 636/722-7111. For other credit cards, call the toll-free number directory at © **800/555-1212.**

If you need emergency cash over the weekend when all banks and American Express offices are closed, you can have money wired to you via **Western Union** (© **800/325-6000;** www.westernunion.com).

Identity theft or fraud are potential complications of losing your wallet, especially if you've lost your driver's license along with your cash and credit cards. Notify the major credit-reporting bureaus immediately; placing a fraud alert on your records may protect you against liability for criminal activity. The three major U.S. credit-reporting agencies are **Equifax** (© **800/766-0008;** www.equifax.com), **Experian** (© **888/397-3742;** www.experian.com), and **TransUnion** (© **800/680-7289;** www.transunion.com). Finally, if you've lost all forms of photo ID, call your airline and explain the situation; they might allow you to board the plane if you have a copy of your passport or birth certificate and a copy of the police report you've filed.

Mail Most mail takes from 2 to 7 days, if air mailed, to reach points between the Cayman Islands and the U.S. mainland. The Cayman Islands don't use postal or zip codes. The main post office in George Town lies at Edward Street and Carnidal Avenue (© **345/949-2474**), between the Royal Bank of Canada and the Bank of Nova Scotia. Even if you don't have a letter to mail, you may want to come here to purchase the Cayman Island's beautiful stamps at the on-site philatelic bureau, open Monday to Friday 8:30am to 5:30pm and Saturday 8:30am to 1pm. For information on post offices on Cayman Brac and Little Cayman, see p. 166 and p. 186, respectively.

A postcard to the United States costs CI20¢ (US25¢). An airmail letter to the U.S. costs CI30¢ (US38¢) per half ounce. Rates to Europe are CI25¢ (US31¢) for a postcard and CI40¢ (US50¢) per half ounce for air-mail letters.

Newspapers & Magazines Published daily, the *Caymanian Compass* is the most popular newspaper on Grand Cayman island. The Friday edition is especially helpful because it lists current and upcoming entertainment events. Rival papers include *New Caymanian,* published every Friday, and *Cayman Net News,* published Tuesday and Thursday. Available at most hotels, *What's Hot* is a free monthly magazine geared to visitors. Copies of the *Miami Herald* and the *International Herald Tribune* are available at the big resorts and at most major newsstands in George Town.

Passports **For residents of the United States:** Whether you're applying in person or by mail, you can download passport applications from the U.S. State Department website at **http:// travel.state.gov**. For general information, call the **National Passport Agency** (© **202/647-0518**). To find your regional passport office, either check the U.S. State Department website or call the **National Passport Information Center** (© **900/225-5674**); the fee is US55¢ per minute for automated information and US$1.50 per minute for operator-assisted calls.

For residents of Canada: Passport applications are available at travel agencies throughout Canada or from the central **Passport Office,** Department of Foreign Affairs and International Trade, Ottawa, ON K1A 0G3 (© **800/567-6868;** www.dfait-maeci.gc.ca/passport).

For residents of the United Kingdom: To pick up an application for a standard 10-year passport (5-year passport for children under 16), visit your nearest passport office, major post office, or travel agency, or contact the **United Kingdom Passport Service** at ⓒ **0870/521-0410** or search its website at www.ukpa.gov.uk.

For residents of Ireland: You can apply for a 10-year passport at the **Passport Office,** Setanta Centre, Molesworth Street, Dublin 2 (ⓒ **01/671-1633;** www.irlgov.ie/iveagh). Those under age 18 and over 65 must apply for a €12 3-year passport. You can also apply at 1A South Mall, Cork (ⓒ **021/272-525**) or at most main post offices.

For residents of Australia: You can pick up an application from your local post office or any branch of Passports Australia, but you must schedule an interview at the passport office to present your application materials. Call the **Australian Passport Information Service** at ⓒ **131-232,** or visit the government website at www.passports.gov.au.

For residents of New Zealand: You can pick up a passport application at any New Zealand Passports Office or download it from their website. Contact the **Passports Office** at ⓒ **0800/ 225-050** in New Zealand or 04/474-8100, or log on to www. passports.govt.nz.

Police   Call ⓒ **911** if you need the police.

Restrooms   There are public restrooms along Seven Mile Beach. Otherwise, public facilities are few and far between. Visitors usually use the facilities of the resorts, although you should technically be a guest or customer (you can always purchase a soft drink or whatever).

Radio   Radio stations in the Cayman Islands mostly play hip music that's popular in Florida. **Radio Z99** (99 on the FM dial), plays Caribbean, pop, easy-listening, and lite rock and roll. **Vibe FM** (98.5 on the FM dial) plays reggae, island/Caribbean, and soul music. **Country Rooster** (101 on the FM dial) plays U.S.-style country-western music.

Safety   See "Health & Safety," earlier in this chapter.

Smoking   Smoking is not regulated as carefully in the Cayman Islands as it is in certain cities of the U.S. However, most hotels, at least the big ones, set aside some rooms for nonsmokers. Restaurants often lack sections set aside for nonsmokers. When being shown to a table, inform the captain or waiter that you want a table as far away from the smoke as possible.

Taxes A government tourist tax of 10% is added to your hotel bill. A departure tax of CI$10 (US$13) is collected when you leave the Caymans, and this tax is included in your plane fare. There is no tax on goods and services.

Telephone To call the Cayman Islands from the States or Canada, dial **1**, then the **345** area code, and the local number. Once you're on the island, to charge a long-distance call to a calling card, here are some access numbers: **AT&T** at ℭ **800/225-5288**; **Sprint** at ℭ **800/877-4646**; and **MCI** at ℭ **800/888-8000**. Call ℭ **411** for directory assistance in the Cayman Islands. Dial ℭ **0** for internal and external operator assistance. Telephone, fax, and telex are offered by **Cable & Wireless** (ℭ **345/949-7800**) at Anderson Square in George Town.

Television The four local television stations are privately run. Most islanders tune in to **CITN**, with its 24-hour transmission of Caribbean news, international events, and entertainment. An affiliate, **CTS**, is aimed at tourists, and repeatedly runs an unhelpful 45-minute newsreel of puffed up promotional material on attractions. The other two channels, **CCT** and **CATN/TV-30**, broadcast religious programs. The larger resorts have satellite or cable TV, offering a wide range of channels.

Time Zone U.S. Eastern Standard Time is in effect year-round; daylight saving time is not observed.

Useful Phone Numbers **U.S. Dept. of State Travel Advisory:** ℭ 202/647-5225 (manned 24 hr.); **U.S. Passport Agency:** ℭ 202/647-0518; **U.S. Centers for Disease Control International Traveler's Hotline:** ℭ 404/332-4559.

Water The water in the Cayman Islands is, for the most part, safe to drink. Two desalination plants on Grand Cayman supply good quality purified tap water to the entire West End, including Seven Mile Beach. If you can determine that you're drinking desalinated water, then it's safe to drink. Just ask. Cayman Brac's desalination plant also supplies purified water to residents, but Little Cayman establishments have their own water systems. If your hotel on Little Cayman relies on rainwater collected in cisterns, it's best to drink only bottled water. When checking into hotels, ask about the water source. Regardless of how fresh the water might appear, never take a drink from a river, spring, or stream.

3

Where to Stay on Grand Cayman

The good news is that the Cayman Islands have some of the finest and most elegant resorts in the Caribbean, opening onto one of the grandest strips of sand in the entire Caribbean Basin.

Now for the bad news: Winter vacations in the Caymans can be pricey affairs. The cost of living here is about 20% higher than in the United States. Because so much food has to be imported from the U.S. mainland, restaurant tabs are second only to the high-priced French islands such as St. Barts and Martinique. But you can make a trip here affordable. The key is to plan in advance and to visit the islands between mid-April and mid-December, when room rates are 20% to 40% lower than they are in winter. In addition, you might consider staying in one of several low-cost or moderately priced lodgings that have opened in recent years. Many of these accommodations include facilities for cooking simple meals. Depending on where you come from, however, so-called moderate or inexpensive hotels in the Cayman Islands might be judged "super-expensive" in other parts of the world, including the United States.

Nearly all the hotels are lined up along Seven Mile Beach. Hotels, unlike many Caymanian restaurants, generally quote prices in U.S. dollars. **So, all prices in this chapter are quoted in U.S. dollars.** When choosing a hotel, keep in mind that the quoted rates do not include the 10% government tax and the 10% hotel service tax.

Consider booking a package tour to make expensive resorts more affordable. See the section "Package Deals" in chapter 2 before you book.

Important: Before you look through this chapter, see our "Tips on Accommodations" in chapter 2 for descriptions of various types of accommodations and tips on saving money.

1 Hotels & Resorts

VERY EXPENSIVE

Hyatt Regency Grand Cayman ✶✶✶   This $80 million resort is the best managed, most luxurious, and most stylish hotel in the Cayman Islands, lying on a lovely stretch of Seven Mile Beach. Located 3.2km (2 miles) north of George Town, the hotel is a major component of the 36 hectare (90-acre) Britannia Resort community, which includes the Britannia Golf Course. The hotel has beautifully landscaped grounds, with dozens of Doric arcades festooned with flowering vines that cascade around reflecting pools and comfortable teakwood settees. Low-rise buildings surround a large, landscaped courtyard that contains gardens, waterfalls, and the main swimming pool.

The moderately sized rooms are luxurious and have private verandas. Each has a king-size bed or two double beds and a spacious bathroom with an Italian marble tub. Two buildings and 44 rooms are devoted to the exclusive Regency Club, where luxury services, such as speedy check-in, are offered. The hotel also offers one- and two-bedroom luxury villas along the Britannia Golf Course or waterway. The villas have their own pool, whirlpool, laundry room, cabana, and patio area.

The Hyatt's many restaurants and bars offer the best hotel food and drink on the island. The Hyatt also offers the most complete watersports facilities and programs in the Caymans, with a Beach Club on the sands and the excellent Red Sail Sports marina offering all kinds of watersports equipment and programs, from sailing to diving.

West Bay Rd. (P.O. Box 1588), Grand Cayman, B.W.I. ℭ **800/233-1234** in the U.S., or 345/949-1234. Fax 345/949-8528. www.hyatt.com. 289 units, 85 villas. Winter $500–$650 double, $585 1-bedroom villa, $755 2-bedroom villa; off-season $220–$285 double, $295 1-bedroom villa, $385 2-bedroom villa. Ask about packages. AE, DC, DISC, MC, V. **Amenities:** 6 restaurants; 4 bars; 6 outdoor pools (1 with swim-up bar); golf; tennis courts (lit for night play); health club; spa; 4 Jacuzzis; extensive watersports equipment; concierge; car-rental desk; business center; shopping arcade; limited room service (6:30am–midnight); babysitting; laundry service. *In room:* A/C, TV, dataport, minibar, coffeemaker, hair dryer, iron, safe.

Westin Casuarina Resort ✶✶✶   The Hyatt has the edge as the best hotel in the Caymans, but this resort runs a close second. Though the Hyatt offers more facilities, the beachfront at the Westin is larger than the Hyatt's beachfront (and much larger than the erosion-prone beach at the Marriott). The Westin lies right on the sands of Seven Mile Beach, with acres of landscaped grounds, a beautiful swimming pool, and lots of sports facilities. Visually, the resort is stylish and pulled-together—a postmodern colonial Caribbean design of cool, coral-limestone blocks and pale turquoise trim. The bedrooms are in five-story wings; most have French doors leading onto balconies. Units are a bit small for such a luxury hotel but are well equipped with quality mattresses and bed linens. Bathrooms are very spacious, with oversize marble tubs. The best rooms have ocean views; the "island view" units look out on the parking lot and main highway, so ask about the view when you reserve. Wheelchair-accessible rooms are available.

The Westin boasts one of the largest pools and poolside decks (450 sq. m/5,000 sq. ft.) in the Caymans, appealingly lined with palm and date trees. Another swimming pool features a waterfall. An 18-hole championship golf course, the Links at Safe Haven, is across the street from the resort. There is an on-site branch of Red Sails Sports, a superb watersports outfitter. The most upscale of the restaurants here is Casa Havana, a dinner-only gourmet restaurant that evokes the glamour of pre-Castro Cuba.

Seven Mile Beach (P.O. Box 30620), Grand Cayman, B.W.I. 🕿 **800/WESTIN-1** in the U.S., or 345/945-3800. Fax 345/949-5825. www.westincasuarina.com. 343 units. Winter $429–$550 double, from $1,050 suite; off-season $236–$297 double, from $735 suite. AE, MC, V. **Amenities:** 3 restaurants; 3 bars; 2 outdoor pools; golf nearby; fitness center; spa; 2 Jacuzzis; watersports outfitter; children's programs; car-rental desk; business center; small shopping arcade; salon; 24-hr. room service; laundry service; same-day dry cleaning. *In room:* A/C, TV, fax, dataport, minibar, coffeemaker, hair dryer, iron, safe.

 ## A Ritzy Preview of Coming Attractions

The Ritz-Carlton chain continues its invasion of the Caribbean with the announcement that it is opening a resort and a series of condos on Grand Cayman by 2004. A nine-hole Greg Norman–designed private golf course and the island's only full-service spa facility will be part of the package. A 366-room resort will be integrated with a 71-unit condo complex. The English colonial architectural and interior design will include white roofs and ivy-covered buildings, all set on 58 tropically landscaped hectares (144 acres) along Seven Mile Beach. Call 🕿 **305/446-0776** for more information.

Accommodations & Dining on Grand Cayman

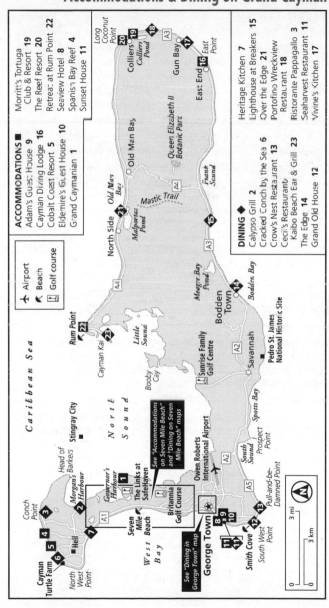

ACCOMMODATIONS ■
Adam's Guest House **9**
Cayman Diving Lodge **16**
Cobalt Coast Resort **5**
Eldemire's Guest House **10**
Grand Caymanian **1**

Morritt's Tortuga Club & Resort **19**
The Reef Resort **20**
Retreat at Rum Point **22**
Seaview Hotel **8**
Spanish Bay Reef **4**
Sunset House **11**

DINING ◆
Calypso Grill **2**
Cracked Conch by the Sea **6**
Crow's Nest Restaurant **13**
Ceci's Restaurant/
Kaibo Beach Bar & Grill **23**
The Edge **14**
Grand Old House **12**

Heritage Kitchen **7**
Lighthouse at Breakers **15**
Over the Edge **21**
Portofino Wreckview Restaurant **18**
Ristorante Pappagallo **3**
Seaharvest Restaurant **11**
Vivine's Kitchen **17**

✈ Airport
⚓ Beach
⛳ Golf course

Caribbean Sea

Head of Barkers

Conch Point

Cayman Turtle Farm

Hell

North West Point

Morgan's Harbour

Governor's Harbour

The Links at SafeHaven

Seven Mile Beach

Britannia Golf Course

West Bay

George Town

Smith Cove

South West Point

South Sound

Prospect Point

Pull-and-be-Damned Point

Owen Roberts International Airport

See "Accommodations on Seven Mile Beach" and "Dining on Seven Mile Beach" maps

See "Dining in George Town" map

Stingray City

North Sound

Booby Cay

Little Sound

Cayman Kai

Rum Point

Sunrise Family Golf Centre

Savannah

Pedro St. James National Historic Site

Spotts Bay

Bodden Town

Bodden Bay

Meagre Bay Pond

Malpartas Pond

Old Man Bay

North Side

Mastic Trail

Queen Elizabeth II Botanic Park

Frank Sound

Long Coconut Point

Colliers Pond

Gun Bay

East End

East Point

Colliers

0   3 mi
0   3 km

63

EXPENSIVE

Holiday Inn ☆ *Kids*   Set near the northern edge of Seven Mile Beach, across West Bay Street from a public beach, this large, five-story hotel is bigger, newer (it opened in November of 2002), and more up-to-date than many of the condos and timeshares nearby. Now firmly entrenched as one of the most recommendable large hotels on Grand Cayman, it has a stone-floored and stone-trimmed lobby, and a pleasing standard-U.S.-hotel design. Bedrooms are larger than you might expect, with big windows, color schemes of turquoise and white, and pale white furniture. Unfortunately, none of the rooms have verandas. Bathrooms with tub or shower are first rate and well maintained. This is a worthy choice for visitors with cars, who can easily drive from the hotel to other, more action-packed sections of West Bay Road.

1590 West Bay Rd., Grand Cayman, B.W.I. ℂ **800/HOLIDAY** in the U.S., or 345/946-4433. Fax 345/946-4434. www.hicaribbean.com. 233 units. Winter $240–$345 double, $530–$930 suite; off-season $160–$190 double, $530 suite. AE, DC, MC, V. **Amenities:** 2 restaurants; 2 bars; outdoor pool; fitness center; laundry service; dry cleaning. *In-room:* A/C, TV, dataport, minibar, fridge, coffeemaker, hair dryer, iron.

Indies Suites ☆ *Kids*   Tucked away behind a Holiday Inn, near the northern terminus of West Bay Road, this is a discreet, quiet, somewhat isolated hotel compound whose rooms are configured as one- or two-bedroom suites with kitchens. Built in 1989, the units surround a long, narrow courtyard that features a gracefully proportioned swimming pool with an ornamental bridge, a gazebo-inspired poolside bar, and carefully manicured palms, flowering vines, and other shrubbery. Because of the relatively low room rates and the fact that each unit features a kitchen (perfect for preparing economical meals), many of the guests are young families with children. Access to the beach, on the opposite side of West Bay Road, requires a 10-minute trek along a macadam-covered access road. Accommodations are comfortable but blandly contemporary, with durable furniture (some of it white-painted rattan). A full range of watersports is available through an on-site branch of Red Sail Sports. Each unit has a bathroom with a shower-tub combination. There's no on-site restaurant, but the restaurant at the Holiday Inn is almost next door, and many restaurants lie within a 10-minute drive.

West Bay Rd. (P.O. Box 2070), Grand Cayman, B.W.I. ℂ **345/945-5025.** Fax 345/945-5024. www.indiessuites.com. 42 units. Winter $299 1-bedroom suite, $360 2-bedroom suite; off-season $180 1-bedroom suite, $215 2-bedroom suite. Rates are based on single or double occupancy. Extra person pays $15 each in any season.

Accommodations on Seven Mile Beach

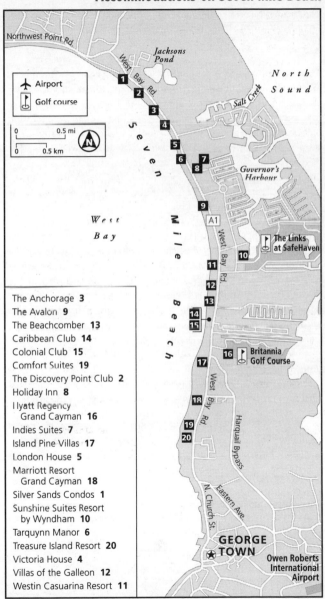

The Anchorage **3**
The Avalon **9**
The Beachcomber **13**
Caribbean Club **14**
Colonial Club **15**
Comfort Suites **19**
The Discovery Point Club **2**
Holiday Inn **8**
Hyatt Regency
  Grand Cayman **16**
Indies Suites **7**
Island Pine Villas **17**
London House **5**
Marriott Resort
  Grand Cayman **18**
Silver Sands Condos **1**
Sunshine Suites Resort
  by Wyndham **10**
Tarquynn Manor **6**
Treasure Island Resort **20**
Victoria House **4**
Villas of the Galleon **12**
Westin Casuarina Resort **11**

Rates include continental breakfast. AE, DC, MC, V. **Amenities:** Poolside bar; outdoor pool; Jacuzzi; watersports outfitter; babysitting; laundry service; coin-op washers and dryers; dry cleaning. *In-room:* A/C, TV, fully equipped kitchen, coffeemaker, iron.

Marriott Resort Grand Cayman ⚑   Under the Hyatt and the Westin Casuarina in the luxury-hotel pecking order, this five-story choice, a 5-minute drive north of George Town, is still among the top ranked hotels on the island. The hotel has an enviable location on Seven Mile Beach, and there's good snorkeling 15m (50 ft.) offshore. However, severe beach erosion, which has been somewhat halted by the construction of breakwaters jutting seaward off the hotel's beach, has limited the appeal of the property's already rather narrow beachfront. There's a feeling of claustrophobia down at the waterfront, though the hotel boasts good watersports facilities. The swimming pool is also small. This hotel is a favorite with large package-tour groups and conventions. Its red-roofed, vaguely colonial design resembles a cluster of balconied town houses. Hotel rooms lie on either side of a long, narrow, hotel-length lagoon whose waters flow downhill between copses of palm trees and banana plants. One of the best features of this hotel is the big, stately, high-ceilinged lobby. Accommodations, which were recently refurbished, open onto the ocean or the courtyard, and are decorated in cool Caribbean pastels. Rooms feature modern art, armoires, large closets, and private balconies. Bathrooms are spacious, with combination tubs and showers.

An oceanfront restaurant, serving decent standard international cuisine, offers three meals a day. Guests can choose to dine inside or out in the open air overlooking the water. Choose this restaurant for its oceanfront view rather than its cuisine.   ~~333-6388~~

West Bay Rd. (P.O. Box 30371), Grand Cayman, B.W.I. ℂ **800/333-3333** in the U.S., or 345/949-0088. Fax 345/949-0288. www.marriott.com. 309 units. Winter $320–$472 double, from $800 suite; off-season $175–$362 double, from $500 suite. AE, DC, MC, V. **Amenities:** 3 restaurants; 2 bars; outdoor pool; health club; Jacuzzi; watersports outfitter; concierge; car-rental desk; business services; limited room service (6am–11pm); babysitting; laundry service; same-day dry cleaning. *In room:* A/C, TV, dataport, minibar, coffeemaker, hair dryer, iron, safe.

Spanish Bay Reef ⚑   This is a small, intimate resort set in an isolated location in the scrublands of the northwestern tip of Grand Cayman. It was the island's first all-inclusive resort. Rather informally run, the pale-pink, two-story stucco units are favored by divers because there's great snorkeling and diving right offshore from the coral beach. The units, which are rather simple, have balconies or patios with garden or ocean views. Some rooms, available by request, offer kitchenettes. Furnishings are Caribbean casual. Beds are comfortable, but bathrooms, containing shower/tub combinations, are a bit cramped. Don't expect grand luxury here: Rooms probably won't appeal to those seeking classic resort-style accommodations and extras.

Rates include all meals and beverages, island sightseeing, entertainment, use of bicycles, introductory scuba and snorkeling lessons, unlimited snorkeling or scuba diving from the shore (including tanks and weight belt), round-trip transfers, taxes, and service. If you're a diver, ask about Certified Divers Packages when making your reservations. Guests lounge around Calico Jack's Poolside Bar, and enjoy an array of dishes (featuring lots of fish) in the Spanish Main Restaurant.

West Bay Rd. (P.O. Box 30867), Grand Cayman, B.W.I. ℂ 800/482-3483 in the U.S., 800/424-5500 in Canada, or 345/949-3765. Fax 345/949-1842. www.cayman resortsonline.com/spanishbay. 66 units. Winter $250–$340 per person (nondiver), $322–$412 per person (diver); off-season $160–$275 per person (nondiver), $230–$347 per person (diver). Children under age 12, $50 each per night in parent's room. Rates are all-inclusive. Ask about dive packages. AE, MC, V. **Amenities:** Restaurant; bar; outdoor pool; Jacuzzi; watersports rentals and lessons; dive shop. *In room:* A/C, TV, dataport, some units contain kitchenettes, hair dryer on request, iron.

Treasure Island Resort 🅰 (Kids)   Set closer to George Town than most of the other mega-resorts on Seven Mile Beach, this is a substantial, very large (the biggest on the island), and durable favorite. It was built in stages around a series of carefully landscaped courtyards, some of which are lavishly landscaped with cascading waterfalls, others centered around swimming pools or gazebo-style bars. The busiest and most charming of the bar lot is the gazebo-based Billy Bones bar, a favorite with Grand Cayman's off-duty lawyers. Accommodations lie within a series of five-story wings and annexes, most facing the landscaped gardens. Rooms have ceramic tile floors, roughly textured white walls, tropical-inspired fabrics in tones of blue and green, and shower-tub combos.

West Bay Rd., Seven Mile Beach, Grand Cayman, B.W.I. ℂ 800/203-0775 or 345/949-7777. Fax 345/949-8672. www.treasureislandresort.net. 278 units. Winter $220–$275 double; off-season $155–$190 double. AE, DC, MC, V. **Amenities:** 2 restaurants; bar; 3 outdoor pools (1 shaped like Grand Cayman itself); kiddie pool; 2 tennis courts (lit for night play); 3 Jacuzzis; watersports outfitter; bike and scooter rental; car-rental desk; salon; limited room service (7am-10pm); babysitting; laundry service; same-day dry cleaning. *In room:* A/C, TV, dataport, fridge, safe.

MODERATE

Cayman Diving Lodge   This casual, laid-back hotel is located on a private coral-sand beach in the southeast corner of the island, 32km (20 miles) east of George Town. It offers good value for experienced divers. Unless you are looking for some real solitude, you are probably better off elsewhere if you're not a scuba diver. Less glamorous than Morritt's, which also lies on the isolated eastern shore of Grand Cayman, the horseshoe-shaped lodge is a two-story blue-and-white building set amid tropical trees. Expect a raffish, free-wheeling ambience and a design that might remind you of a Florida-based waterfront motel from the 1960s, with touches of rural and isolated charm. The lodge's private coral-sand beach boasts a live coral barrier reef just offshore. Package room rates include a daily two-tank morning dive trip of 3½ hours (the three-tank package also includes an afternoon dive). The resort owns two 14m (45-ft.) Garcia dive boats that are very comfortable.

The decor and furnishing in the rooms are somewhat plain, though the ocean view tends to brighten things up. Expect linoleum floors, shower-only bathrooms, and slatted doors. A few units have balconies. The bedrooms have been slightly improved recently, with new beds, furnishings, dressers, and curtains.

Chefs at the lodge's restaurant serve abundant meals and specialize in fish dishes; vegetarian food is also available with advance notice.

East End (P.O. Box 11), Grand Cayman, B.W.I. © **800/852-3483** in the U.S., or 345/947-7555. Fax 345/947-7560. www.divelodge.com. 12 units. Year-round with 2-tank dives, $651 double for 3 nights, $1,042 for 5 nights, $1,494 for 7 nights; with 3-tank dives, $721 double for 3 nights, $1,200 for 5 nights, $1,669 for 7 nights. Rates are per person and all-inclusive. Nondiving plans are available. AE, DISC, MC, V. **Amenities:** Restaurant; bike rental. *In room:* A/C, coffeemaker.

Cobalt Coast Resort *(Finds*   The fans of this resort liken it to a bed-and-breakfast where most of the clients are deeply involved with diving. Most visitors stay for sojourns of at least five nights. Based on the number of awards it has won, and on the loyalty of its oft-returning clientele, it's the best resort for divers on Grand Cayman. Firmly entrenched in the unpretentious residential community of West Bay, beside an isolated stretch of jagged (not at all sandy) coastline, this virtually self-contained community has enormous charm and immediate access to all sorts of thrilling diving options. Don't expect a sandy beach or any strong link to the glittery tourist scene of Seven Mile Beach, whose extreme northern terminus lies 4.8km (3 miles) to the south. The accommodations,

(Kids) Family-Friendly Lodgings

Discovery Point Club (p. 69): This series of condos allows visiting families to create a home away from home in Grand Cayman. The staff does much to welcome families, allowing children under 6 to stay free and providing cribs and rollaways when needed. In the main lobby, the hotel provides games, and kids can watch videos.

Grand Caymanian (p. 70): Families can create an "instant home" in these spacious, well-furnished apartments, which feature well-equipped kitchens for home-cooked meals. The staff organizes many activities for kids.

Holiday Inn (p. 64): At the northern edge of Seven Mile Beach, this is one of the most hospitable hotels welcoming families in the archipelago. It offers everything from special beach gear for kids to cribs.

Indies Suites (p. 64): Often filled with families with children, the accommodations at this somewhat isolated hotel complex—one- or two-bedroom suites with a kitchen—are ideal for self-sufficient visitors. An extra person in a suite pays only $15 in any season.

Silver Sands (p. 79): Right on the beach, this complex of apartments allows large families to lodge all in one place (some accommodations house up to eight people) and to prepare meals in their own fully equipped kitchen. Children up to age 12 stay free with parents.

Treasure Island Resort (p. 67): This is the most family-friendly mega-resort. The large hotel has everything from a kiddie pool to babysitting service. Its artificial rock gardens and waterfalls make it a bit of a Disneyland fantasy for young children.

Villas of the Galleon (p. 79): This is a family favorite on Seven Mile Beach, which provides such extras as baby cribs. Families meet fellow families at this popular outdoor grill.

ranging from oceanfront suites to standard rooms, are supremely comfortable. The hotel's three-story design was inspired by the plantation houses of 18th-century Jamaica, with rooftop spires and balconies that evoke the gingerbread-trimmed architecture of Key

West. Bedrooms are roomy, modern, cozy, and soothing, with Marimekko fabrics from Finland and European plumbing fixtures. Doors can be opened or shut between units to create a variety of floor layout plans. On-site is an excellent restaurant, Duppies, which offers light fare.

Views extend westward from the restaurant's terrace out over the blue sea, and you'll find some of the most spectacular sunsets on Grand Cayman here. One of the keys to this resort's success and sense of intimacy is Arie Barendrecht, a Holland-born entrepreneur and dive enthusiast who works in close conjunction with Divetech, a topnotch, independently operated diving facility on-site. For more about Divetech, refer to chapter 5.

18 Seafan Dr., Boatswains Bay, Grand Cayman, B.W.I. ✆ 800/622-9626, or 345/946-5656 for hotel or 345/946-5658 for Divetech dive center. Fax 345/946-5657 for hotel, or 345/946-5659 for dive center. www.cobaltcoast.com or www.divetech.com. 18 units. Winter $215–$240 double, $295 1-bedroom suite for 2, $425 2-bedroom suite or villa for 4; off-season $160–$190 double, $250 1-bedroom suite for 2, $325 2-bedroom suite or villa for 4. Many dive packages available. AE, DC, MC, V. **Amenities:** Restaurant; bar; outdoor pool; Jacuzzi; watersports outfitter; coin-op washers and dryers. *In room:* A/C, TV, dataport, fridge, coffeemaker, hair dryer, safe.

Comfort Suites   Streamlined, efficient, and cost-effective, this hotel, opened in February of 2000, is one of the more modern lodgings along Seven Mile Beach. Rising five sand-colored stories near the southern end of the fabled beach, it follows a time-tested generic layout that has proven successful in hundreds of other locations within North America. Bedrooms are outfitted in tones of blue and white, and each is standardized in a generic format that, while not particularly Caribbean, is nonetheless very comfortable. Unfortunately, none of the rooms has a balcony or veranda to let the light in. All units have refrigerators, coffeemakers, and microwaves. One- and two-bedroom suites also contain stoves and dishwashers.

West Bay Rd., Grand Cayman, B.W.I. ✆ 800/517-4000 in the U.S., or 345/945-7300. Fax 345/945-7400. www.caymancomfort.com. 109 units. Winter $170–$265 studio for 2, $239–$300 1-bedroom suite for 2, $265–$360 2-bedroom suite for 4; off-season $160–$175 studio for 2, $180–$190 1-bedroom suite for 2; $230 2-bedroom suite for 4. Rates include breakfast. AE, DC, MC, V. **Amenities:** Restaurant; bar; outdoor pool; exercise room; Jacuzzi; watersports outfitter; bike rental; tour desk; car-rental desk; business center; coin-op washers and dryers. *In room:* A/C, TV, dataport, kitchenette in suites, fridge, coffeemaker, safe.

Grand Caymanian ⋆⋆ *(Kids*   This is the most upscale apartment-hotel resort on Grand Cayman's North Sound. The five-star facility was built in 2000 on scrubland that had been shunned by many other building developers. Within a short drive of the island's

biggest golf course (the Links at Safe Haven), facing the narrow and rocky beachfront of North Sound, you'll find an opulent cluster of beige-yellow apartments, each designed in a modernized version of British colonial style. Accommodations occupy a series of two- or three-story wings. Furnishings in each of the units are more elegant than those within the rooms of many of Grand Caymanian's competitors. The granite-trimmed private kitchens are genuinely plush. Sound-insulated doors can be locked and unlocked to allow configurations of units ranging from studios to full-blown two-bedroom suites. All bedrooms include a combination shower and whirlpool tub, plus a veranda or balcony. There is midweek maid service. The social center is a well-designed and pleasant restaurant and bar (Ray's on the Water) that's more casual and relaxed than you might expect for such an upscale venue.

Our objections to this hotel involve landscaping that simply doesn't look finished, a sense that some parts of the complex are still in the process of being built, and a rocky beachfront (which is, nonetheless, good for snorkeling). If none of these aspects bother you, you'll have a fine time sunbathing and enjoying the resort's sense of space and relative isolation.

278 Crighton Dr., Crystal Harbour, P.O. Box 31495 SMB, Grand Cayman, B.W.I. (②) 345/949-3100. Fax 345/949-3161. www.grandcaymanian.ky. Winter $165 studio for 1 or 2 occupants, $235 1-bedroom suite for up to 4, $365–$525 villa for up to 6; off-season $120 studio for 1 or 2 occupants, $185 suite for up to 4, $285–$410 villa for up to 6. AE, DC, MC, V. **Amenities:** Restaurant; bar; outdoor pool; tennis courts (lit for night play); Jacuzzi; watersports outfitter; children's center and programs; concierge; massage. *In room:* A/C, TV, dataport, kitchen, hair dryer, in-room washers and dryers.

Sunset House   Set on a coastal road about 1.2km (¾ of a mile) south of George Town, this is a well-recommended middle-bracket hotel whose rooms are divided among a quartet of two-story pink-sided outbuildings. Accommodations are simple, no-nonsense, and relatively comfortable. This place is favored by divers and snorkelers, who appreciate the jagged, mostly rock shoreline (site of excellent snorkeling possibilities) and the extensive diving programs. You're given a number of options for accommodations here, ranging from the cheapest—a unit opening onto the courtyard—to the most expensive—a roomy suite that contains extras such as private balconies, two double beds, a full kitchen, and a living room (this option is ideal for families or groups of four or more who like to do their own cooking). The midrange standard bedrooms open onto views of the sea and contain more space than the courtyard units.

Don't expect to swim here off sand: You must lower yourself via ladders directly into the sea. Two good reasons for staying here are direct access to the hotel's well-recommended restaurant, Seaharvest (p. 108), and its sprawling bar, My Bar (p. 157), which is especially busy every Friday night. About 80% of the guests staying at the hotel here are scuba enthusiasts; and about 80% of the clients at the hotel's bar and restaurant are full-time island residents.

S. Church St., George Town, Grand Cayman, B.W.I. ℂ **345/949-7111.** Fax 345/949-7101. www.sunsethouse.com. 59 units. Winter $165–$210 double; off-season $130–$170 double. AE, MC, V. **Amenities:** Restaurant; bar; outdoor pool; Jacuzzi; watersports outfitter. *In room:* A/C, TV, dataport, kitchen in apartments, fridge in suites.

Sunshine Suites Resort by Wyndham   Built in 1998 on a flat-as-a-pancake stretch of scrubland that requires a 5-minute trek to the beach, this is a well-designed compound of yellow-fronted buildings that evokes either a private country club or a condo complex, depending on your point of view. Both inside and out, the design reflects British colonial architecture. Because of prices that are relatively reasonable, the suites are usually 85% occupied, regardless of the season. Each of the units has its own kitchenette, so many guests prepare their meals on-site, avoiding the high cost of many of the nearby restaurants. Each of the accommodations is equipped with a midsize private bathroom with tub and shower. Nestled in the compound's center, ringed with festive-looking pavilions painted in tones of pink and purple, are a handful of gazebos and the resort's simple restaurant, the Sunshine Grill.

112 West Bay Rd., Grand Cayman, B.W.I. ℂ **877/786-1110** or 345/949-3000. Fax 345/949-1200. www.sunshinesuites.com. 132 units. Winter $200–$212 studio for 2, $245 1-bedroom suite for 2–4; off-season $130–$150 studio for 2, $175 1-bedroom suite for 2–4. Rates include continental breakfast. AE, MC, V. **Amenities:** Restaurant; bar; outdoor pool; free use of nearby fitness center; watersports outfitter; business center; coin-op washers and dryers. *In room:* A/C, TV, dataport, kitchenette.

INEXPENSIVE

Adam's Guest House *Value*   Tom and Olga Adam advertise their guesthouse as "the best at the lowest." While it may not be the fanciest place to stay, it's among the best values on the island. This 1950s-style West Indian ranch bungalow is located in a residential area a mile south of George Town, which is a long 6.4km (4-mile) haul from Seven Mile Beach. However, there's excellent snorkeling at Smith Cove Bay, only about a 10-minute walk away, and scuba-diving facilities—five different outfits—lie within a 5-minute stroll.

You can stroll over to the restaurant and bar at Seaview Hotel, about 5 minutes away. A supermarket and a drugstore are also nearby, as are some breakfast spots. Two bedrooms offer their own private entrance. The other trio of bedrooms is found in a shared efficiency apartment with access to a fully equipped kitchen and dining room. Each unit is equipped with a small private bathroom with shower stall and tub.

84 Melmac Ave., George Town, Grand Cayman, B.W.I. ⓒ **345/949-2512.** Fax 345/949-0919. www.adamsguesthouse.com.ky. 5 units. Winter $85 double; off-season $75 double. MC, V (accepted only for room deposit; pay with cash or traveler's checks). **Amenities:** Laundry service. *In room:* A/C, TV, fridge.

Eldemire's Guest House   Set within a quiet residential neighborhood on the landward side of South Church Road, 1.6km (1 mile) south of downtown George Town, this is the only bed-and-breakfast inn on Grand Cayman. Homelike and completely unglittery, it's run with a sense of humor by Carol "Tootie" Eldemire Huddleston, the congenial but no-nonsense Jamaica-born entrepreneur who lives just across the street. Tootie's guesthouse has thrived here since 1974, when it was established within a sprawling single-story modern house that was built here that same year. Accommodations lie within either the main house or within a handful of simple outbuildings. Each of the rooms is a simple, sparsely furnished affair, with well-worn furniture and very few frills. Each has a private bathroom with shower, and about half contain a shower-tub combination. There's no swimming pool on the premises, but South Cove Beach lies within a 5-minute walk. Residents of the double rooms have access to the house's communal kitchen, and each of the suites and apartments contains a simple kitchenette.

18 Pebbles Way, George Town, Grand Cayman, B.W.I. ⓒ **345/949-5387.** Fax 345/949-6987. www.eldemire.com. 13 units. Winter $90 double, $95–$105 studio for 1 or 2, $125 1-bedroom apt for 2, $180 2-bedroom apt for 4; off-season $75 double, $80–$90 studio for 1 or 2, $100 1-bedroom apt for 2, $150 2-bedroom apt for 4. **Amenities:** Bike rental; coin-op washers and dryers. *In-room:* A/C, TV, kitchenette in suites and apartments.

Seaview Hotel   This seafront property, a favorite with divers, lies on the south side of George Town, about a 10-minute walk from the downtown area or a 10-minute walk from the beach at Smith Cove. It's about a 2- to 3-minute drive to Seven Mile Beach. One of the island's oldest properties, the hotel still retains its '50s-style look, though it's been improved and upgraded. Bright Caribbean fabrics have enlivened some rooms, and 10 units face the ocean. Rooms range in size from small to medium, but each has a good bed, plus a tiny but well-maintained private bathroom with shower and tub. The on-site pool is large and inviting. The on-site restaurant and bar offers cocktails and three meals a day, with excellent seafood. Boat dives can be arranged, and the place has gear lockers for the storage of diving equipment.

5 S. Church St., George Town, Grand Cayman, B.W.I. ✆ **345/945-0558.** Fax 345/945-0559. 15 units. Winter $119 double; off-season $99 double; suite $200 year-round. MC, V. **Amenities:** Restaurant; bar; outdoor pool; watersports outfitter; babysitting; laundry service. *In room:* A/C, TV, coffeemaker, hair dryer, iron.

2 Condos, Villas & Cottages

VERY EXPENSIVE

The Avalon 🏝🏝 The Avalon, which occupies prime real estate on Seven Mile Beach, is one of Grand Cayman's best condo complexes. It consists of 27 oceanfront 3-bedroom/3-bathroom units, 17 of which can be rented. It's about a 5-minute drive from George Town, only a short distance from restaurants. The Avalon has an architectural style and grace that's lacking in many beachfront properties. The well-appointed, spacious units have a tropical motif. Each condo has a fully equipped open kitchen, king or twin beds, and a large, screened lanai that overlooks a stretch of the beach. Oversized tubs and separate shower stalls are in each bathroom. Cribs can be provided.

West Bay Rd. (P.O. Box 31236), Grand Cayman, B.W.I. ✆ **345/945-4171.** Fax 345/945-4189. www.cayman.org/avalon. 17 units. Winter $680 apt for 4, $800 apt for 6; off-season $480 apt for 4, $540 apt for 6. AE, DISC, MC, V. **Amenities:** Outdoor pool; tennis courts (lit for night play); fitness center; Jacuzzi; private garage. *In room:* A/C, TV, coffeemaker, kitchenette, iron.

The Beachcomber In the center of Seven Mile Beach, this is one of the older (1978) condo complexes, but it's still well maintained and inviting. The fabled sands of Seven Mile Beach lie right outside your rental. You're made to feel welcome immediately upon your arrival, as you are given a piece of rum cake and discount coupons for some shops and attractions. One of the newer features of the complex is free admission to the World Gym, right down the street from the condos. The condos are spacious but rather simply furnished. Each is a two-bedroom apartment that sleeps four people comfortably and six people in a somewhat more cramped fashion. Tile floors and rattan furnishings make up the decor, and each unit opens onto a view of the sea from a screened-in private patio. There is good snorkeling on the reef right offshore. For those who want to make use of their kitchenettes, at least for preparing simple meals, there is a grocery store across the street. Even if you don't have a car, you'll find a deli, three dive shops, liquor stores, and scooter rental nearby. The restaurants and bars of the Westin and Hyatt are also within walking distance.

Seven Mile Beach (P.O. Box 1799), Grand Cayman, B.W.I. ℂ 345/945-4470. Fax 345/945-5019. www.beachcomber1.com/location.html. 24 condos. Winter $445–$605 double, extra person $35; off-season $275–$395 double, extra person $25. MC, V. **Amenities:** Outdoor pool; babysitting; laundry facilities. *In room:* A/C, TV, kitchen, outside grill.

Colonial Club 𝄞𝄞   The pastel-pink Colonial Club occupies a highly desirable stretch of the famous Seven Mile Beach. Built in 1985, it's a rather standard three-story condominium development about 6.4km (4 miles) north of George Town and some 10 minutes from the airport. First-class maintenance, service, and furnishings are provided in the apartments, all of which have kitchen fans, maid service, and laundry facilities. Units come with three bedrooms and three bathrooms, which are well maintained and feature a shower stall.

West Bay Rd. (P.O. Box 320W), Grand Cayman, B.W.I. ℂ 345/945-4660. Fax 345/945-4839. 24 units. Winter $470–$530 apt for 2, $520–$590 apt for 3–4, $570–$650 apt for 5–6; off-season $260–$340 apt for 2, $310–$390 apt for 3–4, $360–$440 apt for 5–6. Minimum stay 5 nights Dec 16–Apr 15. AE, MC, V. **Amenities:** Outdoor pool; tennis court (lit for night play); Jacuzzi. *In room:* A/C, TV, kitchenette, iron, safe.

Retreat at Rum Point   This secluded, remote group of condominiums, located on Rum Point peninsula, opens onto 390m (1,300 ft.) of white sandy beach. The beach, shaded by casuarina trees, is a bit narrow and can hardly compare to the wide sands of Seven Mile Beach, but the place draws tranquility seekers. The retreat is a 35-minute drive from George Town or the airport. Private condos that are owner-occupied for part of the year are rented. Each condo has been individually decorated by its particular owner, and most feature typical Caribbean decor, with wicker and rattan. All units contain private balconies. Each condo has a fully equipped kitchen, including washers and dryers. Parties ranging from two to six can be accommodated here in one-, two-, or three-bedroom beachfront condos. All units receive maid service. The Hyatt Rum Point Club is right next door, offering a beach bar and a beach barbecue, and the Red Ginger Restaurant and Lighthouse Restaurant are within walking distance. Right next door to the Retreat is an office of Red Sails Watersports, an excellent watersports outfitter.

North Side (P.O. Box 46), Grand Cayman, B.W.I. ℂ **866/947-9135** or 345/947-9135. Fax 345/947-9058. www.theretreat.com.ky. 23 units. Winter $395–$450 double, $595 triple; off-season $295–$350 double, $450 triple. AE, DISC, MC, V. **Amenities:** Outdoor pool; tennis court (lit for night play); fitness center; sauna; watersports outfitter; racquetball court. *In room:* A/C, TV, kitchen, coffeemaker, hair dryer, iron, washer and dryer.

EXPENSIVE

Caribbean Club *ᏀᏀ*   Located right at the midpoint of gorgeous Seven Mile Beach, the low-key Bermudan-looking Caribbean Club is an exclusive compound of well-furnished villas, each with a full-size living room, dining area, patio, and kitchen. The villas are owner-occupied for part of the year, and are rented when the owners are away. The Caribbean Club's only serious competition is the comparable Colonial Club. The Caribbean Club has a long list of faithful repeat visitors who would stay nowhere else, although the complex is hardly deluxe. The pink villas are 4.8km (3 miles) north of George Town, either on or just off the beach. Naturally, the six oceanfront villas are more expensive than the others. Accommodations are furnished by each individual owner, and often feature tropical furnishings. Villas offer open verandas (often with barbecues), spacious closets, fully equipped kitchens, and combination bathrooms (tub and shower). At the core of the colony, the two-story club center has tall, graceful arches and picture windows that look out onto the grounds, which are planted with palm trees and flowering shrubs. The staff is one of the best and most helpful on the island. Maid service can be arranged upon request.

West Bay Rd. (P.O. Box 30499), Grand Cayman, B.W.I. ℂ **345/945-4099.** Fax 345/945-4443. www.caribclub.com. 18 units. Winter $260–$460 1-bedroom villa, $375–$525 2-bedroom villa; off-season $180–$335 1-bedroom villa; $280–$375 2-bedroom villa. AE, MC, V. No children under age 12 Jan 3–Mar 15. **Amenities:** Tennis court; laundry service. *In room:* A/C, TV, kitchen, coffeemaker, iron.

The Discovery Point Club *ᏀᏀ* *(Kids)*   Located at the far end of the northern stretch of Seven Mile Beach, in West Bay (9.7km/6 miles from George Town), this tranquil group of condos is composed of ocean-bordering suites. Some of the best snorkeling along the beach is found just off the shores here. When you tire of snorkeling, you can retreat to the club's freshwater pool or heated Jacuzzi. The accommodations here are definitely upmarket and are superior to the units offered by many competitors along the beach. Condos feature tasteful, comfortable furnishings and well-maintained private

bathrooms with tubs and showers. Each rental also boasts a screened-in patio. Each unit is decorated by the individual owner and all come with fully equipped kitchens. Children under 6 stay free, and cribs and rollaways are available. Each condo receives maid service. Built in 1987, the condos were last renovated in 2002.

West Bay Rd., West Bay (P.O. Box 439), Grand Cayman, B.W.I. © 345/945-4724. Fax 345/945-5051. www.cayman.org/discoverypoint. 47 units. Winter $225 studio for 2, $395 1-bedroom unit, $455 2-bedroom unit; off-season $125 studio for 2, $205 1-bedroom unit, $240 2-bedroom unit. AE, DISC, MC, V. **Amenities:** Outdoor pool; 2 tennis courts (lit for night play); Jacuzzi; laundry services; coin-op washer and dryers. In room: A/C, TV, kitchen, hair dryer, safe.

Island Pine Villas 🌴 Right on Seven Mile Beach, this unpretentious villa complex is comfortable and casual, though it's far less elegant than either the Colonial Club or the Caribbean Club. Inside and outside, it looks like a Days Inn motel along the Florida Turnpike. It is a family-friendly complex of one- or two-bedroom condos close to George Town. The units are well furnished with fully equipped kitchens, well-kept bathrooms with shower units, and daily maid service. There's a choice of queen- or king-size beds, and the best accommodations overlook the beach.

Seven Mile Beach (P.O. Box 30197-SMB), Grand Cayman, B.W.I. © 345/949-6586. Fax 345/949-0428. www.islandpinevillas.com. 40 units. Winter $235–$270 double; off-season $140–$180 double. AE, MC, V. **Amenities:** Watersports outfitter; laundry service. In room: A/C, TV, kitchenette, iron.

London House 🌴 At the tranquil northern end of Seven Mile Beach, London House is a good choice if you'd like your own upscale apartment. Each unit has a fully equipped kitchen, spacious living and dining areas, and a private patio or balcony overlooking the water. Floral prints, rattan, tile floors, and Caribbean pastels set a tropical tone in most units. Ceiling fans supplement the air-conditioning, and daily maid service is available. Each room has well-maintained bathrooms equipped with shower stalls.

The complex has its own seaside swimming pool (try to get a room away from the pool if you're bothered by noise, as parties are sometimes staged on the pool patio), plus a volleyball court. There's a stone barbecue for private poolside cookouts and there are also many restaurants nearby.

Seven Mile Beach, Grand Cayman, B.W.I. © 345/945-4060. Fax 345/945-4087. www.londonhouse.com.ky. 21 units. Winter $335–$375 1-bedroom apt, $355–$475 2-bedroom apt, $925 3-bedroom apt; off-season $285–$305 1-bedroom apt, $295–$360 2-bedroom apt, $775 3-bedroom apt. Extra person $20 per day. AE, MC, V. **Amenities:** Outdoor pool; babysitting; laundry. In room: A/C, TV, kitchen, fridge, coffeemaker, hair dryer, washers and dryers.

Morritt's Tortuga Club & Resort ✺   Located on 3.2 beachfront hectares (8 acres), this is one of the most appealing resorts on the island's isolated eastern fringe. This condo complex, painted a conch-shell pink, was built in the Antillean plantation style from the remains of a former hotel. The waters here offer some of the island's best diving, with nearby offshore reefs teeming with marine life. The resort is home to watersports outfitter Cayman Windsurfing, which offers snorkeling and windsurfing, and rents sailboats and catamarans. Tortuga Divers, also on the premises, offers diving courses at the resort.

About a 42km (26-mile) drive from the airport, the complex is composed of clusters of three-story beachfront condos opening onto the water. Many are rented as timeshare units. Each of the comfortably furnished apartments has a fully equipped kitchen, although many guests opt for meals in the resort's restaurant. Each unit has a small bathroom containing a shower/tub combination.

East End (P.O. Box 496GT), Grand Cayman, B.W.I. © **800/447-0309** in the U.S., or 345/947-7449. Fax 345/947-7299. www.morritt.com. 178 units. Winter $195–$205 studio, $275–$295 1-bedroom apt, $375–$405 2-bedroom apt; off-season $145–$155 studio, $185–$220 1-bedroom apt, $255–$285 2-bedroom apt. AE, DISC, MC, V. **Amenities:** 2 restaurants; 3 bars; outdoor pool; tennis court; watersports outfitter; activities desk; coin-op washer and dryers. *In room:* A/C, TV, dataport, kitchenette.

The Reef Resort ✺ *(Finds*   A bit of a discovery, this well-maintained and exceedingly comfortable timeshare/condo complex is located in the less trampled East End, a 32km (20-mile) drive from the airport. Guests who stay here will need a car, as the property lies about a 45-minute ride from George Town. There is a wide range of spacious beachfront units, from luxury studios to suites. The studio units are the smallest, and feature their own balcony, a full bathroom, an oversize Jacuzzi, and a kitchenette. Two people can be accommodated here comfortably, and honeymooners often choose these studios. The one-bedroom suites are mainly the same as the studios except that they are larger and feature two pull-out Murphy beds in living room, which makes these units suitable for four guests. Families often book the suites. The largest, best, and most expensive of the accommodations are the two-bedroom villas, which are a combination of the one-bedroom suite and the studio. The spaciousness of these accommodations makes them a favorite with larger families. The long roster of activities here, from stargazing to diving instruction, is sure to keep you occupied.

Colliers Bay, Queen's Hwy., East End (P.O. Box 3865), Grand Cayman, B.W.I. © 800/ 232-0541 in the U.S., or 345/947-3100. Fax 345/947-9920. www.royalreef.com. 30 units. Winter $195 studio, $275 1-bedroom suite, $410 2-bedroom villa; off-season $140 studio, $195 1-bedroom suite, $295 2-bedroom villa. AE, MC, V. **Amenities:** Restaurant; bar; 3 outdoor pools; tennis courts (lit for night play); fitness center; spa; Jacuzzi; watersports outfitter; concierge; limited room service (7:30am–9pm); babysitting. *In room:* A/C, TV (VCR in suites and villas), kitchenette, fridge, coffeemaker, hair dryers available on request, iron, safe.

Silver Sands Condos ⚡ *(Kids)*   A good choice for families, this modern eight-building complex is arranged in a horseshoe pattern on the beach, 11km (7 miles) north of George Town. The well-maintained apartment blocks are grouped around a freshwater pool and contain either two-bedroom/two-bathroom or three-bedroom/three-bathroom units. The two-bedroom units can hold up to six people, and the three-bedroom units can house up to eight guests. Each apartment has a balcony, a fully equipped kitchen (great for preparing economical family meals), and a small bathroom with shower. There is maid service for all units on every day except Sunday. In all, this is a smoothly run operation, which, in spite of its high rates, satisfies most guests.

West Bay Rd. (P.O. Box 205GT), Grand Cayman, B.W.I. © **800/327-8777** in the U.S., or 345/949-3343. Fax 345/949-1223. www.silversandscondos.com. 15 condos. Winter $450 2-bedroom apt, $545 3-bedroom apt; off-season $260–$325 2-bedroom apt, $395 3-bedroom apt. Additional person $25 extra. Children age 12 and under stay free in parent's unit. Minimum stay 7 nights in winter, 3 nights in off-season. AE, MC, V. **Amenities:** Outdoor pool; 2 tennis courts; coin-op washers and dryers; volleyball courts. *In room:* A/C, TV, kitchen, iron.

Victoria House ⚡   Spanning 105m (350 ft.) of prime oceanfront along Seven Mile Beach, this condo complex consists of one-, two-, and three-bedroom apartments, each with a screened porch, a fully equipped kitchen, and a bathroom containing a shower unit. Apartments are tastefully furnished in a tropical motif. There is daily maid service. The resort is known for its trademark hammocks strung between the palms fronting the beach.

Seven Mile Beach, near West Bay (P.O. Box 30571-SMB), Grand Cayman, B.W.I. © **866/422-9626** in the U.S., or 345/945-4233. Fax 345/945-5328. www.victoria house.com. 25 units. Winter $295 1-bedroom apt, $365 2-bedroom apt; off-season $195 1-bedroom apt, $225 2-bedroom apt. AE, MC, V. **Amenities:** Tennis court (lit for night play). *In room:* A/C, TV, kitchen.

Villas of the Galleon ⚡ *(Kids)*   This condo complex is on the widest strip of sand along the Seven Mile Beach, across the road from the Links at Safe Haven golf course. The facades of the stucco cottages look a little battered, but once you go inside, you'll find impressive, well-maintained rooms. Rattan furnishings and pastels, along with creamy tiles, evoke the easy, breezy Caribbean lifestyle. Each of the rentals contains one, two, or three bedrooms along with fully equipped kitchens. The closets are especially large. Each villa opens onto a private balcony or patio overlooking Seven Mile Beach and the ocean. The villas lie just 2 blocks from grocery and liquor stores and several top restaurants. Families like to check in here because each unit comes with baby cribs and rollaways. You'll find beach towels, patio furniture, beach loungers, and outdoor grills. There is daily maid service.

Seven Mile Beach (P.O. Box 1797), Grand Cayman, B.W.I. ℂ 345/945-4433. Fax 345/945-4705. www.villasofthegalleon.com. 59 villas. Winter $345–$385 1-bedroom, $440–$490 2-bedroom, $620–$675 3-bedroom, extra person $40; off-season $275–$295 1-bedroom, $315–$350 2-bedroom, $430–$465 3-bedroom, extra person $30. AE, DISC, MC, V. **Amenities:** Coin-op washers and dryers. *In room:* A/C, TV, kitchen, coffeemaker, hair dryer.

MODERATE

The Anchorage   On a tranquil section of Seven Mile Beach, this complex offers well-furnished, privately owned and individually decorated villas. Each unit has two bedrooms, two baths (showers only), and kitchens, and each can accommodate up to four persons (great for two couples traveling together or for a family with kids). Units opening onto the garden are the least expensive; you pay more for oceanfront accommodations. Each villa has a screened porch or balcony overlooking the beach. There's good snorkeling right offshore.

Seven Mile Beach, Grand Cayman, B.W.I. ℂ 800/433-3483 in the U.S., or 345/945-4088. Fax 345/945-5001. www.destination.ky/anchorage. 15 units. Winter $265–$450 2-bedroom apt; off-season $170–$290 2-bedroom apt. AE, MC, V. **Amenities:** Outdoor pool; tennis court; watersports can be arranged; limited business services; coin-op washers and dryers. *In room:* A/C, TV/VCR, kitchen, iron.

Tarquynn Manor   Opening onto one of the loveliest stretches of Seven Mile Beach, this condo complex is a breezy, airy Caribbean place. The compound consists of two- or three-bedroom air-conditioned apartments, all of which are roomy and well furnished, with fully equipped kitchens. Even when you fill a unit with the six-person maximum, you'll find the large living area spacious. Each unit has a small bathroom with a shower stall.

Seven Mile Beach (P.O. Box 30435 SMB), Grand Cayman, B.W.I. ℂ 866/596-8367 in the U.S., or 345/945-4038. Fax 345/945-5062. www.tarquynn.com. 19 units. Winter $325 up to 4 persons, $430–$475 up to 6 persons; off-season $265 up to 4 persons, $350 up to 6 persons. AE, DISC, MC, V. **Amenities:** Outdoor pool; watersports outfitter. *In room:* A/C, TV, kitchenette, hair dryer, iron.

4

Where to Dine on Grand Cayman

On his trip to the West Indies in 1859, Anthony Trollope, the British novelist, was not impressed with the food his plantation-owning hosts served him. Ignoring the rich bounty of their islands, including local fruits and vegetables, they fed him canned potatoes, "tinned meats," and cheeses imported from England. At the time, these British expats felt that if a food item didn't come from their homeland, it wasn't worth putting on the table.

Regrettably, Trollope did not visit the Cayman Islands as part of his sojourn. Had he paid a call, he would have found that the Caymanians were eating what they raised. Or, more accurately, what they caught. There was little reliance on imported goods. Today, Caymanian cuisine continues to take advantage of the islands' natural bounty.

1 A Taste of the Caymans

Many chefs in the Cayman Islands rely on international recipes for their restaurant offerings, and some Caymanians claim that you have to be invited to a local home for the real homestyle island cuisine. That is not true. There are still many restaurants featuring West Indian cooks who prepare food as their grandmothers did, and we've recommended several of these restaurants. Unless a restaurant is devoted to a foreign cuisine, such as Italian, many Cayman dishes still appear regularly on menus. You'll usually find two or three local dishes, if not more, on most menus.

SEA TURTLE   Turtle meat that appears on menus in the Cayman Islands is from a local turtle farm, which raises turtles specifically for commercial purposes.

QUEEN CONCH   The national food of the Cayman Islands is conch. The firm white meat of this mollusk—called the "snail of the sea"—is enjoyed throughout the islands. Actually, conch tastes

---

Tips Which Dollar? Yours or Mine?

Make sure you know which currency the menu prices are printed in. If the currency is not written on the menu, ask the waiter if the prices are in U.S. dollars or Cayman Island dollars.

---

somewhat bland—until local chefs get their hands on it. Locals eat it as a snack (it's often served at happy hour in taverns and bars), as a main dish, in salads, and as an hors d'oeuvre.

Pacific Coast residents may think conch tastes like abalone. It does not have a fishy taste, like halibut, but it has a chewy consistency, which means that a chef must pound it to tenderize it, the way one might pound Wiener schnitzel. Every cook has a different recipe for making conch chowder. A popular version includes tomatoes, potatoes, sweet peppers, onions, carrots, salt or pork bacon, bay leaves, thyme, and (of course) salt and pepper. In addition to conch chowder, you will find conch soup.

Conch fritters, shaped like balls, are served with hot sauce and are made with finely minced peppers, onions, and tomato paste, among other ingredients. They are deep-fried in oil.

Cracked conch (or "fried conch," as the old-timers used to call it) is prepared like a breaded veal cutlet. Pounded hard and dipped in batter, it is then sautéed. Conch is also served steamed, in Creole sauce, curried, "scorched," creamed on toast, and stewed. You'll even see "conch burgers" listed on menus.

Marinated conch is frequently enjoyed right on the water, courtesy of the numerous Caymanian sea captains who operate North Sound excursions that include lunch. They will scoop a conch right out of the sea, remove it from its shell (an art unto itself), slice it up, and serve it with lime juice and onions—as fresh as it can possibly be. The lime juice tenderizes the flesh, eliminating the need for pounding it. Similar to the preparation of Mexico's ceviche, marinated conch is found in many restaurants.

THE MAIN EVENT   Red snapper, mahimahi (which is also called dorado or dolphin), swordfish, yellowfin tuna, and grouper are the most commonly available fish. Imported fish such as salmon appear on some restaurant menus, but it's unlikely you'll find them in restaurants serving local cuisine.

The most elegant item you'll see on nearly any menu is the local spiny lobster. A tropical cousin of the Maine lobster, it is also called

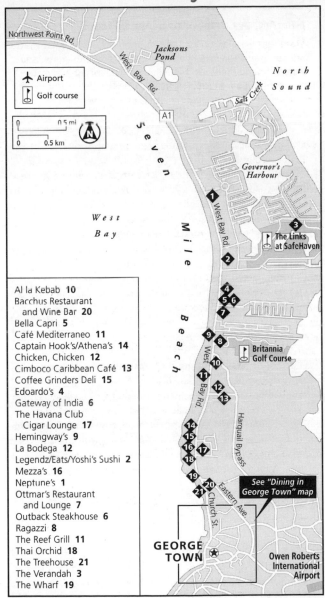

Northwest Point Rd.

Jacksons Pond

West Bay Rd.

North Sound

Salt Creek

A1

Airport

Golf course

0   0.5 mi
0   0.5 km

N

Governor's Harbour

West Bay

Seven Mile Beach

West Bay Rd.

The Links at SafeHaven

Britannia Golf Course

Harquail Bypass

See "Dining in George Town" map

Eastern Ave.

Church St.

GEORGE TOWN

Owen Roberts International Airport

Al la Kebab **10**
Bacchus Restaurant
   and Wine Bar **20**
Bella Capri **5**
Café Mediterraneo **11**
Captain Hook's/Athena's **14**
Chicken, Chicken **12**
Cimboco Caribbean Café **13**
Coffee Grinders Deli **15**
Edoardo's **4**
Gateway of India **6**
The Havana Club
   Cigar Lounge **17**
Hemingway's **9**
La Bodega **12**
Legendz/Eats/Yoshi's Sushi **2**
Mezza's **16**
Neptune's **1**
Ottmar's Restaurant
   and Lounge **7**
Outback Steakhouse **6**
Ragazzi **8**
The Reef Grill **11**
Thai Orchid **18**
The Treehouse **21**
The Verandah **3**
The Wharf **19**

> *Fun Fact* **A Caymanian Dinner, Please**
>
> If you're staying at one of the many condos and villas that pepper Grand Cayman, you can call a private caterer and order an island dinner to be delivered. One of the best caterers is **Burton Ebanks (© 345/949-7222)**.

crayfish or rock lobster. Only the tail is eaten. You get fresh lobster only when it is in season, from the beginning of April until the end of August. Otherwise it's frozen.

Caymanian lobster, in spite of its cost, is not always prepared well. Sometimes a cook leaves it in the oven for too long and the meat becomes tough and chewy. But when prepared right, it is absolutely delicious, and worth the exorbitant cost.

Chicken and pork, the meats that are most often prepared island-style, are frequently roasted, grilled, curried, or "jerked"—that is, rubbed with spices and slow-smoked over a low fire, preferably made with pimento wood, for hours. Each cook has his or her own special spice blend, but jerk spices usually include allspice, hot Scotch bonnet pepper, thyme, nutmeg, salt, garlic, onion, and green onion. Other popular meat dishes that are easily found at restaurants serving island cuisine include braised beef liver, curried goat, oxtail, and salt beef and beans.

The most frequent companion for main dishes is "rice and peas," a dish that's also popular in Jamaica, which is actually composed of rice and red beans cooked in coconut milk. Every cook adds his or her own touch to the pot, including sweet peppers and tomatoes, hot peppers, onions and thyme, beef, bacon, ham bone, or any combination of these and other ingredients. Along with rice and peas, ripe plantains (larger, less sweet relatives of the banana) are fried or baked with brown sugar and served alongside main dishes.

2 Expensive Restaurants

Also see the map "Accommodations & Dining on Grand Cayman" on p. 63.

Cecil's Restaurant/Kaibo Beach Bar & Grill ***CCC*** INTERNATIONAL   Collectively, these restaurants are often referred to simply as "the Kaibo Yacht Club," a term that can be misleading, since the marina facilities offered here are less comprehensive and formal than those available at more lavish marinas closer to George Town.

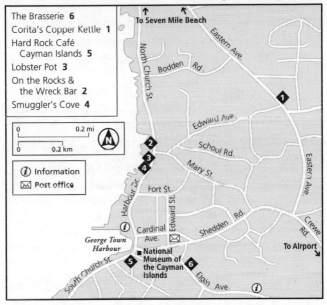

Dining in George Town

The Brasserie **6**
Corita's Copper Kettle **1**
Hard Rock Café
  Cayman Islands **5**
Lobster Pot **3**
On the Rocks &
  the Wreck Bar **2**
Smuggler's Cove **4**

Nonetheless, the charm and quality of this bar and restaurant put it head and shoulders above other Cayman Islands yacht club dining and drinking establishments. This place offers superb food and a fun, gregarious atmosphere. The management's lighthearted but intensely professional approach to the restaurant business has helped transform this compound into a Sunday afternoon beachfront hangout that some Caymanians drive long distances to reach.

Some aspects of the place might remind you of a beach compound in Polynesia, thanks to flaming torches, multilevel terraces, beach cabanas roofed in palm thatch, and a clientele that, especially on weekends, might remind you of South Beach in Miami during the Winter Music Conference. It's easy to get hooked on the compound's beach-level bar (p. 154). But if you're looking for cuisine that's much more sophisticated than what's available in the beachfront bar, we recommend that you climb a flight of exterior steps for one of the best meals on Grand Cayman. Here, within Cecil's Restaurant, you'll find decor that evokes a combination of pagan temple, treehouse, and Palladian villa, with the "bones" of a clipper ship (mast, rudder, and part of the rigging) suspended from the ceiling.

Tips **The High Price of Imported Ingredients**

Because many ingredients must be shipped in to the Cayman Islands, restaurants here are among the most expensive in the Caribbean. Even so-called moderate restaurants can become expensive if you order steak or lobster. For the best taste and value, opt for West Indian fare.

As you eat, some of the most lazily hypnotizing ceiling fans on Grand Cayman circulate the air beneath the soaring ceiling.

The energetic and personable Jerry Mixon is the creative genius behind the cuisine at this place. Mixon was trained at upscale restaurants in New Orleans, and spent an extensive part of his training with mega-chef Paul Prudhomme. Begin your meal with Louisiana crab cakes served with a Creole rémoulade sauce, or spectacular baked oysters topped with spinach and cheese. Main courses include pan-seared tuna with a honey-sesame-soy-ginger sauce; seared catfish with a Louisiana crawfish sauce; and voodoo chicken, blackened and served with Creole sauce. The grilled filet steak, stuffed with blue cheese and served with onion sauce and the potato of the day, is spectacular.

In the Kaibo Yacht Club, North Side. ℂ **345/947-9975**. Reservations recommended in Cecil's, not necessary at the beach bar. Platters, salads, and sandwiches in the Kaibo Beach Bar and Grill CI$6.50–CI$10 (US$8.15–US$13); main courses in Cecil's CI$20–CI$33 (US$25–US$41). AE, MC, V. Kaibo Beach Bar and Grill daily 11am–11pm; Cecil's Tues–Sun 6–11pm.

Cracked Conch by the Sea *ℛ* SEAFOOD   Long a culinary landmark, this popular restaurant, located near the famous turtle farm in West Bay, serves some of the island's freshest seafood and some of the most succulent turtle steak in the Caymans. The menu is one of the largest on the island, featuring burgers, chicken, steaks, and even a vegetarian pasta of the day along with the specialties mentioned above. The inevitable namesake conch appears in various tasty combinations. Food is freshly prepared—nothing is frozen. The decor is a bit corny, particularly the cement floor made to look like "authentic" wood planking from a pirate ship. There's a patio bar overlooking the sea, and a walkway so you can watch fish feeding at 8pm every evening. Quite justifiably, the restaurant's Sunday brunch has many fans.

West Bay Rd., near Cayman Turtle Farm. ℂ **345/945-5217**. Reservations recommended. Main courses CI$18–CI$34 (US$22–US$42); Sun brunch CI$13 (US$16). AE, MC, V. Daily 11:30am–10pm; Sun brunch 10am–3pm.

Grand Old House ✿✿✿ AMERICAN/CARIBBEAN/PACIFIC RIM This former plantation house lies amid old, distinguished trees 1.6km (a mile) south of George Town, past Jackson Point. Built on bedrock near the edge of the sea, 129 ironwood posts support the main house and a bevy of gazebos. The Grand Old House is the island's premier caterer, hosting everything from lavish weddings and political functions to informal family celebrations.

Chef Tell Erhardt put the restaurant on the Cayman culinary map, so the place is often called Chef Tell's. And though the former TV celebrity chef is long gone, the Grand Old House has suffered no decline in food or service. The same menu has been retained, but it's been slightly updated by the new chef, Indian-born Kandaphil Matahi. Appetizers remain the most delectable on the island, including coconut beer-battered shrimp and home-smoked marlin and salmon. For your main dish, dig into fresh seafood and lobster prepared in a coconut-flavored curry sauce with tropical chutney, or Cayman-style turtle steak served in a spicy tomato sauce.

Petra Plantation, S. Church St. ℂ 345/949-9333. Reservations required. Main courses CI$19 CI$33 (US$23 US$41). AE, DISC, MC, V. Mon–Fri 11:45am–2pm; daily 6–10pm. Closed Sept.

Hemingway's ✿✿ SEAFOOD/INTERNATIONAL The finest seafood on the island can be found 3.2km (2 miles) north of George Town at Hemingway's, which is named after the novelist and inspired by Key West, his one-time residence. The restaurant is set within a modern replica of a high-ceilinged villa, in a section of the Hyatt Resort that fronts the sea. You can either dine within the airy interior, or on the wind-sheltered outdoor terrace, with a vista of the swimming pool and a narrow-angled view of the sea. The menu is among the most imaginative on the island and has won acclaim from *Gourmet* magazine. Appetizers include pepperpot soup and gazpacho served with a black-bean relish. The catch of the day, perhaps snapper or wahoo, emerges grilled to your liking. You can also order roasted rack of lamb served on fruit compote with caramelized-onion mashed potatoes. Want something even more imaginative? Try grouper stuffed with crabmeat, or Cuban-spiced tenderloin served on white-bean-and-fennel ragout.

In the Hyatt Regency Grand Cayman, West Bay Rd. ℂ 345/949-1234. Reservations recommended. Lunch CI$9.75–CI$15 (US$12–US$19); dinner CI$22–CI$29 (US$27–US$36);. AE, DC, DISC, MC, V. Daily 11:30am–2:30pm and 6–10pm.

The Lighthouse at Breakers ✿ CARIBBEAN/ITALIAN/SEAFOOD You'll recognize this place by the theme-ish, two-story lighthouse that rises abruptly from a rocky stretch of coastline on Grand Cayman's southern coast, a 25-minute drive east of George Town. In distinct contrast to the more informal restaurant, The Edge, which lies a short distance to the west, this place exudes propriety and upscale comfort. You can dine within the carefully manicured, nautically inspired interior, or head out to a T-shaped dock that juts seaward directly above the water. Resting on the pier are dining tables, each shaded from the daytime glare with parasols. The restaurant has a creative menu, featuring fresh local seafood and Italian dishes. The well-trained chef, backed up by a skilled staff, offers well-prepared meals that attract both locals and visitors. You can enjoy such tempting appetizers as portobello mushroom carpaccio with shaved Parmesan, or tuna sushi rolled in sesame seeds. For your main course, opt for the tender veal chop topped with Gorgonzola and pancetta, or a mixed seafood grill in a lemon-butter sauce. Pastas are strongly represented on the menu, and fettuccine Mediterranean, made with seasonal vegetables, is a particular favorite. The restaurant has one of the best wine cellars on island.

Breakers. ℂ 345/947-2047. Reservations recommended. Lunch main courses CI$6.95–CI$14 (US$8.70–US$18); dinner main courses CI$15–CI$40 (US$19–US$50). AE, MC, V. Daily 11:30am–4pm and 5:30–10pm.

Lobster Pot ℛ SEAFOOD/INTERNATIONAL

Though not as good as Hemingway's, Lobster Pot is still an island favorite. It overlooks the water from its second-floor perch on the western perimeter of George Town, near what used to be Fort George. True to its name, it offers lobster prepared in many different ways: Cayman style, bisque, and salad. Conch schnitzel and seafood curry are on the menu, along with turtle steak from turtle grown commercially in the Cayman Islands. The seafood is sometimes a bit overcooked for our tastes, but most dishes are right on the mark. This place is also known for its prime beef steaks. For lunch, you might want to try the English fish and chips, the seafood jambalaya, or pasta. The Lobster Pot's pub is a pleasant place for a drink—you may even find someone up for a game of darts.

N. Church St. ℂ 345/949-2736. Reservations required in winter. Main courses CI$16–CI$32 (US$20–US$40). AE, MC, V. Mon–Fri 11:30am–2:30pm; daily 5–10pm.

Neptune's ℛ ITALIAN/SEAFOOD

Set in a simple concrete building near the northern end of West Bay Road, this is one of a few genuinely appealing and relatively affordable Italian restaurants on Grand Cayman. There's no view of the sea, but the you'll get the feeling that you're at the seashore, thanks to a decor featuring very pristine ceramic tiles, a color scheme of blue and white, and a mural of cavorting mermaids. Tables on the large outdoor terrace are centered around a human-sized statue of the Neptune, Greek god of the sea. Menu items include a wide array of all the usual pastas, plus some nonstandard choices such as Spaghetti alla Courtney, made with eggplant, fresh tomatoes, garlic, and mozzarella cheese; and Spaghetti Bella Pesaro, made with grilled zucchini and fresh clams. The seafood here is especially tempting, including such dishes as shrimp with garlic butter, balsamic vinegar, and fresh herbs; mixed seafood curry; and grilled red snapper served with lobster, shrimp, and tomato-flavored cream sauce.

Trafalgar Place (across from the Seven Mile Public Beach), West Bay Rd. © 345/946-8709. Reservations recommended only Fri Sat at dinner. Lunch pastas and main courses CI$9.95–CI$13 (US$12–US$16); dinner pastas and main courses CI$14–CI$30 (US$18–US$38). AE, DC, MC, V. Mon–Sat 11:30am–2:30pm; daily 5:30–10pm.

Ottmar's Restaurant and Lounge 🦀🦀 INTERNATIONAL/FRENCH/CARIBBEAN   One of the island's top restaurants, Ottmar's is outfitted in a French Empire style, with lots of paneling and rich upholstery, and plenty of space between tables. There's a formal bar/lounge area decorated with deep-sea fishing trophies. This is the domain of Austrian expatriate Ottmar Weber, who abandoned the Austrian kitchens of his youth to roam the world, taking culinary inspiration wherever he finds it. The results are usually pleasing. The Indonesian *rijstafel* (a meal composed of many small dishes served with rice) with seafood in a mild curry sauce comes as a delightful surprise, as does a dish called mahimahi Chapultapez, which originated with the Aztecs and is a tender filet of fish stuffed with avocado purée, spinach, red and green peppers, mushrooms, and onions, baked with Monterey cheese. You can also order a Swiss cheese fondue or jumbo shrimp lightly poached in white wine with lobster sauce. Lunch is served at the Waterfall Restaurant. Ottmar's offers a professional welcome and attentive service. Every Friday from 5 to 8pm is happy hour on the waterfront terrace, with live entertainment and free hors d'oeuvres, in addition to raffles for various prizes.

West Bay Rd. (side entrance of Grand Pavilion Commercial Centre). © 345/945-5879. Reservations recommended. Main courses CI$19–CI$32 (US$24–US$40). AE, MC, V. Daily 6–11pm.

Over the Edge CARIBBEAN/INTERNATIONAL   If you liked this establishment's sister restaurant, The Edge, in Bodden Town (p. 97), you might want to venture even farther afield and drop into Over the Edge, The Edge's more remote and even more raffish twin. This restaurant is something of a mecca for residents of the sparsely populated North Side, who gravitate here for an ambience that's the opposite of what you'll find at the glossy venues of West Bay Road and downtown George Town. A bar with a raucous crowd greets you at the entrance. There's an interior dining room whose walls block out the sometimes-ferocious winds that batter this place during storms. Outside, you'll find a wharf-style terrace whose pilings extend straight down into the seabed. The views from the terrace have been described as mystical, especially on calm, moonlit nights. Lunches are relatively simple affairs, focusing on Cayman-style steamed fish, pan-fried conch steak, turtle steak with port sauce, sandwiches stuffed with either tuna or mahimahi, and chef's salads. Dinners are more elaborate, featuring well-prepared dishes such as charbroiled rock lobster tail, lobster Thermidor, savory jumbo shrimp in Pernod sauce, grilled wahoo, and grilled breast of chicken with Dijonnaise sauce. Though most of the regulars seem to stick to beer, visitors often order the house drink, a creamy chocolate Mudslide-type concoction priced at CI$7 (US$8.75).

Old Man Bay, North Side. ℂ 345/947-9568. Lunch sandwiches, salads, and platters CI$4.95–CI$13 (US$6.20–US$16); dinner main courses CI$18–CI$32 (US$22–US$40). AE, MC, V. Daily 7am–10pm (bar stays open till 1am).

Portofino Wreckview Restaurant ⋩ ITALIAN/INTERNATIONAL/CARIBBEAN   In 1962, an American cargo ship, the *Liberty,* sank during a storm on a reef close to Grand Cayman's eastern shore. Today, split into three thoroughly rusted separate sections that rest in shallow water, it provides a focal point for the panoramas that open before you from the terrace of this pleasant and well-managed restaurant. This is the most popular independent restaurant on Grand Cayman's East End, drawing clients from the hotel and resort complexes nearby who are looking for a break from their in-house restaurants. Wall murals, frescoes of grape arbors, and blue and white tiles provide a lighthearted reference to southern Italy. If you want to dine outside, a terrace, painted in cheerful tones of pink and blue, gives you the opportunity to soak in the sunlight, salt air, and wreck views. You might begin a meal here with a satay (skewer) of beef or chicken, served with a cucumber-and-peanut sauce, then follow with a savory version of *zuppa di pesce* (fish soup); breaded conch steak served in traditional East End style; turtle steak; any of several kinds of pasta; shrimp *fra diavolo;* and the house specialty, baked seafood portofino, which combines lobster, tiger

Kids   Family-Friendly Dining

Café Mediterraneo (p. 95): The wide array of pizzas and pastas and the convenient hours, beginning in the late morning and lasting throughout the day, make this is a favorite of many families, both local and visiting.

Chicken, Chicken (p. 103): Families on a budget often head here to order an entire roasted chicken or two (each chicken serves about three diners), served with side dishes, for the low cost of CI$24 (US$30).

Outback Steakhouse (p. 100): This member of an international chain enjoys the same family patronage in the Caymans that it does back in the States. Your budding little Crocodile Dundee will find much to delight him or her here, including coconut shrimp or chicken cooked on the barbie.

shrimp, scallops, and mousseline potatoes au gratin. Lunches are simpler than dinners, focusing on salads, sandwiches, pastas, and grilled fish.

In Colliers, East End. ① **345/947-2700.** Reservations recommended. Lunch platters CI$6–CI$13 (US$7.50–US$16); dinner main courses CI$14–CI$30 (US$18–US$38). AE, MC, V. Daily 11:30am–5pm and 5:30–10pm.

The Reef Grill _☆☆☆_ SEAFOOD   Located in the heart of Seven Mile Beach, this is one of the island's finest restaurants. The moment your first dish from the seductive menu arrives, you'll know you've made a good choice. Prepared with quality ingredients, the cuisine is flavorful and imaginatively presented. We'd rate The Reef Grill's appetizers as the best on island. The seafood chowder is memorable, as are the other appetizers, including a carpaccio of raw beef with arugula and aged Parmesan, shrimp and chicken spring rolls, and hot fried calamari with jalapeño mayonnaise. Pastas can be served as an appetizer or main course. Our favorite is the lobster-filled ravioli with brandy, diced tomatoes, and a creamy seafood essence. The chef's fish dishes are excellent, especially the signature red snapper with a chili-laced vinaigrette, the seared red snapper filet baked in banana leaves with scallions, and the jumbo shrimp sautéed with artichokes, black olives, and sun-dried tomatoes. For meat eaters, a winning choice is the oven-roasted, 14-ounce, center-cut pork chop glazed with Jack Daniels. You dine under the stars, listening to some of the most talented local musicians playing soca and calypso. The helpful, experienced staff will guide you through one of the Cayman's best wine lists. As for desserts, what Cayman chef can top the almond-and-chocolate mousse served as a finale?

In the Royal Palms, Seven Mile Beach. 🅒 345/945-6358. Reservations required. Main courses CI$19–CI$34 (US$24–US$43). AE, DC, MC, V. Daily 6:30–10pm.

Ristorante Pappagallo 🅖 NORTHERN ITALIAN/SEAFOOD
One of the island's most memorable restaurants lies on a 6-hectare (14-acre) bird sanctuary overlooking a natural lagoon, 15 minutes north of George Town. The restaurant's designers incorporated Caymanian and Aztec weaving techniques into its thatched roof, which gives the place a tropical feel. Glass doors, black marble, and polished brass add an Edwardian opulence to the mix. Although the restaurant's name means "parrot" in Italian, it is decorated with live jewel-toned macaws that are carefully cared for and caged. You might launch your repast with seafood chowder (which the chef spices with aged rum in old island style), or duck foie gras terrine and pear compote, drizzled with a port wine sauce. Pastas can be ordered as appetizers or main courses. There's none finer than the penne sautéed with lobster and cherry tomatoes in a peppery vodka-and-tomato cream sauce. The fish dishes are limited, but the selections are top-notch, especially the delectable mahimahi sautéed with garlic, scallions, and parsley in a white wine–lemon sauce. A few meat dishes are offered, the most authentic of which is peppered West Indian pork tenderloin with an apple bourbon sauce and mashed potatoes laced with onion seed.

At Villas Pappagallo, Conch Point, Barkers (near the northern terminus of West Bay Rd. and Spanish Cove, 13km/8 miles north of George Town). 🅒 345/949-1119. Reservations required. Main courses CI$7–CI$31 (US$8.75–US$39). AE, MC, V. Daily 6–10pm.

The Wharf 🅖 CARIBBEAN/CONTINENTAL Centered
around a gazebo and festooned with twinkling lights, this well-recommended waterfront restaurant sits on the northern fringe of George Town, at the point where the city limits meet the southern tip of Seven Mile Beach. Large, prosperous looking, and well manicured, with hints of European flair, this is a solid, well-rehearsed restaurant where you could take your spouse or partner, your most important business contacts, or your investment counselor for an evening of well-prepared cuisine in an uncontroversial setting. There's an air-conditioned interior area, a strolling guitarist, and a

series of outdoor, oceanfronting wooden decks that gradually descend to a gingerbread-trimmed open-air bar. Lunch offerings might include chicken wraps, fish and chips, steak sandwiches, and meal-sized salads, sometimes garnished with grilled chicken or shrimp. Dinner items are more elaborate. Try, for example, such flamboyant dishes as basil-and-pistachio-nut-crusted sea bass served with a creamy champagne sauce, or a "symphony" of seafood that includes pan-fried dolphin (dorado, not Flipper), sea scallops, and jumbo shrimp served with a zesty red-pepper sauce. Only in the Caymans can you get a local version of chunky turtle-and-lobster pie topped with a mashed potato crust. Another winner is the Wharf Grill, combining a tender grilled veal scaloppini with fresh sea scallops and a potato gratin.

Every evening at 9pm, an employee heads to a point near the gazebo-style bar and throws kitchen scraps to the teeming schools of prehistoric-looking tarpon who glide beneath the restaurant's piers.

West Bay Rd. ℂ 345/949-2231. Reservations recommended for dinner. Lunch main courses CI$7–CI$16 (US$8.75–US$20); dinner main courses CI$18–CI$30 (US$23–US$38). AE, MC, V. Lunch only from Dec 15–Apr 15, Mon–Fri 11:30am–2:30pm. Dinner daily year-round 6–10pm.

3 Moderately Priced Restaurants

Bacchus Restaurant and Wine Bar ⍟ CONTEMPORARY AMERICAN   Located in the center of George Town and surrounded by office buildings and shops, this restaurant does most of its business at lunchtime and during the late afternoon, after the nearby businesses have closed. Dozens of regulars enjoy cocktails here after work, making late afternoon an especially good time to get an insight into the inner life of Grand Cayman. The restaurant and bar are decorated like a warm, welcoming tavern, with exposed brick and dark mahogany paneling. Lunches here are simple, quick, and efficient, focusing on salads, sandwiches, light platters, and soups. Dinners are more elaborate, and can be accompanied by glasses of any of eight house wines, which are priced from CI$5 to CI$7 (US$6.25–US$8.75) a glass. Other cocktails, such as a melon-flavored piña colada (called a Midori Colada) cost from CI$6.50 to CI$7.50 (US$8.15–US$9.40) each. If you just want to nibble on bar snacks and tapas and hang out at the bar, consider ordering the jerk chicken quesadilla, the flash-fried calamari with jerk-seasoned tartar sauce, or an antipasto platter. Main courses at dinner might include well-prepared versions of partially seared tuna tataki; baked portobello mushrooms with Gorgonzola cheese; roasted and olive-crusted rack of lamb; and braised salmon with seaweed salad.

3 Front St., George Town. ℭ 345/949-5747. Main courses CI$17–CI$24 (US$21–US$30). AE, DC, DISC, MC, V. Mon–Fri 11am–1am; Sat 3pm–midnight.

Bella Capri ITALIAN   Cozy, warm, and attractive, this restaurant serves well-prepared Italian food to a mixed clientele of local residents and the occupants of the many hotels and condos that line either side of West Bay Road. You'll find two separate dining rooms here, both outfitted in tones of forest green and white, with exposed wine racks. The menu features conservative but well-flavored versions of Italian staples as you might find them in their homeland. The best dishes are lobster penne in a tomato-flavored chardonnay sauce; crepes stuffed with chicken, mushrooms, and a Parmesan-flavored cream sauce; imaginative pumpkin dumplings with caramelized walnuts and a mixture of Cambazola cheese and Parmesan cheese; linguine del mar pasta topped with fresh seafood; and Jumbo Shrimp Old Pompeii in a sauce of pinot grigio wine, garlic, and lemon. Also available are juicy grilled Black Angus filet steaks, and a seared version of pepper-encrusted tuna tataki with watercress, arugula, and portobello mushrooms. Lunch is only served on Friday, when guests come for the lunch buffet, which features the restaurant's Italian specialties and is acknowledged as one of the island's best luncheon values.

Adjacent to the Strand Shopping Center, West Bay Rd. ℭ 345/945-4755. Reservations recommended. Fri lunch buffet CI$8.95 (US$11) per person; dinner main courses CI$14–CI$29 (US$18–US$36). AE, DC, MC, V. Fri 11:35am–2:30pm; daily 5–10pm.

The Brasserie ⭐⭐ CONTINENTAL/INTERNATIONAL   Elegant and stylish, this restaurant is removed from the tourist hubbub of Seven Mile Beach and other tourist-geared areas. It was built in the mid-1990s as part of a glistening office compound that is one of the most architecturally avant-garde office building complexes in the Cayman Islands, with a low-slung pavilion surrounded by soaring branches of, among others, the Union Bank of Switzerland and the Canadian National Bank. Because of its location, many of its clients are likely to be financiers and insurance-industry executives entertaining one another or their clients.

Expect a Caribbean colonial decor with high ceilings, artfully carved teakwood and mahogany furniture, spinning ceiling fans, and a cool, breezy layout that might evoke an upscale private club in a long-gone British colonial empire. The Brasserie serves one of the most appealing tapas menus on the island. Tapas choices might include lamb and pinenut sausages with Dijon mustard, fish ceviche, and roasted red-pepper salad. Lunches focus on upscale and upbeat salads such as a black and white sesame-crusted fresh tuna tataki with seaweed, watercress, and miso-ginger slaw, and pastas such as a ravioli of the day. Dinners are more formal and more expensive, with main courses that include roasted Cornish game hen with lemon-and-rosemary sauce, and rack of lamb with an herbed brioche-and-pomegranate sauce.

Cricket Square, Elgin Ave. (C) **345/945-1815.** Reservations recommended, especially at lunch. Lunch salads and platters CI$7–CI$14 (US$8.75–US$18); dinner main courses CI$10–CI$27 (US$13–US$33); tapas CI$3 (US$3.75) each. AE, MC, V. Mon–Fri 11:30am–2:30pm; bar and tapas menu daily 5–10:30pm; dinner daily 6–10:30pm.

Café Mediterraneo (Kids) ITALIAN   This tavern and trattoria is managed by France-born Bruno Deluche, who spent enough time in Italy to know how a trattoria should operate. The result is a hideaway pocket of South European service and cuisine that's tucked into a modern shopping center. The decor includes a mock version of a garden in Naples, banquettes patterned after grottos, and murals showing the highlights of both Monte Carlo and Capri. It's all very tongue-in-cheek, but despite a whiff of corniness, the food is well prepared and flavorful, and the place is genuinely popular, especially with families, who are drawn to its pizzas and pastas. Expect a menu with seven kinds of pizza; a long list of pastas and risottos, including an excellent version of tortellini stuffed with cheese and served with mushrooms, sweet peas, and ham in a creamy sauce; lobster flambéed in brandy; and a mixed grill that includes a beef filet, a lobster tail, and shrimp.

In the Galleria Plaza, West Bay Rd. (C) **345/949-8669.** Reservations recommended only at dinner on Fri–Sat. Pizzas, pastas, and main courses CI$12–CI$24 (US$15–US$30); Sun brunch CI$15 (US$19). AE, DC, MC, V. Daily 11am–1am; Sun brunch 11am–3pm.

Calypso Grill (★) (Finds) CARIBBEAN/INTERNATIONAL   At first glance, you might think this is little more than a waterfront shack, or perhaps a repair shop for the motorboats that are launched from an immediately adjacent concrete ramp. But once you enter, you'll find a charming, funky, and slightly psychedelic bar and restaurant that absolutely drips with Creole colors and a sense of whimsy. If the wind isn't too brisk, you can sit on a wooden deck directly above the water, watching workaday fishing craft depositing

their loads at West Bay's busiest fishing port. The venue is very authentic—a far cry from the congestion and glitter of Seven Mile Beach. But despite its highly appealing raffishness, this place isn't without its touches of elegance. Perch at the rectangular bar here for a cocktail or any of 14 kinds of wine by the glass, or opt for a full meal. The best menu items are marinated conch; Cuban-style shrimp with sherry-flavored cream sauce; fresh fish (ask the waiter what's available) that can be blackened, grilled, or sautéed; roasted rack of lamb with rosemary-and-port-wine sauce; and garlic shrimp linguine. Favorite desserts include mango crepes and sticky toffee pudding.

Morgan's Harbour, West Bay. (✆ 345/949-3948. Reservations recommended. Main courses CI$16–CI$28 (US$19–US$35). AE, DC, MC, V. Tues–Sun 11:30am–3pm and 6–10:30pm.

Captain Hook's/Athena's CARIBBEAN/GREEK/INTERNA-TIONAL   Located on West Bay Road, immediately adjacent to the entrance to the also-recommended Treasure Island Resort (p. 67), this dining complex boasts some of the most clever and appealing restaurant themes on Grand Cayman. Except for a tucked-away bar area that's devoted exclusively to sushi, about half of the restaurant revolves around American/Caribbean cuisine served in a romanticized version of a pirates' lair. The other half focuses on Greek cuisine and boasts a decor that evokes a romantic *taverna* in the Greek islands. This section features what's probably the most romantic and visually stunning interior on Grand Cayman, with elaborately handcrafted murals showing pre-Raphaelite interpretations of Hellenistic water nymphs, toga parties, and cavorting cherubs dangling from swings. The best way to choose which area you want to dine in is to wander through both halves of the restaurant (there's an interconnecting door), and then opt for the section that entices (and/or amuses) you the most. Either menu can be served in either area.

Sushi—incongruously served from a bar top that's otherwise devoted to a "ho-ho-ho and a bottle of rum" theme—is very fresh here, and less expensive that what you'll find at some competitors on other parts of Seven Mile Beach. Feeling Greek? Tasty menu items include moussaka, four kinds of souvlaki, roasted "tavern-style" lamb, grilled pork chops, seafood brochettes, and chargrilled octo-pus. Want something more Caribbean? Try savory conch fritters; coconut shrimp; quesadillas with jerk chicken, lobster, or shrimp; zesty chargrilled barbecued ribs; or flavorful Caribbean-style curried pork or chicken.

In the Treasure Island Resort, West Bay Rd. ⓒ **345/949-7777**. Lunch main courses CI$6–CI$11 (US$7.50–US$14); dinner main courses CI$14–CI$30 (US$18–US$38); sushi rolls CI$4–CI$8 (US$5–US$10). AE, DC. MC, V. Daily 11:30am–4:30pm and 5–10pm.

Crow's Nest Restaurant ⭐ *Value* CARIBBEAN   With a board-walk and terrace jutting onto the sands, this informal restaurant has a view of both Sand Cay and a nearby lighthouse. It's on the island's southwesternmost tip, a 4-minute drive from George Town. Crow's Nest Restaurant is one of those places that evoke the Caribbean "the way it used to be." There's no pretense here—you get good, honest Caribbean cooking, featuring grilled seafood. Try a daily special or perhaps the sweet, tender Caribbean lobster. Other dishes include grilled tuna steak with ackee (a fruit) and Jamaican chicken curry with roasted coconut. If it's available, try the banana toffee pie for dessert.

South Sound. ⓒ **345/949-9366**. Reservations recommended. Main courses CI$15–CI$25 (US$19–US$31). AE, DISC, MC, V. Daily 11:30am–3pm and 5:30–10pm.

The Edge *Finds* CARIBBEAN/INTERNATIONAL   This place is regarded as an escape for pressurized local "urbanites" who work at one of the island's many corporations. It lies just east of the center of Bodden Town, on a narrow stretch of land between the coastal road and the sea, within a building that you might think at first is nothing more than a glorified trailer. It's probably the most informal venue on the island, with enough beachcomber memorabilia to remind even the most high-powered executive that London and New York are, indeed, very far away. You can dine inside or on a deck whose pilings go directly into the seabed. Lunches are simple, featuring burgers, conch fritters, grilled pork chops, salads, and the traditional Jamaican dish of ackee with saltfish. The dinner menu includes conch and turtle steaks, grilled filets of very fresh snapper or tuna; and breast of chicken Dijonnaise. Everybody's favorite drink here is a mudslide—made with Kahlua, Frangelico, Bailey's, whipped cream, and cinnamon—but be warned in advance that more than one of these creamy, semihallucinogenic drinks will com-pletely spoil your appetite for dinner. Come here for a respite from the glitter of George Town, and be prepared to be as "raffish-chic" and unpretentious as possible.

Bodden Town. ⓒ **345/947-2140**. Lunch main courses CI$7.75–CI$13 (US$9.70–US$16); dinner main courses CI$18–CI$32 (US$22–US$39). AE, DC, MC, V. Daily 7am–1am.

Edoardo's ITALIAN   This restaurant completely lacks a view, and its location within a shopping center on the landlocked side of West Bay Road is less than glamorous, but this Austrian-owned trattoria-cum-tavern draws a loyal patronage from full-time residents of Grand Cayman, many of whom make dining here on Friday and Saturday nights their culinary respite from a week of home-cooked meals. Food is served in generous portions in a no-nonsense, dark-paneled setting that might have been imported directly from a bar and grill in the suburbs of, say, Detroit or Pittsburgh. However, considering that many of the clients aren't particularly interested in a restaurant theme of "Caribbean romance" (they're probably sick of that restaurant theme anyway), no one seems to care.

Begin your meal with zesty grilled shrimp and calamari in a garlic-and-lemon-flavored sauce, or barbecued Cajun prawns. Pastas come in dozens of different varieties; a favorite is pasta tossed in a basil sauce with red potatoes. Mussels are piled high in a dish with your choice of four sauces—white wine with garlic, spicy marinara, saffron-flavored cream, or red-wine sauce—and served as either a starter or a main course. The best meats and fish are a savory snapper *livornese* (made with capers and black olives); veal Edoardo (scaloppine topped with Parma ham and fontina cheese), and tenderloin of beef wrapped in bacon and served with Cambazola cheese and red-wine demi-glace. If you're in the mood for pizza, there are a dozen types, plus the option of building your own pizza from about 20 toppings, including blackened chicken and shrimp.

Coconut Plaza, West Bay Rd. (℃ **345/945-4408.** Reservations recommended on weekends. Pizzas CI$12–CI$18 (US$15–US$22); main courses CI$17–CI$25 (US$21–US$31). AE, DC, MC, V. Mon–Sat 11:30am–2:30pm; daily 5:30–10:30pm.

Gateway of India (Value INDIAN   Although some island restaurants might feature an Indian dish on their menus from time to time, this is the only purely Indian restaurant in the Cayman Islands, and as such, it's often sought out as a change of pace by diners who have had their fill of Caribbean cuisine. It shares the back side of a clapboard-covered building with Bella Capri, an Italian restaurant that is also recommended (p. 94). The decor is warm, folkloric, and charming, with the interior illuminated with lanterns made from embroidered fabric. Dishes are, as a matter of policy, prepared with a "medium" degree of spiciness, which you can doctor by instructing the staff (most of whom come from either Goa or Bombay) according to your wishes. There's a wide array of meat, fish, and vegetarian dishes to choose from, but ongoing favorites include chicken *korma* in a mild curry sauce; chicken *tikka masala,* cooked in a medium-spicy tomato-flavored butter sauce; and lamb *shahi korma,* served in a creamy curry sauce. All main courses come with saffron-flavored rice, pickles, yogurt, salad, and Indian breads. The lunch buffet is one of the genuinely excellent meal values on Grand Cayman.

Adjacent to the Strand Shopping Center, West Bay Rd. ✆ **345/946-2815.** Reservations not necessary. Lunch main courses CI$6.95–CI$15 (US$8.70–US$19); lunch buffet CI$8.95 (US$11); dinner main courses CI$8.95–CI$26 (US$11–US$32). AE, DC, MC, V. Mon–Fri 11:30am–2:30pm; daily 5:30–10pm.

The Havana Club Cigar Lounge ✿ *(Finds* CUBAN/CARIBBEAN

No other restaurant on Grand Cayman celebrates Cuban mystique with as much joy and abandon. You'll find a richly paneled bar on one side of the venue and a small-scale dining room on the other, both of them permeated with the kind of permissive gallantry you might have expected in Old Havana prior to Fidel Castro. If you don't like cigar smoke, this place will not particularly please you. But if you revel in an venue filled with cigars, aged rum, *mojitos* (drinks made with a blend of sugar, mint leaves, lime juice, rum, ice, and soda water), and Cuban food, where an attractive staff will attend to your needs, you might absolutely, positively adore it.

The food served here is savory, well prepared, and deeply committed to the culinary traditions of Cuba. Menu items include conch fritters; raw marinated fish *(ceviche);* lobster with coconut-flavored curry sauce; and a mixed grill Old Havana, composed of slices of grilled beef, pork, and chicken, served with black beans, rice, and Cuban-style Creole sauce. Throughout most of the week, this is strictly an upscale bar with an attached restaurant, but on Friday, and to a lesser degree on Saturday, clients might actually get up and dance (see p. 155 for a lengthier description of the bar). Don't overlook the possibility of buying some unusual items here: A display case in the back sells aged, top-of-the-line rums and a huge array of all-Cuban cigars (which Americans must smoke in the Cayman Islands because they are illegal in the U.S.).

In the Regency Court Building, West Bay Rd. ✆ **345/945-5391.** Reservations recommended only Fri and Sat nights. Lunch main courses CI$11–CI$12 (US$13–US$15); dinner main courses CI$16–CI$20 (US$20–US$25). AE, DC, MC, V. Mon–Fri 11:30am–1am; Sat–Sun 11:30am–midnight.

La Bodega LATINO/CARIBBEAN

A touch of Iberia reigns here, thanks to massive ceiling beams, terra-cotta floor tiles, a bar crafted from mosaics, thick stucco-covered walls, and paintings which might have been inspired by the reawakening of Madrid during the late 1990s. Many clients come here for the bar, eventually moving on to dinner almost as an afterthought when they are finished with their stiff drinks. See p. 155 for a more detailed description of the bar. This well-managed restaurant's theme evokes a rustic *pueblo* somewhere in the Spanish-speaking world. Menu items are well prepared and flavorful, especially the corn-crusted Caribbean snapper, chili-and-honey-cured Chilean salmon, and rum-infused tenderloin of pork with mole. A special favorite is grilled and roasted local wahoo fish served with conch-stuffed ravioli and chardonnay-flavored lime butter.

In the West Shore Shopping Plaza, West Bay Rd. 🅲 **345/946-8115.** Reservations recommended only for dinner Fri–Sat nights. Lunch main courses CI$7–CI$15 (US$8.75–US$19); dinner main courses CI$17–CI$28 (US$21–US$35). AE, DC, MC, V. Mon–Fri 11:30am–11pm (bar open until 1am); Sat 11:30am–midnight; Sun 5:30–11pm (bar open until midnight).

Outback Steakhouse *(Kids* AUSTRALIAN   This is the Cayman branch of the hugely successful international chain that taught many a North American family how to order dinner in Australian vernacular. The dining room and bar are comfortable, relaxing, and as big and open as the great Australian interior. The rooms are sheathed in dark paneling and decorated with touches of brass and tons of "down under" memorabilia. You'll be steered toward the bar while you wait for your table (reservations aren't accepted), where Australia-centric drinks include glasses of Australian merlots and chardonnays, beers, and specialty cocktails laced with Aussie humor (the vodka-and-schnapps-based Wallaby Darned is a favorite). The menu features the kind of savory, hearty fare you'd associate with a barbecue in Sydney. The best examples include shrimp, ribs, or chicken on the barbie; coconut shrimp; Aussie cheese fries; a Queensland salad that incorporates seasoned chicken with cheeses, bacon, tomatoes, and toasted almonds; rib-eye steak; porterhouse steak (which weighs in at a gut-stretching 20 ounces); and pastas. A favorite dessert, cheesecake with either raspberry or caramel sauce, is named in honor of everybody's favorite Aussie singer, Olivia Newton-John.

In the Strand Shopping Center, West Bay Rd. 🅲 **345/945-3108.** Reservations not accepted. Lunch platters (takeout only) CI$8.75–CI$9.25 (US$11–US$12); dinner main courses CI$12–CI$26 (US$15–US$33). AE, DC, MC, V. Lunch (takeout food only) Mon–Fri noon–3pm; dinners (in-house) Sun–Thurs 5:30–10pm; Fri–Sat 5:30–11pm.

Ragazzi ITALIAN   This is one of our favorite Italian restaurants on Seven Mile Beach. It's located between two banks, in a shopping center that's adjacent to the entrance to the Hyatt Hotel on West Bay Road. You can dine on a narrow terrace in front, but the real glamour of this place will strike you when you walk inside, where you'll find a very large Northern Italian–style blue-and-gold room with granite trim. This place is hip, fun, stylish, and breezily upscale, drawing a clientele of worldly residents, many of whom work in the financial services industries. Lunches are lighter and less formal than dinners, with a medley of very fresh salads, about a dozen pastas (including a version with crayfish and crabmeat), unusual pizzas (including an "Austrian" version with brie cheese and smoked Parma ham) and elegant platters of mostly white-meat and fish dishes such as chicken scaloppine with marsala-and-mushroom sauce, and sautéed mahimahi with capers and chardonnay sauce. Dinners offer savory items such as a blue-crab spring roll, lobster quesadillas, rosemary-marinated duck breast with an orange demi-glace, and walnut-crusted sea bass served in a rum-flavored banana sauce.

Buckingham Square, West Bay Rd. ℭ **345/945-3484.** Reservations recommended only for dinner Fri–Sat. Lunch main courses CI$7–CI$17 (US$8.75–US$21); dinner main courses CI$11–CI$27 (US$14–US$34). AE, DC, MC, V. Daily 11am–4:30pm and 5–11pm.

Smuggler's Cove ℛ INTERNATIONAL   Part of the charm of a meal at this restaurant, located at the edge of George Town, is gazing at the party-colored lights that decorate the adjacent shoreline. The venue is airy, breezy, and ultracomfortable, and hundreds of financial, sports-industry, and music-industry folk have enjoyed savory meals here since the place was founded in the late 1990s. There's a stylish, warm, and comfortable dining room, but—depending on the weather—the most desirable place to sit is on the crescent-shaped concrete deck that was poured directly onto an almost lunar-looking landscape of treacherously jagged rocks that front the ocean. The view encompasses the wide-open ocean, but directly in front of you, as you dine, you might get a close-up look at about a half dozen of the world's biggest cruise ships. Menu items are served in generous portions. Some of the island's most enticing and imaginative dishes are served here, along with old favorites. The mesquite-grilled jerk duck served with a wild berry sauce is remarkable. The catch of the day, a combination of two fresh Caribbean fish with two matching sauces, is also mesquite grilled. The grilled and spicy pork tenderloin comes marinated with Cayman Scotch bonnet peppers, and the seared Chilean salmon filet comes in a crispy and flavorful potato-and-leek shell with a ginger drizzle and a hint of lemon grass.

N. Church St., South George Town. ℂ 345/949-6003. Reservations required. Main courses CI$18–CI$29 (US$23–US$36). AE, MC, V. Mon–Fri 11:30am–2:30pm. Daily 5:30–10:30pm.

Thai Orchid THAI   This is the only spot on Grand Cayman that serves the intricately flavored and sometimes fiery cuisine of Thailand. The interior is graceful, elegant, and rather formal and upscale-looking, with black lacquer furniture and lots of Thai paintings. The waitresses are beautifully outfitted in formal Thai costumes, many of them pink. This place is genuinely well liked by many island diners, who come here for their favorite dishes, including a divine Thai-style lobster and squid with red-curry sauce, Pad Thai (rice noodles with shrimp and bean sprouts), stir-fried chicken with cashews and bell peppers, curries, Thai-style spring rolls, and a deep-fried whole red snapper topped with Thai-style chili sauce (the best dish, in our opinion). A lunch buffet is offered on Tuesdays and Thursdays.

In the Queen's Court Shopping Plaza, West Bay Rd. ℂ 345/949-7955. Lunch main courses CI$10–CI$13 (US$13–US$16); lunch buffet (served Tues and Thurs) CI$12 (US$15); dinner main courses CI$16–CI$21 (US$20–US$26). AE, DC, MC, V. Mon–Sat 11:30am–2:30pm; daily 6–10pm.

The Verandah ⍟ INTERNATIONAL   Set on the upper level of the clubhouse that overlooks the Links golf course at Safe Haven (the only 18-hole golf course on Grand Cayman), this restaurant is the kind of hip, elegant, cutting-edge eatery that you might expect to find in South Beach, Miami. At least some of the allure derives from the attractive and charming staff. Within a soaring four-sided postmodern structure with beautifully grained paneling, you'll have an experience that's both "fine dining and fun dining" at the same time. Views extend out over the driving ranges, a saltwater lagoon, and vistas of the North Sound. Cuisine, as envisioned by Scottish-born chef Johnny Aitken, is among the most creative and cutting-edge on the island. The best examples include shrimp rolls with sweet chili sauce; smoked breast of duck with caramelized orange sauce and rosemary-permeated muffins; a carpaccio of locally caught and locally smoked marlin, served with a honey-flavored horseradish sauce; honey-roasted duck breast with yam cakes and

Scotch bonnet relish; tenderloin of pork white beans; and seared red snapper with sautéed *cho-cho* (a hybrid vegetable that resembles a cross between an apple and a potato), served with cornmeal flan and chili oil.

Above the clubhouse of the Links golf course at Safehaven, off West Bay Rd. © 345/943-2000. Reservations recommended. Lunch main courses CI$12–CI$15 (US$15–US$19); dinner main courses CI$17–CI$25 (US$21–US$31). AE, DC, MC, V. Mon–Fri 11:30am–2:30pm and Mon–Sat 5:30–10pm. From West Bay Rd., turn inland just opposite the site for the new Ritz-Carlton Hotel.

4 Inexpensive Restaurants

Al la Kebab KEBABS   If you're in the mood for a convivial outdoor snack with the young, the restless, and the wasted, consider driving over to this late-night joint for kebabs, which is open after most of the other restaurants on Grand Cayman have closed for the night. The setting is a vividly painted clapboard shack plunked down in a parking lot adjacent to the island's biggest theater. There's no dining room here, but the dashboard of your car can work quite nicely as a table. The tasty, juicy kebabs are seasoned with fresh herbs and grilled to perfection. They come in lamb, chicken, or beef, and can be doused with any of the half-dozen varieties of sauce. Your hosts are Alan Silverman, Laura Wintermut (both from Canada), and their Caymanian partner, Frank McCoy.

Lawrence Blvd., adjacent to the cinema, across from World's Gym. © 345/943-4343. Kebabs CI$5.50–CI$6.50 (US$6.90–US$8.15). No credit cards. Mon–Fri 6pm–4am; Sat 6pm–1am.

Chicken, Chicken *(Kids* *(Value* AMERICAN   This venue completely lacks glamour, but within its cheerful and unpretentious premises (it looks like the interior of a brightly painted Creole cottage), you can feed an entire family for less money than at virtually any other restaurant on Grand Cayman. The specialty here, and the only available main course, is tender, richly seasoned, perfectly cooked chicken. As many as 40 chickens at a time rotate enticingly in the glare of the island's biggest, and most theatrical, rotisserie, prominently positioned near the restaurant's entrance. Each chicken is flavored with herbs and a touch of garlic. After placing your order at the stand-up counter, you can opt to dine in the restaurant (which most people do at lunchtime), or you can haul your chicken away for consumption somewhere else (which most customers do later in the day). The chicken (breast, thigh, or whole roasted birds, depending on your order) is accompanied by corn bread and your choice of cole slaw, rice, or beans. Again, don't expect romance or anything flashy—this is a venue that's family-friendly, efficient, uncomplicated, and cheap.

In the West Shore Shopping Plaza, West Bay Rd. ℂ **345/945-2290**. Lunch CI$6.25–CI$7.25 (US$7.80–US$9.05); dinner CI$8–CI$9 (US$10–US$11). AE, DC, MC, V. Daily 11am–10pm.

Cimboco Caribbean Café INTERNATIONAL   This is one of the most charming spots on Grand Cayman for a light, simple meal. Whimsical and tongue-in-cheek, it occupies a modern building very close to Grand Cayman's only movie theater. The venue is deceptively simple: You might imagine at first glance that you're in a brightly colored cafe that just serves coffee and drinks, but a quick glance at the menu reveals a sophisticated medley of pizzas, salads, Caribbean-style rotis (pancake-type bread with various fillings), and a full bar serving the kinds of the fiesta-colored drinks that you might expect at a breezy bar beside the beach. The caramelized scallops served with mango-flavored salsa are an excellent starter. Caesar salads can be garnished with grilled chicken or grilled shrimp. Pizzas can be livened up with all sorts of toppings, including slices of jerk chicken and lamb sausage. Other offerings include pastas (such as a three-cheese chicken fettuccine), and an oft-changing array of daily specials. Canada-born Tom and Meg Lasley are your charming and hardworking hosts.

In the Marquee Shopping Center, near the corner of the Harquail Bypass and West Bay Rd. ℂ **345/947-2782**. Reservations recommended for parties of 6 or more. Pizzas, burgers, and platters CI$7.75–CI$17 (US$9.70–US$21). AE, MC, V. Daily 11am-10pm.

Coffee Grinders Deli *(Value* SANDWICHES/SOUPS/PASTRIES This is the largest, cleanest, and busiest deli and pastry shop on the island, with a solid reputation for fresh and imaginative soups and sandwiches. Sandwiches are ordered at the glass-fronted display case, made while the customer waits, and consumed at luncheonette-style tables. A meal here is the perfect antidote to the increasingly high restaurant tabs that are becoming the norm on Grand Cayman. Soups might include, depending on the day of the week and the mood of the chef, corn and chicken enchilada, cream of leek and potato, and lobster-tomato bisque. Some excellent sandwich options are roast turkey with chunky apple-celery-and-lemon-flavored mayonnaise, a Cuban-style Reuben, and (perhaps best of all) a Louisiana-style muffuletta—a sourdough roll topped with olives, tomatoes, roasted turkey, and Havarti cheese.

In the Seven Mile Shopping Centre, West Bay Rd. (📞 345/949-4833. Reservations not accepted. Sandwiches, salads, and platters CI$6.95–CI$9.75 (US$8.70–US$12). No credit cards. Mon–Sat 7am–6pm; Sun 8am–3pm.

Corita's Copper Kettle 🍴 (Value CARIBBEAN/AMERICAN

This place is usually packed in the mornings, when you can enjoy a full American breakfast or a wide selection of West Indian breakfast specialties, including green bananas served with fried dumplings, fried flying fish, and Corita's Special (ham, melted cheese, eggs, and fruit jelly all presented on a fried fritter). The lunch menu is diverse, including salads; chicken and beef platters; and conch, turtle, or lobster prepared as burgers or served up in a hearty stew.

In Dolphin Center. (📞 345/949-7078. Reservations required. Main courses CI$7–CI$14 (US$8.75–US$18); lunch CI$6.50–CI$8.50 (US$8.15–US$11). No credit cards. Mon–Sat 7am–5pm.

Hard Rock Cafe Cayman Islands AMERICAN   In terms of the dollar amount of business it generates, this restaurant blows every other eatery in George Town way out of the water. Most of the restaurant's business is conducted at lunchtime, when long lines of hungry cruise-ship passengers are handled efficiently, and vast quantities of party-colored drinks, commemorative T-shirts, and American-derived comfort food are sold at speeds and quantities that would make any restaurant in the world deeply envious. On the street level, you'll find a faux-Victorian bar, a T-shirt boutique, and a waiting area for diners. The dining room lies at the top of a wide staircase on the building's second floor. If you have to wait for a table (you won't usually need to wait more than 10 or 15 minutes), there's no lack of visual distraction here—the walls are covered with references to pop icons and music-industry memorabilia. You'll spot framed photographs of Mick Jagger and Bob Marley, outfits worn by Madonna and Buddy Holly, and more. Suspended from the ceiling, just above the stairwell that leads up to the dining room, is part of a 1959 pink Cadillac.

The establishment's most popular drink is the Hurricane, which is made from three kinds of rum and three kinds of fruit juice. It sells for between CI$6.25 and CI$9.95 (US$7.80–US$12), depending on what size you order. Menu items include burgers, Reuben sandwiches, meal-sized salads, steaks, pastas, Pig Sandwiches (barbecued pork with french fries), fish and chips, and a particularly comforting version of meatloaf. Evenings here, after the departure of the cruise ships, are much less crowded than lunchtime.

43 S. Church St., George Town. 🕾 **345/945-2020.** Reservations not accepted. Lunch and dinner main courses CI$8–$CI$22 (US$10–US$27). AE, DC, MC, V. Daily 9am–10pm.

Heritage Kitchen 🅰 *(Finds* CAYMANIAN   Before the advent of most of the fancy restaurants that now dot the edges of West Bay Road, many Caymanians lived on a diet of fried fish, deep-fried fritters, and "fish tea," a hearty seafood soup thickened with mashed plantains. A handful of native cooks survive from the era prior to mass tourism, and at least some of them have achieved local fame and widespread approval. One of these is Tunny Powell, a native Caymanian who sets up an informal takeaway restaurant every weekend in a battered, wood-sided building that was originally a garage. During opening hours, as many as a dozen cars at any time might be parked on the shoulder of Boggy Sand Road, located in a residential neighborhood in the district of West Bay. Don't expect grandeur, but know in advance that you're approaching something of a cultural icon here.

There are only two menu choices available: Styrofoam containers filled with spicy, steaming fish tea (a fish soup enriched with plantains and potatoes) and Styrofoam containers filled with fried fish (usually mahimahi, dolphin, or kingfish), served with large, fluffy fritters and wrapped in newspaper. Bring your own beer, or buy sodas or fruit juice here. There are a handful of battered plankwood tables and benches on-site, and of course, the charming and irrepressible Tunny Powell is always available with his pithy insights into development and recent changes in the Cayman Islands.

A nearby storeroom, loaded with rusted and dusty industrial artifacts and minor curiosities, functions as an informal museum, which may or may not be open at the time of your visit depending on the mood and inclination of Mr. Powell. The charge for entrance into the museum is CI$3 (US$3.75); but in many cases, the entrance fee is waived. Boggy Sand Road is interesting in and of itself—it's a prestigious residential street that's home to some genuinely interesting buildings, both compact and historic, and very large and modern.

11 Boggy Sand Rd., near the junction, marked with a traffic light, of Church St. and West Bay Rd., in the district of West Bay. 🕾 **345/949-3477.** Fish tea CI$3 (US$3.75) per pint; deep-fried fish with fritters CI$8 (US$10) per portion. No credit cards. Fri 1pm–2am; Sat 10am–1am; Sun 9am–4pm.

Legendz/Eats/Yoshi's Sushi 🅰 INTERNATIONAL   This is the best arranged, most diverse, and most entertaining restaurant compound on Grand Cayman. It contains three distinctly different environments, including the tongue-in-cheek retro Eats cafe; the cool, hip, and permissive sports and singles bar Legendz for mature adults; and the minimalist Yoshi's Sushi. Legendz serves a two-fisted international menu of steaks, pastas, salads, and seafood. Eats presents a menu of burgers, milkshakes, omelets, and fries to match the candy-colored luncheonette decor that was clearly inspired by teeny-boppers from the age of Elvis. (If you've never seen leopard skin–patterned Formica countertops, you must have a look.) Yoshi's Sushi offers well-presented portions of sashimi, tempura, and sushi in the most soothing of the restaurants in the trio. Come to this complex of restaurants at any hour of the day for a medley of different kinds of food. Expect lots of bar traffic later in the evening. See p. 157 for more information on the bar here.

West Bay Rd. ℂ 345/945-5288. Reservations recommended only for Yoshi's Sushi. Breakfast combos and omelets CI$5.45–CI$7.95 (US$6.80–US$9.95); burgers, pizzas, salads, and platters CI$5.95–CI$19 (US$7.45–US$24); sushi meals CI$15–CI$19 (US$19–US$24). AE, DC, MC, V. Kitchen service daily 6:30am–11:30pm; bar service Sun–Fri 11:30am–1am, Sat 11:30am–midnight.

Mezza's INTERNATIONAL Hip, breezy, and urban, this restaurant sits one floor above a landmark liquor store and microbrewery (Big Daddy's and the Old Dutch Brewery). Much of the beer produced at the brewery is sold within Mezza's. This is a venue that you might expect to encounter in South Beach, Miami. All eyes are drawn to the large rectangular bar area, a magnet for available and restless expatriates serving time in the Cayman's tourism, insurance, or banking industries. Mugs of Old Dutch beer cost from CI$2.50 to CI$4 (US$3.15–US$5), and come in at least six colors ranging from pale to dark amber. Lunches are simple, featuring steak sandwiches, burgers, Caesar salads, and seafood linguines. The dinner menu is more artful, with dishes that include sautéed shrimp with wine sauce and asparagus, grilled swordfish with papaya salsa, sautéed lobster with curry-flavored cream sauce, marinated conch, and fettuccine with jerk chicken.

West Bay Rd., above Big Daddy's Liquor Store, a few steps south of Treasure Island Resort. ℂ 345/949-8511. Reservations recommended only on Fri–Sat nights. Lunch main courses CI$6–CI$11 (US$7–US$14); dinner main courses CI$9–CI$19 (US$11-US$24). AE, MC, V. Mon–Fri 11:30am–1am; Sat 11:30am–midnight; Sun 11am–11pm.

On the Rocks & the Wreck Bar INTERNATIONAL This amiably battered and completely unpretentious bar and grill is the unofficial Grand Cayman gathering place for Australians and their fans.

It's divided into two semiautonomous units, a restaurant (whose decor might remind you of a slightly rundown seaside luncheonette on Cape Cod), and a bar, whose almost-black wood paneling keeps out most direct sunlight, even during the glare of noon, much to the relief of clients nursing hangovers from the night before. From the windows of the restaurant, you'll get a sometimes alarming close-up view of as many as six of the world's biggest cruise ships moored close to shore. Menu items include standard salads, burgers, pastas, fish and chips, grilled fish, and steaks. The fish and chips—a huge and appealingly greasy platter of whatever fish is fresh that day—is the most famous dish on the menu, often ordered by day-trippers who have heard about the restaurant and the dish from other cruise-ship passengers who have visited before. Other popular dishes are burgers, and a Cajun-inspired version of pasta made with blackened red snapper. Several times a year, the place celebrates "Australia Day," when everybody seems to talk like Crocodile Dundee and Australian beers sell at a discount.

N. Church St. 🕐 **345/949-6163** (restaurant) or 345/949-8060 (bar). Burgers, sandwiches, and platters CI$9–CI$23 (US$11–US$29). AE, MC, V. Restaurant Mon–Fri 9:30am–10pm; Sat–Sun 8:30am–1pm; bar remains open until at least midnight.

Seaharvest Restaurant 🍴 INTERNATIONAL This place hosts a pleasing mix of local residents and short-term visitors, all enjoying well-prepared cuisine whose origins range from Europe to India. Low-slung, pink-sided, and separated from the rocky and jagged shoreline by a rectangular swimming pool, this very appealing restaurant is associated with the also-recommended hotel Sunset House (p. 71). You won't notice the restaurant from South Church Street, since it's hidden behind rows of greenery and separated from the hotel by a parking lot. Within a plush, high-ceilinged dining room that's accented with bubbling aquariums and elaborate draperies, you can enjoy lunch fare that includes burgers, salads, pastas, coconut shrimp, salmon poached with orange slices—our favorite—and "calypso chicken" (which is stuffed with ham and cheese, dredged in coconut flakes, and served with a raspberry-mango sauce). Dinners are more elaborate, featuring dishes like grilled shrimp wrapped in bacon and served with a honey-flavored mustard sauce, roasted breast of duck with a Thai chili sauce, chicken tikka masala, and several different versions of lobster. Lamb *banjara,* slow-cooked with pounded spices in the tradition of the southern Indian city of Hyderabad, is an excellent choice if you like Indian food.

At the Sunset House, S. Church St. ℂ **345/949-7111**. Reservations recommended only at dinner Fri–Sat. Lunch CI$7.95–CI$13 (US$9.95–US$15); dinner main courses CI$13–CI$23 (US$16–US$29). AE, DC, MC, V. Daily 11:30am–10pm.

The Treehouse ℛ INTERNATIONAL   Perched on a spit of land that juts seaward, just a few minutes' walk north from the center of George Town, this bar and restaurant manages to be both hip and upscale at the same time. As you approach it, you'll see caged macaws and trees festooned with strings of lights. The less formal area of the restaurant is at street level, where access to the beach, the piers, and the wharves that surround this place is relatively easy. Various tapas, including coconut shrimp, conch fritters, steamed mussels, tuna sashimi, and baked brie, are served in the downstairs venue. The more formal dining area is situated upstairs, in a room with big windows that encompass views of the sea, the land, and the lights of George Town—select your seat according to what you want to view. Light menu offerings include an absolutely superb hamburger served with jalapeño jack cheese, bacon, and fried onions; a Cajun snapper sandwich; a jerk pork-loin sandwich; and a grilled chicken sandwich. Savory platters include chicken curry, filet mignon with a cabernet-flavored mushroom cream sauce, surf and turf, rack of New Zealand lamb with a Dijon mustard and port-wine glaze, and mahimahi in banana leaves with lime, cilantro, chilies, and coconut milk. This is the type of place where you would be equally comfortable entertaining a business client or a date.

N. Church St. (across from Kirk's Supermarket), George Town. ℂ **345/945-0155**. Tapas CI$3–CI$10 (US$3.75–US$13); sandwiches and salads CI$6–CI$10 (US$7.50–US$13); main courses CI$12–CI$28 (US$15–US$35). AE, DC, MC, V. Restaurant daily 11am–10pm; bar Mon–Fri 11am–1am, Sat–Sun 11am–midnight.

Vivine's Kitchen ℛ *Finds* WEST INDIAN   Native Caymanian Vivine Watler runs this charming restaurant from a terrace beside her home on an isolated stretch of road in the East End. Identifiable by the large signs in psychedelic colors, it beckons to motorists who appreciate a bit of local color in a landscape that's otherwise isolated and a bit lonely. You'll dine at plastic tables that are set either on a cement-floored terrace surrounded by lattices, or amid sea grapes, close to the edge of the sea. Don't underestimate the local fame of this place within Caymanian society: When we were last here, an eminently respected middle-aged hostess arrived from faraway West Bay, having driven almost 2 hours (each way) to retrieve a pot full of Vivine's conch stew, with the intention of serving it at a dinner party for old-time Caymanians who missed "cooking the way it used to be." Menu items are written on a blackboard, and change with the availability of ingredients. The tastiest items are fried fish, chicken and chips, cheeseburgers, tuna sandwiches, turtle stew, whelk stew, barbecued ribs, and pork chops. Dessert choices almost always include "heavy cakes" (made from raw grated cassava, yam, or breadfruit). No liquor is served, but drinks include fresh juice made from mangos, tamarinds, and carrots, as well as old-fashioned lemonade. Wednesday night is the most popular night of the week here, with a seafood buffet served between 6:30 and 9pm. The buffet, priced at CI$16 (US$20) per person, features different preparations of turtle, lobster, conch, and fried fish.

Gun Bay, East End. ② 345/947-7435. Main courses CI$4–CI$10 (US$5–US$13). No credit cards. Daily 10am–8pm (except Wed buffet, which lasts until 9pm).

5

Beaches, Scuba Diving & Other Outdoor Pursuits

Almost-guaranteed sunshine, one of the world's most beautiful beaches, and the Caribbean's best scuba diving and snorkeling have put Grand Cayman on the tourist map, where it seems permanently anchored.

Grand Cayman has a number of smaller beaches, but it's so-called **Seven Mile Beach** (actually 8.9km/5½ miles) is the major attraction, with its vast expanses of powdery white sand. Unlike the beaches on some islands to the south, such as Jamaica, Seven Mile Beach is litter-free and also relatively free of annoying peddlers hawking souvenirs.

The beach is so big that there's always plenty of room for everybody, even in the midst of the winter tourist season and at the peak of the cruise-ship arrivals. Most of Grand Cayman's hotels, restaurants, and shopping centers are found along this much-frequented strip of beach. Many scuba-diving outfitters are also located here.

Along with swimmers and beach buffs, scuba divers are attracted to the Cayman Islands in droves and from around the world. As diver Bob Soto puts it, "If there's any spot on the planet that God created just for divers, it is Grand Cayman." One-third of all visitors to the Cayman Islands arrive here to go scuba diving or snorkeling.

There are more than 200 named and explored dive sites in the Cayman Islands. The dive outfitters (see below) are familiar with the best of them and will guide you to what interests you the most. The Cayman Islands, unlike some other islands in the West Indies, have the most reliable outfitters in the Caribbean, rivaled only by those on the little island of Bonaire. Some of the most dramatic dive sites have not been thoroughly explored (and unfortunately aren't on the itineraries of most dive outfitters), owing to the massive coral reef and drop-off that surrounds not only Grand Cayman but Cayman Brac and Little Cayman.

Even if you're not a scuba diver or snorkeler, you'll find many other attractions on the water, including fishing, boating, kayaking, water-skiing, and windsurfing. If you're a landlubber, there's always hiking, golfing, and horseback riding. But most landlubbers never seem to leave Seven Mile Beach. *Note:* All prices in this chapter are given in U.S. dollars.

1 Hitting the Beaches

One of the finest beaches in the Caribbean, Grand Cayman's **Seven Mile Beach** ⟨★★★⟩ boasts sparkling white sands rimmed with Australian pines and palms. (Technically, the beach is named West Bay Beach, but everybody calls it Seven Mile Beach.) This haven of white, white sands stretches all the way from George Town to Long Point. It tends to be crowded near the big resorts, but the beach is so big that you can always find some room to spread out your towel.

Because the beach is on the more tranquil side of Grand Cayman, there is no great tide and the water is generally placid and inviting, ideal for families, even those with small children. A sandy bottom slopes gently to deep water. The water is great for snorkelers and swimmers of most ages and abilities, and it's so clear that you can easily see what's swimming around below you.

Along the stretch of the beach, from one end to the other, there are hotels and condos, many with beachside bars that you can visit. All sorts of watersports concessions can be found along this beach, including places that rent snorkel gear, boats, windsurfers, wave runners, paddlecats, and aqua trikes (these two latter are floating pedal toys).

The hotels that line the beach have bars and restaurants open to nonguests. Most of these hotels also have watersports and beach kiosks where you can book for parasailing or windsurfing experiences, or rent snorkeling equipment for a morning, an afternoon, or the full day.

Of all the bars and restaurants strung along the beach strip, one of the friendliest is the **Beach Club Hotel & Dive Resort,** West Bay Rd. (© **345/949-8100**), which welcomes nonguests. The restaurant is open daily from 7:30am to 9pm and the beach bar is open Monday to Friday 10am to 11pm and Saturday and Sunday 11am to 11:45pm. For divers, a special offer here is a certified boat diving package costing $72 per person, including a two-tank boat dive. The on-site dive shop is open daily from 7am to 5pm.

Grand Cayman also has a number of minor beaches, although they pale in comparison to Seven Mile Beach. Visit these if you want to escape the crowds. Beaches on the east and north coasts of Grand Cayman are good—filled with white sand and protected by an offshore barrier reef, so waters are generally tranquil.

In total contrast to the glitz and glitter of Seven Mile Beach, an attractive little beach lies on the west side of George Town. **Smith Cove Public Beach** is located between Coconut Harbour and Cayman Coves. The sandy strip is small but top-notch. It's a good spot for snorkeling and makes a nice venue for a picnic, as trees shade the picnic tables. There are changing facilities and bathrooms here.

On North Sound along the northern coast, **Rum Point** lies 40km (25 miles) north of George Town and offers one of the best beaches in Grand Cayman, though it is also one of the most remotely located. You can reach the beach by taking the *Rum Pointer* ferry (p. 51). Calm, clear waters make this tree-shaded beach an excellent spot for swimming. Snorkeling is also good here, with rainbow-hued fish and swaying sea fans composing the majority of the underwater life. There are changing facilities here, along with public toilets and showers. On-site is the Wreck Bar if you want a drink. Saturday afternoon from 2 to 5:30pm is the big time here, with a barbecue and live entertainment right on the beach. The watersports operation here is run by Red Sail Sports (see below).

One of our favorite beaches is on the north coast, bordering the **Cayman Kai Beach Resort,** directly to the southwest of Rum Point. This beach is a Caribbean cliché of charm, with palm trees and beautiful sands. You can snorkel along the reef to Rum Point. The beach is also ideal as a Sunday-afternoon picnic spot. Bathrooms and changing facilities are available here. **Awesome Charters** (✆ **916/406-9345**) leads deep-sea fishing, bonefishing, and snorkeling trips here.

The best windsurfing is found in the East End, at the beach near the settlement of **Colliers,** reached along Queen's Highway and lying near Morritt's Tortuga Club.

2 Scuba Diving & Snorkeling

What they lack in nightlife the Cayman Islands make up in watersports, especially diving and snorkeling. Coral reefs and coral formations encircle all three islands and are filled with loads of marine life, which scuba divers and snorkelers are forbidden to disturb. *Important:* For our recommendations of the best scuba-diving and snorkeling sites, be sure to refer to chapter 1, "The Best of the Cayman Islands."

The full diving scene in the Cayman Islands would fill a book unto itself, and has done just that. If you're a serious diver, pick up one of three comprehensive guides published: *Diving Cayman*

Islands by Jesse Cancelmo (Aqua Quest Publications, 1997), *The Dive Sites of the Cayman Islands* by Lawson Wood (Contemporary Books, 2001), and *The Cayman Islands Dive Guide* by Stephen Frink and William Harrigan (Abbeville Press Publishers, 1999).

It's easy to dive close to shore, so boats aren't necessary, although there are plenty of diving boats available. For certain excursions, we recommend a trip with a qualified dive master. There are many dive shops for rentals, but they won't rent you scuba gear or supply air unless you have a card from one of the national diving schools, such as NAUI or PADI. Hotels also rent diving equipment to their guests, and will arrange snorkeling and scuba-diving trips.

Universally regarded as the most up-to-date and best-equipped watersports facility in the Cayman Islands, **Red Sail Sports** maintains its headquarters at the Hyatt Regency Grand Cayman, West Bay Road (© **877/REDSAIL** in the U.S., or 345/945-5965; www.redsail.com). Other locations are at the Westin Casuarina (© **345/949-8732**) and at Rum Point (© **345/947-9203**). Red Sail has a wide range of offerings, including deep-sea fishing, sailing, diving, and more.

Red Sails offers certified divers a variety of boat dives each day. A two-tank morning or afternoon dive goes for $85, with a one-tank afternoon boat dive costing $55. Special dives include a one-tank Stingray City dive for $60 and a one-tank night dive for $60. Full PADI open-water certification costs $500, and all types of scuba gear can be rented.

Red Sails offers the most comprehensive watersports program on the island, including all equipment rentals for everything from a banana-boat tube ride to kayaking and water-skiing.

The company also offers boating trips, including parasailing excursions. Catamaran sails are offered, the most popular being a 4 ½ hour jaunt to Stingray City, with lunch and snorkeling included, that goes for $75 for adults or half price for children 12 and under. Two-hour sunset sails along the North Sound cost $30 for adults or half price for children 12 and under, and you can also book a dinner catamaran cruise for $65 for adults or half price for children 12 and under. Glass-bottom boat snorkeling trips are offered at $40 per person with equipment included. And these are only some of the offerings. Although there are many other outfitters on the island (see below), Red Sails will be able to handle most of your needs above and below the water.

Divetech, Cobalt Coast Resort, 18 Seafan Dr., Boatswains Bay (© **866/622-9626** in the U.S., or 345/946-5658; www.divetech.com) is one of the genuinely excellent dive operations in the

Cayman Islands. It's one of the best organized and most attentive outfitters, with a fine reputation and a location near deep marine walls and drop-offs that divers find superb—in fact, the best shore diving on island. The operation is headquartered in a clapboard-covered cottage on the grounds of the recommended Cobalt Coast Resort (p. 68), on Grand Cayman's most northwestern tip, far from the touristic glitter of Seven Mile Beach. Don't come here expecting a sandy beach: The coastline is treacherously jagged, covered with bruising rocks that can puncture the side of any watercraft that ventures too close. Consequently, Divetech boats moor at a massive 36m (120-foot) concrete pier that juts seaward. From here, within a relatively short distance, divers have access to a cornucopia of dive options that are difficult to duplicate anywhere else.

Many, but not all, of the Divetech's clients opt to stay at its well-recommended associated hotel, Cobalt Coast. (Those who don't stay at Cobalt Coast must either drive or make special arrangements for transportation from hotels on other parts of the island.) Prices are invariably cheaper when they're clustered within one of the resort's many dive packages, but for a rough idea of prices, a two-tank dive for certified divers costs $85, and a 3½ hour resort course for a first-timer goes for $100. Open-water certification costs $425. Guided shore dives are $35 during the day or $45 at night. Canadian-born Nancy Romanica is the organization's founder and creative force. She's also an authority on the curious pastime known as free-diving, recommended only for very experienced divers, where aficionados (without scuba tanks) reach alarming depths using only their carefully trained lung capacities. The cost for a guided free dive and a lesson (usually taught by Nancy herself) is $100 per person for a half day and $200 per person for a full day.

Ocean Frontiers, East End (© **345/947-7500;** www.ocean frontiers.com), specializes in scuba diving and snorkeling trips in the East End, where divers find some of the best coral reefs in the Caribbean, including such shipwreck sites as HMS *Convert* and *Marybelle.* This is the best outfitter for experienced divers. Taking out small groups, Ocean Frontiers avoids the crowds along Seven Mile Beach. It offers regular scuba diving: $60 for one tank, $85 for two tanks, and $129 for three tanks. Snorkeling is also offered on Wednesday, a half day costing $35. Equipment can be rented.

The most enduring and longest-established dive operator in Grand Cayman is **Bob Soto's Diving Ltd.** (© **800/262-7686** in the U.S. or 345/949-2022 to make reservations). Owned by Ron Kipp, the operation includes full-service dive shops at Treasure

Island, the SCUBA Centre on North Church Street, and Soto's Coconut in the Coconut Place Shopping Centre. This is the best outfitter for novices. A full-day resort course, designed to teach the fundamentals of scuba to beginners who know how to swim, costs $120: The morning is spent in the pool and the afternoon is a one-tank dive from a boat. All necessary equipment is included. Certified divers can choose from a wide range of one-tank ($55) and two-tank ($85) boat dives daily on the west, north, and south walls, plus shore diving from the SCUBA Centre. A one-tank night dive costs $60. Nondivers can take advantage of daily snorkel trips ($30–$50), including excursions to Stingray City. The staff is helpful and highly professional.

Don Foster's Dive Cayman, North Church Street, George Town (© **345/907-9821**), dating from 1982, is one of the best and most respected dive outfitters. A big, well-run operation, it features one-tank dives for $45 and two-tank dives for $75. Night dives cost $55, with a resort course going for $75 and open-water certification costing $450. The outfitter also features snorkeling from 2 to 4:30pm daily at Stingray City, at a cost of $30 per person. Equipment can be rented.

Seven Mile Watersports, West Bay Road (© **345/949-0332; www.7mile.ky**), operates from the Seven Mile Beach Resort and Club and is particularly sensitive to the requests of individual divers. The outfitter takes out only 15 divers at a time in its 12m (40-ft.) dive boat. Most of its diving jaunts are to the north wall. A one-tank boat dive costs $55, with a two-tank dive going for $75. A special feature is a three-tank dive, including lunch, for $150. A one-tank dive at Stingray City costs $55 per person. There is also a snorkel excursion, called the Sunset Trip, which makes stops at Stingray City, the Coral Gardens, and the Barrier Reef. Offered each Tuesday, it leaves at 3pm and lasts until dusk. The Sunset Trip costs $40.

Off the Wall Divers, West Bay Road (© **345/945-7525**), also caters well to the individual diver as it specializes in custom dive jaunts for groups of 2 to 10 (no more) divers. The outfitter offers training resort courses and full certifications, plus Nitrox certifications. A one-tank dive goes for $45, two tanks for $70, and three tanks for $115, with a PADI open-water certification course costing only $375. Resort scuba courses cost $95, and equipment rentals, including dive computers, are available.

Another good dive outfit, **Tortuga Divers** (© **345/947-2097**), operates out of Morritt's Tortuga Club and Resort at East End. This outfitter caters to both experienced or novice divers, offering two daily dive jaunts at 9am and 2pm. Half-day or full-day snorkeling

(Moments Your Temporary Caymanian Pet:
A Stingray

The offshore waters of Grand Cayman are home to one of the most unusual (and ephemeral) underwater attractions in the world, **Stingray City** 🐟🐟. Set in the sun-flooded, 4m-deep (12-ft.) waters of North Sound, about 3.2km (2 miles) east of the island's northwestern tip, the site originated in the mid-1980s when local fishermen cleaned their catch and dumped the offal overboard. They quickly noticed scores of stingrays (which usually eat marine crabs) feeding on the debris, a phenomenon that quickly attracted local divers and marine zoologists. Today, between 30 and 50 relatively tame stingrays hover in the waters around the site for daily handouts of squid from increasing hordes of snorkelers and divers. To capitalize on the phenomenon, various outfitters lead expeditions from points along Seven Mile Beach, traveling around the landmass of Conch Point to the feeding grounds. One well known outfit is **Treasure Island Divers** (✆ **345/949-4456**), which charges divers $60 per one tank and snorkelers $35. Trips are made daily at 1pm. (Be warned that stingrays possess deeply penetrating and viciously barbed stingers capable of inflicting painful damage to anyone who mistreats them. Above all, the divers say, never try to grab one by the tail. Despite the potential dangers, divers and snorkelers seem amazingly adept at feeding, petting, and stroking the velvety bodies of these bat-like creatures while avoiding unpleasant incidents.)

adventures can also be arranged, and all types of gear can be rented on the premises. The morning scuba dive costs $85, the afternoon dive goes for $60. A half day's snorkeling costs $60, going up to $75 for a full day.

Although nearly every scuba outfitter also offers snorkeling tours, the best outfitter just for snorkeling (no scuba trips) is **Captain Marvin's,** Cayman Falls Shopping Center, Seven Mile Beach (✆ **345/945-4590**). A 2-hour trip costs $30 for ages 12 and over, and $20 for ages 4 to 11, including stops at Stingray City and the Barrier Reef. A 3-hour trip goes for $35 for ages 12 and over, or

$17.50 for ages 4 to 11. All prices include snorkel gear and instruction if required, and food for feeding the stingrays. Boats range in size from 9m to 14m (30 ft.–45 ft.). Captain Marvin, who launched his tours with a borrowed sailboat in the '50s, is now one of the leading charter boat operators in Grand Cayman.

Captain Bryan's, North Church Street in George Town (© **345/ 949-0038**), features snorkeling, fishing, and sailing trips on 15m (50-ft.) boats. Sunset sails and private snorkeling charters are also available. Most watersports buffs use these services for snorkeling, a half-day trip costing $30, and a full day going for $60.

Captain Crosby's Watersports, Coconut Place, West Bay Road (© **345/945-4049**), was a pioneer of snorkeling trips to Stingray City. The outfitter still conducts either half-day ($34) or full-day ($44) trips to the site on a 12m (40-ft.) trimaran. A freshly prepared seafood lunch is part of the package. Bonefishing and reef-fishing trips can also be arranged.

In addition to the above outfitters, you'll find dozens of kiosks along Seven Mile Beach offering snorkeling gear.

3 More Fun in the Surf

BOAT RENTALS & SUBMARINE RIDES

Many travelers dream of sailing their own boat beneath an azure Caribbean sky, without the company of a crew. Alas, unless you're a very experienced sailor, and unless you can afford it, it might not be feasible to rent one of the very large sailing vessels that are the norm at most boat-charter outfits, and which often require a substantial cash deposit before a newcomer will be entrusted to take it out onto the deep blue. However, there are numerous ways for less experienced sailors to rent small boats

Small (about 3.3m/11-ft.-long) sailcraft are the specialty at the **Cayman Islands Sailing Club,** Spinnaker Road, Red Bay, near the hamlet of North Sound (© **345/947-7913**). On a sun-baked, gravel-covered compound, isolated from the traffic and congestion of West Bay, you'll find a two-story warehouse crafted from wood planks and corrugated metal panels, a clubhouse with its own trophy-filled bar, and an inventory of about 70 small-scale sailboats, usually Picos, Lasers, or (least high-tech of all) simple sailing dinghies, each suitable for either one or two persons. Most boats here rent for 2-hour periods, during which you can do some quality brisk sailing in Grand Cayman's North Sound. Boat rentals are $25 per hour. Rentals are available every day from 9am to 5pm, and

Finds   Wreck of the Ten Sails

The date was February 8, 1794. Captain William Martin was steering the lead ship, HMS *Convert,* when the vessel hit a reef. The captain fired a cannon to signal a fleet of other merchant vessels about the treacherous reefs that lay ahead. The captains of the other ships mistook the signal for a warning of an impending pirate attack. One vessel after another in the convoy of 58 merchants ships, most of them square-rigged sailing vessels bound for Europe, met the same fate as the *Convert* in the rough, pitch-black seas.

In all, 10 ships were wrecked that disastrous night. By some miracle, villagers of the East End of Grand Cayman managed to save all 400 or so sailors and officers wrecked that night, bringing them ashore in canoes.

Four of the ships were eventually salvaged, and the other vessels sunk to the bottom of the sea. The cannons from the wrecked ships were eventually salvaged and sent to England as scrap.

In the little community of Gun Bay in the East End, a monument can be seen commemorating that tragic maritime event. The statue was dedicated by Queen Elizabeth II on her visit to Grand Cayman in 1994. A local legend— untrue—maintains that King George II gave the Caymanians tax-free status because of their heroic rescue. If you'd like to explore this shipwreck site, it is often included in the diving programs offered by Ocean Frontiers (p. 115).

require at least a rudimentary level of prior sailing experience. If you don't feel completely proficient, you can sign up for a series of five sailing lessons, each lasting 2 hours, for a fee of around $625.

Atlantis Adventures (Cayman) Ltd. (for information and reservations from the U.S., dial © **800/887-8571;** from the Cayman Islands or other parts of the world, dial © **345/949-7700;** www. atlantisadventures.net) is the better-established of two outfits on Grand Cayman that promise to take you, safely and panoramically, beneath the surface of the waves. The company offers three distinctly different underwater tours, any of which will provide views of the remarkable geology beneath sea level around Grand Cayman. None of the three excursions requires any advance diving experience or skill. Each trip departs from a clearly signposted building set directly on the waterfront of George Town, immediately south of the cruise-ship piers.

The cheapest submarine experience, limited to relatively shallow waters, is offered within the *Seaworld Explorer* semi-submarine. Developed in Australia for viewing marine life above the Great Barrier Reef, this is a steel-hulled watercraft that only appears unusual beneath the waterline (it looks like a regular boat from above). In the ship's lowest level, in cramped proximity to up to 45 other passengers, you'll be seated next to long rows of windows that angle downward for panoramic views of the deep. Because the ship never descends beneath the surface of the sea, a ride within its hull is best suited for viewing sun-flooded underwater reefs, shipwrecks, and objects lying no more than 7.5m (25 ft.) beneath the surface. Part of the attraction of this trip derives from the scuba divers who dispense scraps of fish to all manner of hungry marine life, including Bermuda chubs, sergeant-majors, and angelfish. One-hour boat rides are priced at $34 per adult, with children aged 2 to 12 paying half price.

The second option is offered aboard the *Atlantis* submarine, a fully submersible craft holding 48 passengers. A 1¼-hour tour priced at $84 per person descends to depths of 30m (100 ft.). Children aged 4 to 12 pay half price, and teenagers (ages 13–18) are charged $59 each. No children under 4 are allowed on board. There's a lot to see underwater at this depth, and there's still enough sunlight to allow for the growth of thousands of kinds of plant life, vital for the sustenance of thousands of species of fish. This is the most popular, and perhaps the most visually rewarding, of the submarine experiences, with lots of plant and marine life visible through the windows.

Most unusual and expensive of all is a ride aboard the *Atlantis Deep Explorer,* a yellow-hulled two-passenger submarine that carries two well-funded passengers at a time to depths of between 240m and 300m (800 ft. and 1,000 ft.) beneath the waves. Unlike the *Atlantis* submarine, whose counterparts appear in other destinations, this is the only submarine in the world that offers descents to these depths to members of the general public.

The environment at these depths is harsh, cold, and unforgiving, with life forms becoming increasingly sparse as depths increase. There's very little light and very little plant life, and you might have difficulty gaining visual perspective as your mini-sub free-falls through progressive layers of water temperatures. Below about 180m (600 ft.), the water only supports weird, palm tree–shaped creatures known as crinoids that are of distinct interest to zoologists and botanists, but not all that dramatic to laypersons. Crinoids resemble a miniature version of a palm tree, but are colored an iridescent pale gray because they're completely devoid of chlorophyll. If you opt for this deep ride, be prepared to be uncomfortable, cramped, and claustrophobic, and be aware that the submarine's captain and guide may or may not be articulate, or even particularly informative, about your underwater sightings. Also be prepared to pay a steep price for your descent to the dark and chilly deep. A descent to 240m (800 ft.) costs US$345, and a descent to 300m (1,000 ft.) costs $450. Frankly, the difference in what you'll see at each of those depths isn't distinct. Know in advance that the deep dive will require a 15-minute transit, by motorboat, from the point of departure to the submarine (the company operates two of them), which is usually moored several hundred feet offshore.

The less-recommended competitor of the Atlantis submarines is the 60-passenger *Nautilus,* Bush Centre, George Town (© **345/945-1355;** www.nautilus.ky), a semi-submarine with a protected glass hull that cruises 1.5m (5 ft.) below the sea's surface. The craft, named after Jules Verne's futuristic vessel, departs from Rackham's Dock behind Rackham's Pub in George Town. The trips, which include commentary, take visitors to the *Cali* and *Balboa* shipwrecks and on to Cheeseburger Reef, where passengers can view divers feeding the fish. Departures are daily at 11am and 3pm, with the afternoon tour allowing passengers 30 minutes of snorkel time. The morning tour takes 1 hour and the afternoon tour takes 1½ hours. The morning tour costs $35 for adults and $15 for children 3 to 12 (children under 3 are free), with the afternoon tour going for $39 for adults and $19 for children 3 to 12 (children under 3 are free).

WINDSURFING

Avid windsurfers rate the 6.4km (4 miles) of reef-protected shallows off East End as the best location for windsurfing. Prevailing winds there are 24kmph to 40kmph (15 mph–25 mph) from November through March, with 6- to 10-knot southeasterly breezes in summer months.

The best outfitter to hook you up with windsurfing gear and lessons is **Cayman Windsurfing** at Morritt's Tortuga Club (© **345/947-7492**), in the East End of the island, an hour's drive from George Town. Open daily from 8:30am to 5pm, it charges $35 per hour or $85 for 3 hours for windsurfing gear. If your stamina demands 5 hours, the cost goes up to $130. Windsurfing lesson packages are also offered, beginning at $35 for 30 minutes and going up to $280 for 7 days, including training classes. Snorkeling equipment can also be rented here at a cost of $15 for 24 hours.

4 Other Outdoor Pursuits

FISHING Grouper and snapper are most common catches for those who bottom-fish along the reef. Deeper waters turn up barracuda and bonito. Sportsfishermen from all over the world come to the Caymans with hopes of hooking one of the big ones: tuna, wahoo, or marlin. Most hotels can make arrangements for charter boats; experienced fishing guides are also available. **Red Sail Sports** (p. 114) offers deep-sea-fishing excursions in search of tuna, marlin, and wahoo on a variety of air-conditioned vessels with an experienced crew. Tours depart at 7am and 1pm, last half a day, and cost $600 (a full day costs $800). The fee can be split among four to six people.

FITNESS CENTERS The original fitness center on the island, **World Gym,** West Bay Road (℃ **345/949-5132**), is still going strong. You'll find it behind a branch of Wendy's on Seven Mile Beach. It features such state-of-the-art equipment as Nautilus and cardiovascular machines, plus activities such as aerobics on a sprung wood dance floor, bodybuilding, jujitsu karate, massages, weights and the like, with five personal trainers on call. A one-day pass costs $20. The center is open Monday to Friday 5:30am to 9pm, Saturday 8am to 6pm, and Sunday 8am to 4pm.

A competitor is **Fitness Connection,** Glen Eden Road, South Sound (℃ **345/949-8485**), which is a full-service facility with a lot of extras—even high-gyrating belly dancing and tap dancing. Of course, regular gym workouts are offered, along with personal training and yoga. The admission cost is $31 for everybody (aerobics and dance classes are included in this fee), plus an additional $9 for use of special facilities and for special programs. The complex is open Monday to Friday from 8am to 6pm and Saturday 9am to 1am.

GOLF The best course on the island, the **Britannia Golf Club,** next to the Hyatt Regency on West Bay Road (℃ **345/949-8020**), was designed by Jack Nicklaus and incorporates three different courses in one: a 9-hole championship layout, an 18-hole executive setup, and a "Cayman" course. The last course was designed for play with the Cayman ball, which goes about half the distance of a regulation ball. Greens fees are a pricey $110 to play 18 holes or $70 for 9 holes. Cart rentals are included, but club rentals cost $20 for 9 holes or $40 for 18 holes. All of these courses are of medium difficulty. Reserve at least 24 hours in advance.

Constantly windswept, the **Links at Safe Haven** (© 345/949-5988) is a par-71, 6,605-yard course designed by Roy Case and set in an environment that's tantamount to a botanical garden. On-site are a clubhouse, pro shop, and restaurant. Greens fees are $120 per person for 18 holes, with mandatory golf carts included. Clubs are $15 to $35, depending on the type. The golf course lies across Seven Mile Beach Road, opposite from the Westin Casuarina. Reserve at least 24 hours in advance.

A smaller, less important course is the **Sunrise Family Golf Centre,** Sunrise Landing, Savannah (© 345/947-4653), lying a 15-minute drive east of George Town. This is a 9-hole, par-3 golf course, with a full-length driving range and clubhouse. Greens fees are $21, with club rentals available for $10. A pro on hand offers golf lessons for $69 per hour.

Golf courses in Grand Cayman are open daily from 8am to 6pm. Many golfers like to avoid the intense noonday sun.

HORSEBACK RIDING   Nicki's Beach Rides (© 345/945-5839) collects riders anywhere in the vicinity of Seven Mile Beach and takes them on early-morning or late-afternoon rides on the beach, with some riding on trails that cut inland. Nicole Eldemire ("Nicki") is a font of information about life in Grand Cayman, and she adds to the enjoyable experience of horseback riding with her anecdotes about island life and its flora and fauna. You're in the saddle for 1½ hours for $65 per person. Sunset rides can also be arranged if at least 6 riders are interested.

Honeysuckle Trail Rides, Savannah (© 345/947-7976), will also arrange to pick you up if you're staying in the vicinity of Seven Mile Beach. This outfitter offers morning and sunset rides lasting 1½ hours at a cost of $60 per rider. Both Western and English tack are offered.

TENNIS   Many of the big resorts have their own tennis courts available to guests. However, if yours does not, you can go to the **Cayman Islands Tennis Club** (© 345/949-9464), open daily from 8 to 11am and 2 to 9pm. The charge for playing is $12 per person. The club rents equipment and also offers various lessons. It lies in back of the Grand Cayman Rugby Club on South Sound Road.

Exploring Grand Cayman

What attractions does Grand Cayman have other than Seven Mile Beach? Admittedly, this golden strip of sand is its most fabled lure, but if you can tear yourself from the sandy strip, there are a number of attractions, many of which may pleasantly surprise you. As one villa owner, who had been living in Grand Cayman for 3 years, told us, "There is more to see and more diversity here than my wife and I ever realized when we first came from Florida to settle permanently."

The most interesting sections of George Town can be explored on foot in an hour or so (see below), although you could spend hours shopping in the town. Your options for exploring the island in greater depth are to take a guided tour, or to rent a car or a scooter and set out.

Most visitors drive north of George Town along West Bay Road and the fabled Seven Mile Beach, which is the most heavily developed part of Grand Cayman. Those seeking a more in-depth look at the less touristed areas can take our guided tour of the East End, going all the way from George Town to Rum Point in the north.

In the East End you find such attractions as blowholes (rock formations that produce huge spouts of water when waves hit) and botanical gardens, plus some of the remains of Grand Cayman's early settlements. Of course, it's always fun to break up a drive across the island with a swim in the Caymans' warm waters or a picnic on a secluded beach somewhere.

1 The Top Five Attractions

Cayman Turtle Farm 🐢🐢   This is the only green-sea-turtle farm of its kind in the world. The islands once had a multitude of turtles in the surrounding waters (which is why Columbus called the islands "Las Tortugas"), but today these creatures are sadly few in number, and the green sea turtle has been designated an endangered species (you cannot bring turtle products into the United States). The turtle farm exists to provide the local market with edible turtle meat (preventing the need to hunt them in the wild) and to replenish the

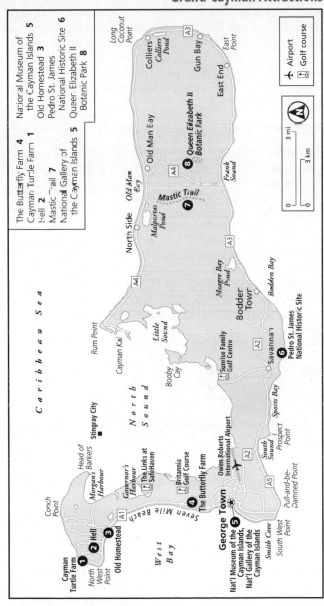

Grand Cayman Attractions

The Butterfly Farm **4**
Cayman Turtle Farm **1**
Hell **2**
Mastic Trail **7**
National Gallery of
the Cayman Islands **5**

National Museum of
the Cayman Islands **5**
Old Homestead **3**
Pedro St. James
National Historic Site **6**
Queen Elizabeth II
Botanic Park **8**

✈ Airport
Golf course

Caribbean Sea

Long Coconut Point

Colliers

Colliers' Pond

A3

Gun Bay

East Point

East End

Old Man Bay

Queen Elizabeth II Botanic Park **8**

Frank Sound

A4

Mastic Trail **7**

North Side

Old Man Bay

Malportas Pond

A4

Meagre Bay Pond

A3

Bodden Bay

Bodden Town

Rum Point

Cayman Kai

Little Sound

North Sound

Booby Cay

Sunrise Family Golf Centre

Savannah

A2

Pedro St. James National Historic Site **6**

Spotts Bay

South Sound

Prospect Point

Head of Barkers

Morgan's Harbour

Governor's Harbour

The Links at Safehaven

Britannia Golf Course

The Butterfly Farm **4**

Owen Roberts International Airport

A2

A5

Pull-and-be-Damned Point

George Town **5**

Nat'l Museum of the Cayman Islands,
Nat'l Gallery of the Cayman Islands

Smith Cove

South West Point

Conch Point

Stingray City

A1

Seven Mile Beach

West Bay

North West Point

Cayman Turtle Farm **1**

Hell **2** **3**

Old Homestead

0   3 mi

0   3 km

125

waters with hatchling and yearling turtles, with the hope that one day their population in the sea will regain its former status. Visitors can observe turtles in every stage of development in 100 circular concrete tanks. Turtles here range in size from 6 ounces to 600 pounds. At a snack bar and restaurant, you can sample turtle dishes if you wish.

Northwest Point. ✆ 345/949-3893. Admission US$6 for adults, free for children 12 and under. Daily 8:30am–5pm.

Queen Elizabeth II Botanic Park ☆☆

On 24 hectares (60 acres) of rugged wooded land off Frank Sound Road, North Side, this park offers visitors a short walk through wetland, swamp, dry thicket, mahogany tree stands, and patches of orchids and bromeliads. The trail is 1km (⅗ths of a mile) long. You'll likely see chickatees, which are freshwater turtles found only on the Caymans and in Cuba. Occasionally you'll spot the rare Grand Cayman parrot, or perhaps the anole lizard, with its cobalt-blue throat pouch. Even rarer is the endangered blue iguana. There's a visitor center with changing exhibitions, plus a canteen for food and refreshments. The botanic park also includes a heritage garden with a re-creation of a traditional Cayman home, garden, and farm; a floral garden with .6 hectares (1½ acres) of flowering plants; and a .8-hectare (2-acre) lake with three islands, home to many native birds.

Off Frank Sound Rd., North Side. ✆ 345/947-3558. Admission CI$6 (US$7.50) for adults, CI$4 (US$5) for children 6–12, free for children 5 and under. Daily 9am–6:30pm.

National Museum of the Cayman Islands ☆

Set directly on the waterfront, in a George Town neighborhood that's more densely packed with cruise-ship passengers than any other area on the island, this museum is housed in a dignified clapboard-covered building that's one of the oldest on the island, and one of the few to have survived the disastrous hurricane of 1932. The 6,000-square-foot interior is a repository for the lore, history, and memorabilia of the Cayman Islands. Many older islanders feel that the importance of local history is being ignored by the younger generations of Caymanians; thus, you might find more passion and ferocious national pride associated with the exhibits inside this place than you might have expected. Exhibits focus on the sociological, archeological, and mercantile history of the Caymans, with a heavy emphasis on the hardships suffered by the Caymanians prior to the advent of tourism and the modern-day financial-services industries. The formal exhibits feature more than 2,000 items depicting the natural, social, and cultural history of the Caymans, including an assortment of

Caymanian artifacts that were collected by islander Ira Thompson beginning in the 1930s. The museum also incorporates a gift shop, a theater, and a cafe.

S. Church St. (Harbour Dr.) © 345/949-8368. Admission CI$4 (US$5) adults, CI$2.50 (US$3.15) children under 12, free for children under 6. Mon–Fri 9am–5pm; Sat 10am–2pm.

Pedro St. James National Historic Site ⭐   This is a restored great house dating from 1780, when only 400 people lived on Grand Cayman. It outlasted all the island's major hurricanes but was destroyed by fire in 1970. It has been rebuilt and is now the center-piece of a heritage park with a visitor center and an audiovisual the-ater that presents laser light shows. Because of its size, the great house was called "the Castle" by generations of Caymanians. Its pri-mary historic importance dates from December 5, 1831, when res-idents met here to elect Cayman's first legislative assembly, making the house the cradle of the island's democracy. The great house sits atop a limestone bluff with a panoramic view of the sea. Guests enter via a $1.5 million visitor center with a multimedia theater (shows run 10am–4pm), a landscaped courtyard, a gift shop, and a

---

Overrated **Try to Avoid Going to Hell**

This is the most overblown and fundamentally most irri-tating attraction on Grand Cayman. "Hell" is a tiny village in a desolate area, lying just under a kilometer (about half a mile) from the sea. Covering about a quarter hectare (half acre) of jagged limestone in West Bay, near the island's most northwesterly point, Grand Cayman's earliest settlers (who wisely avoided this area) labeled this inhos-pitable location as "hellish"... *ergo,* Hell.

Don't even think of walking upon the terrain: First of all, it's restricted. If you defy the signs and take a walk, you have a good chance of spraining your ankles or gashing up your shins. A jagged lunar landscape of somber-toned gray rock, it evokes a treacherous coral formation—the kind that could easily tear open the hull of the sturdiest water-craft—that happens to be above the surface of the water. Except for birds, most animals tend to avoid the place.

The big "attraction" here is a little post office where you can get your cards and letters postmarked from Hell.

cafe. You can take a guided tour of the premises (call to find out what time the tour will be conducted) or you can explore the site on a self-guided tour. Check out the house's wide verandas, rough-hewn timber beams, gabled framework, mahogany floors and stair-cases, and wide-beam wooden ceilings. Guides in 18th-century costumes are on hand to answer questions.

Savannah. ☎ 345/947-3329. Admission CI$6.75 (US$8) for adults, CI$3.20 (US$4) for children 6–12, free for age 5 and under. Daily 9:30am–5pm.

Old Homestead ⋇   This pink-and-white cottage from 1912 is the most photographed building in Grand Cayman. Once known as the "West Bay Pink House," it's constructed of wattle and daub with ironwood posts. With its white trim and green shutters, it is the most inviting and picture-postcard-ready house in Grand Cayman. MacLure Bothwell, one of eight children who were "brung up" at the house, has restored the building to its former condition. The original furnishings are intact, including wood stoves, kerosene lamps, and mahogany beds. You're taken on an evocative and nos-talgic tour of the property, one of the few remaining examples of the Cayman Islands "the way they used to be."

West Bay Rd., West Bay. ☎ 345/949-7639. Admission US$5. Mon–Sat 8am–5pm.

2 Other Attractions

Mastic Trail ⋇ *(Finds)*   A great deal of Grand Cayman is difficult to penetrate. However, the Mastic Trail, stretching for 3.2km (2 miles), provides a rare chance to experience a fascinating journey into Cay-man's wild interior, an area where woodland has been left virtually undisturbed for 2 million years. Guided walks along the length of the trail take 2½ to 3 hours. The trail came to the attention of much of the world in 1995 when *Islands* magazine chose it as a finalist in their annual Ecotourism competition.

Mastic Trail is home to a wide variety of plants and animals unique to the Cayman Islands. Fauna includes the stripe-headed tanager, the Cuban tree frog, and the racer snake, along with vari-ous species of birds. The trail is also home to large populations of trees that have vanished from more accessible places due to logging in the 18th and 19th centuries. You will be walking through one of the last remaining examples of the Caribbean's dry, subtropical for-est. Throughout much of the West Indies, these types of forests have been the victims of particularly intense deforestation.

One part of the trail goes through a black mangrove swamp. The highlights of this part of the trail are the mastic trees, from which the trail takes its name. This type of tree is famous for the veins on its self-peeling bark, and there is both a black mastic tree and a yellow one on the trail. Near the end of the trail you'll reach the highest point in Grand Cayman, a hill—locals call it "The Mountain"—that rises 18m (60 ft.).

Birders will find that the ideal time to walk the trail is from October to early December, when you will be able to observe the seasonal migrations of various birds. If you want to see the tree orchids, visit the trail in June and early July. The trail offers much to see year-round. Avoid the trail when it's raining intensely since the route is subject to flooding.

Don't be deceived by the shortness of the trail. Along the way you'll pass through difficult terrain, especially in the boggy wetlands. Most of the soil lies on karst rock, which can be unkind to hikers. Before setting out, learn to identify the innocent-sounding "maiden plum," a species of tree with purplish fruits that tends to grow close to the path. The sap from this tree can cause a nasty rash.

Although it isn't necessary to tour the trail with a guide, taking a guided walk is highly recommended, as guides can spot and identify the various flora and fauna. Geddes Hislop, who used to work for the National Trust, and his wife, Janet, conduct the best guided walks along Mastic Trail. Excursions are booked through their company, Silver Thatch Excursions (© **345/945-6588**), and cost US$45 per person.

The Butterfly Farm Lovers of the beautiful, elusive butterfly flock to Grand Cayman's latest attraction. You'll have the opportunity to enter an area enclosed in mesh where butterflies from all over the world flutter freely.

There is a wealth of information on the butterfly life cycle here. We learned that females perpetuate the butterfly world, as the males spend most of their lives getting drunk on rotten fruit. The males flit about showing off their vivid, beautiful wings, trying to attract the females (who are usually drably colored in comparison).

The farm also features several species of moth, including the Atlas moth, the largest moth in the world. With a typical wingspan of 36cm (14 in.), it's the size of a small bird.

Guided tours take you through the farm. The staff will answer all the questions—and then some—that you may have about the butterflies.

Harquail Bypass (opposite the cinema). © **345/946-3411**. Admission US$15 adults, US$9 children of any age with parents; free for children under 3. Daily 7:30am–4pm (last admission 3:30pm).

Offshore Investments in the Cayman Islands

Thanks partly to a crackdown from U.S. banking and drug enforcement authorities, and partly to (U.S.-sponsored) pressure from the British Central Bank, things have gotten very squeaky clean these days in George Town. Because of legislation enacted in 2000 and 2001, owners—corporate or individual—of bank accounts are required to complete page after page of documentation about the source and origin of their funds.

If you're curious about investing your (legit) money here, you might want to attend one of the frequent investment seminars hosted by the Hyatt Regency Grand Cayman (© 345/945-1234 for more information).

National Gallery of the Cayman Islands   This gallery is the only noncommercial venue for the exhibition of art in the Cayman Islands. The kindly curator here is quick to tell you that the premises that the gallery presently occupies are temporary; a move to bigger, more impressive digs is expected sometime before 2005. In the meanwhile, however, the compact but efficient museum mounts about seven fine-art exhibitions per year, each containing about 60 works. About 30% of art here is by local artists.

Harbour Place, S. Church St., George Town. © 345/945-8111. Free admission (but donations are welcome). Mon–Fri 8:30am–6pm; Sat 11am–4pm.

3 Driving Tour 1: George Town to Rum Point

Start:	George Town
Finish:	Rum Point
Time:	2–2½ hours
Best Time:	Daylight hours from 9am to 5pm
Worst Time:	When rains have been, or are, heavy

Leave George Town on Route A2 heading in the direction of Owen Roberts International Airport. At a point 4.8km (3 miles) east of George Town, A2 is marked as Crewe Road as it heads immediately east to become Red Bay Road, along which lies:

Driving Tour 1: George Town to Rum Point

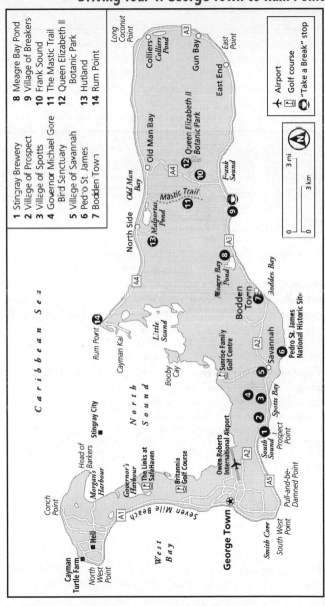

1 Stingray Brewery
2 Village of Prospect
3 Village of Spotts
4 Governor Michael Gore Bird Sanctuary
5 Village of Savannah
6 Ped'o St. James
7 Bodden Town
8 Meagre Bay Pond
9 Village of Breakers
10 Frank Sound
11 The Mastic Trail
12 Queen Elizabeth II Botanic Park
13 Hutland
14 Rum Point

✈ Airport
⛳ Golf course
☕ "Take a Break" stop

❶ Stingray Brewery

This is one of the only home breweries in the Cayman Islands, and visitors are introduced to the trio of beers made here. Each of these beers is sold at bars, hotels, and restaurants throughout the Caymans. Both Durty (3%) and Dark (6%) are sold on draught only. The most popular beer is the bottled Premium (4%). You can take a free tour of the brewery, with samples of beer distributed at the end. Brewing days are Monday and Thursday, and bottling takes place on Wednesday. Visiting hours are Monday to Friday 9am to 5pm, Saturday 10am to 5pm. Call ✆ **345/947-6699** for more information.

After visiting the brewery, continue driving east on Red Bay Road (which is what A2 is called at this point) through the:

❷ Village of Prospect

There is little to see in this village, but it is interesting to note that you're passing through what is thought to be the site of the first settlement in Grand Cayman. Settlers established a fort and an outpost here some time in the latter half of the 1700s, which was "ancient history" in terms of the Caymans. You can see a little monument marking the site of Prospect Fort, the oldest fort on the island. The village, which lies to the immediate east of Red Bay Road along Prospect Point Road, has been mostly abandoned since 1932. The village's church, opening onto the coast, was left to decay. Nearby, the Watler Family Cemetery dates from the 1800s and is under the protection of the National Trust. The cemetery is open to the public and you can still see stone gravestones—some curiously shaped like small homes. Caymanians called these family plots "Gardens of Memories." Of interest to most visitors is the good sandy beach lying just around the point at Prospect. Both divers and snorkelers are drawn to the beach and sea here. Beach shelters and public toilets are available.

As you continue east along Jack Road (A2) (Red Bay Rd. turns into Jack Rd. at the Village of Prospect), you'll pass through:

❸ Village of Spotts

Like Prospect, Spotts is another historic village. It is currently a private residential area, although the government has plans to turn the coast into a public seaside park and to develop the area as a cruise-ship docking space should the waters at George Town be too rough for smooth landings. A sandy public beach is nestled here between the rocks and is good for swimming. There is also an old cemetery here, with 18th-century grave markers painted white.

From Spotts, you can take a short detour to the north along Governor Spotts Newlands Road to reach:

❹ Gov. Michael Gore Bird Sanctuary

This bird sanctuary is open all day and is particularly interesting to visit from April to June, when it is at its most beautiful and shelters the most birds. At various times of the year, more than 60 species—both land and water birds—inhabit the sanctuary. It is a birder's delight. At least a quarter of the native birds of the Caymans can be seen here, and many of them use the freshwater pool at the center of the .8-hectare (2-acre) refuge. Birds can be viewed from an observation platform and from the walkways that lace the sanctuary. Admission is free.

Double back to the main road (A2) and continue east to the:

❺ Village of Savannah

This village contains a 1940s schoolhouse that was restored by the National Trust. It's open to the public only by reservation, so call ☎ **345/949-0121** if you're interested. Frankly, we don't think it's worth the bother. We recommend you pass through the village, as there is little of interest here. After you've left town, a crossroads to the left, called Hirst Road, takes you to the Sunrise Golf Centre, a 9-hole, par-3 course that's open to the public.

At the golf course, turn right onto Pedro Castle Road, which leads to the historic 18th-century plantation great house:

❻ Pedro St. James

This national historic site is one of the major attractions of Grand Cayman. For complete details, refer to the description of Pedro St. James on p. 127. You can either visit "the Pedro St. James" now or return at some point later if you don't want to stop during your driving tour.

Back on the main road, A2 continues east and is named Poinciana Road before becoming Shamrock Drive. Shamrock Drive leads to:

❼ Bodden Town

This is more of a village than a town, where single-story homes with corrugated-iron roofs and wooden verandas evoke British colonial architecture. Once called "South Side," Bodden Town was the first capital of Grand Cayman. "Respectable settlers" (or so the history books tells us) made the town their home back in the 1700s. Over time, Bodden Town's power and prestige was transferred to George Town in the west.

Because it doesn't have the commercial interest of George Town or the touristed frenzy of Seven Mile Beach, Bodden Town still retains some of its traditional aura.

Bodden Town is named for Gov. William Bodden, who was chief magistrate (which is virtually the same as a governor) of the island from 1776 to 1823. Because he did much to improve the life of the islanders, Governor Bodden is known today as "the Grand Old Man of Grand Cayman."

You can visit Guard House Park, opposite Manse Road, where an old guard house once stood. The guard house protected the western approach to town, with its cannons pointed down a rocky gorge toward the sea. The two cannons that stand here today are from the ships involved in Cayman's most famous disaster, the Wreck of the Ten Sails (p. 119). In a patriotic gesture, the Caymanians sent their antique cannons to England in the darkest days of World War II to be melted down and rebuilt into modern weapons.

Another small battery of cannons once stood on Gun Square, Bodden Town's second defense point, guarding the eastern approach to the town. Two of the original cannons are still in place. Behind Gun Square is Mission House, its first floor constructed in the 1840s, making it one of the oldest buildings in the Caymans.

Leaving Bodden, drive along A2 1.6km (1 mile) east to:

⑧ Meagre Bay Pond

This is a small wildlife sanctuary that was once frequented by hunters seeking mallard and teal ducks. Today, the government protects the area. The freshwater pond dries out in the winter months and fills up again in the summer. Early morning or late afternoon is the best time to view this waterfowl breeding area, with its various flocks of shore birds and migratory wading birds, including willets, stilts, ibis, herons, grebes, egrets, and cormorants. Though the government owns this mangrove-fringed lagoon, the land around it is private, so there is no public footpath to the sanctuary. You'll have to park off the side of the road and watch the birds from a distance.

Continue following the same road to the east. The road now changes its designation from A2 to A3. Follow A3 east to the:

⑨ Village of Breakers

The village of Breakers would hardly merit your attention were it not for The Lighthouse Restaurant at Breakers (see below and p. 87 for a complete review).

TAKE A BREAK
The Lighthouse Restaurant at Breakers (✆ 345/947-2047) is the ideal luncheon venue for those traveling the southern coast. Its combination of Caribbean and Italian food, with an emphasis on the catch of the day, is delicious. The lighthouse was purposely built as a restaurant, with a terrace opening onto views of the sea.

From here, continue east on A3, which winds its way to the beautiful:

⑩ Frank Sound

The Sound can be seen to your right as you drive along. You might want to stop off and go for a quick swim along the narrow sands of the sound. Part of the beach is set against a backdrop of Australian pines. A boat launch ramp leads into the shallow and calm waters, which are protected by a reef. The sands and waters here are idyllic for beachcombing, swimming, or even bonefishing.

Near the boat ramp a road turns north, cutting down considerably on the driving time. This road, Frank Sound Drive, takes you to two of the major attractions of Grand Cayman: the Mastic Trail and Queen Elizabeth II Botanic Garden, both previously reviewed under "The Top Five Attractions."

It's also possible to continue to the East End following A3 all around the coast. This is an interesting drive, although it's devoid of specific attractions, except for the blowholes near the hamlet of High Rock, where onshore sprays of water shoot up like geysers, creating a roar like a lion.

If you want to stick to the main tour, take Frank Sound Drive immediately north until you come to:

⑪ The Mastic Trail

These 400 hectares (1,000 acres) and the beautiful walking trail that traverses them are adventures unto themselves and are described more fully on p. 128. If you want to finish the driving tour and get back to George Town in the late afternoon, you might skip the Mastic Trail for the moment and continue on your way. If you have time to negotiate the trail, you can find it just off Mastic Road, which is located to the left of Frank Sound Drive near the little fire station.

After leaving the entrance to the trail, you can continue north on Frank Sound Drive for 2.6km (1.6 miles) to the entrance of:

⑫ Queen Elizabeth II Botanic Park

Named in honor of Her Majesty, this park and botanical garden is fully described on p. 126. If you're pressed for time and want to complete the driving tour, you may want to plan a leisurely visit to the park for another day.

After passing the entrance to the park, Frank South Drive continues north to the northern coast. Turn left on A4. With the sea on your right and the marshy interior on your left, you can drive along to the west, enjoying the fresh air and the scenery. A4 at this point is also known as Ralph Drive. A possible stopover, if you want a cool drink, is the little town of:

⑬ Hutland

This community takes its name from the huts that were constructed in the area by early settlers who farmed the land. This is one of the last havens for the endangered whistling duck, the only duck that breeds in the Caymans. Consider stopping off at Charlie and Elaine Ebanks's home, North Side (© 345/947-9452). The Ebanks welcome visitors to their grounds and always seem happy to show people around. Charlie makes and sells hand-carved birdhouses and waurie boards (which are similar to backgammon boards). The property is signposted just off the main road. Mr. Willy, Charlie's brother, supervises a whistling duck feeding at 4:30pm daily, just down the road.

From Hutland, A4 runs all the way west to:

⑭ Rum Point

This area has a good beach and is a fine place to end your island tour. Rum Point got its name from the barrels of rum that once washed ashore here after a shipwreck. Today, it is dreamy and quaint, surrounded by towering causarina trees blowing in the trade winds. Most of these trees have hammocks suspended from their trunks, and you can hop into one and leisurely enjoy the surroundings. Featuring cays, reefs, mangroves, and shallows, Rum Point is a refuge that extends west and south for 11km (7 miles). It divides the two "arms" of Grand Cayman. The sound's many spits of land and its plentiful lagoons are ideal for snorkeling, swimming, wading, and birding. It you get hungry, drop in to the Wreck Bar for a juicy burger.

After visiting Rum Point, you can head back to George Town by backtracking on the route that got you here.

4 Driving Tour 2: George Town to West Bay

Start:	George Town
Finish:	Batabano
Time:	½ hour
Best Time:	Daily between 10am to 4pm (traffic is less heavy during those hours)
Worst Time:	When many cruise ships are docked (Seven Mile Beach roads are the most crowded at this time). You can ask when cruise ships are coming in at the tourist bureau.

This second driving tour is shorter and takes you north of George Town to West Bay, one of the oldest and most colorful districts in the Caymans, inhabited for 2 centuries.

Driving Tour 2: George Town to West Bay

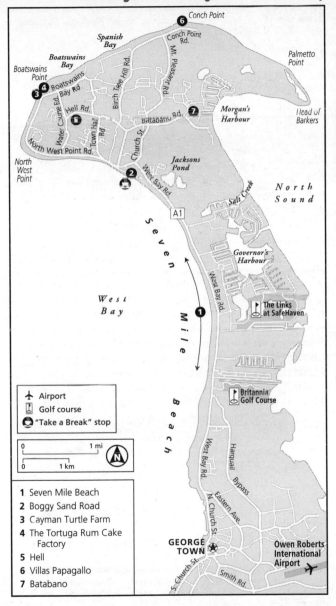

Conch Point

6

Spanish
Bay

Conch Point
Rd.

Palmetto
Point

Boatswains
Bay

*Boatswains
Point*

4

3

Boatswains
Bay Rd.

Birch Tree Hill Rd.

Mt. Pleasant Rd.

Head of
Barkers

Morgan's
Harbour

7

Hell Rd.

Water Course Rd.

5

Batabano Rd.

Town Hall
Rd.

Church St.

North West Point Rd.

*North
West
Point*

2

West Bay Rd.

*Jacksons
Pond*

Salt Creek

*North
Sound*

A1

*West
Bay*

Seven Mile Beach

1

*Governor's
Harbour*

West Bay Rd.

The Links
at SafeHaven

Britannia
Golf Course

✈ Airport

⛳ Golf course

☕ "Take a Break" stop

0		1 mi
0		1 km

N

West Bay Rd.

Harquail
Bypass

N. Church St.

Eastern Ave.

**GEORGE
TOWN** ✈

S. Church St.

Smith Rd.

**Owen Roberts
International
Airport** ✈

1 Seven Mile Beach
2 Boggy Sand Road
3 Cayman Turtle Farm
4 The Tortuga Rum Cake
  Factory
5 Hell
6 Villas Papagallo
7 Batabano

From the center of George Town, follow North Church Street north to the intersection with A1 coming up from the south. Hug left and continue along West
Bay Road north. This will take you along:

❶ Seven Mile Beach

This is the fabled beach that put Grand Cayman on the tourist maps
of the world. True, it doesn't really stretch for 7 miles (11km). Most
locals claim it's only 5½ miles (8.8km) long, but that's still a whole
lot of beach.

The southern part of the sandy stretch is the most heavily developed, saturated with condos, villas, restaurants, hotels, apartment
buildings, a number of shopping centers, and fast-food dives.

This is the most congested part of Grand Cayman and the speed
limit here is only 40kmph (25 mph). Joggers, motorists, cyclists,
and just plain walkers clog the streets throughout the day and for
most of the evening.

There are no specific attractions along the beach itself, so you can
continue your drive without stopovers.

West Bay Road (also called A1) eventually leads to North West Bay Road. With
Jackson's Pond on your right, you'll approach Cemetery Road and a fire station.
At this junction, turn left along:

❷ Boggy Sand Road

This scenic coastal road contains some of the most traditional historic Cayman houses and churches. Many visitors pass it by and
drive on the main road, but this route is well worth exploring.

Vibrant tropical plants surround many of the old gingerbread-style
fishermen's cottages, which date from the first two decades of the 20th
century. You can stop at Grandma Julia's Beach if you'd like to go for a
swim. The beach is raked every morning in the old-fashioned manner.

TAKE A BREAK
Along the beach, you'll see a little hut painted a stark blue with
gingerbread trim. Called **Heritage Kitchen,** it's an outdoor cafe
selling traditional "fish tea" and a seafood broth, along with fish
fritters cooked over an open grill placed over an old iron drum.

It's a great place to relax in the shade and take in views of the water.
The fried fish isn't bad, either. It's open Friday, Saturday, and Sunday. See
p. 106 for more details.

At the end of Boggy Sand Road, you will connect once more to West Bay Road,
which you can continue to follow by heading west and then north, bypassing
such geographic landmarks as Dolphin Point and North West Point. North West
Point Road will lead you by the:

❸ Cayman Turtle Farm

This is one of the major sights on Grand Cayman. Established in 1968, it's the world's only commercial green-sea-turtle farm, where you can observe turtles in all stages of development. See p. 124 for more details.

Right next door to the turtle farm is:

❹ The Tortuga Rum Company

Many of the rum cakes that visitors purchase as souvenirs in George Town stores are made on-site at this large bakery. You can watch the process of making rum cake through glass windows and sample some of the various flavors of rum cake before making your purchase. The factory charges no admission and receives guests Monday to Friday from 8am to 5pm, Saturday 8am to 2:30pm.

If you'd like to stop for lunch nearby, drop in at Cracked Conch by the Sea, near the turtle farm. For a complete review of the restaurant, see p. 86.

After leaving the Tortuga Rum Cake Factory or the Cracked Conch, follow North West Point Road to the junction with Water Course Road, and head south on Water Course Road. At the junction with Hell Road, continue east on Hell Road to:

❺ Hell

This is the most overrated tourist trap in the Cayman Islands (p. 127). It's a rugged outcrop of iron shore with a bleak lunar landscape that does indeed look like the charred remains of Hellfire. Grab some souvenirs if you must, and then press on to the greater charms of West Bay. Hell is said to be the setting for some scenes in Defoe's *Robinson Crusoe*, but some biographers dispute this claim.

Leave Hell by traveling east along Reverend Blackman Road until you reach the junction with Birch Tree Hill Road. Take Birch Tree Hill Road north until you reach the northern coastline at Spanish Bay. Continue east along this road (whose name changes from Birch Tree Hill Road to Conch Point Road), bypassing Spanish Bay Reef Hotel. At the end of the road you come to:

❻ Villas Papagallo

Here you'll find a complex of private villas and the Papagallo Restaurant, a good choice for lunch but closed at dinner. You can get out of your car here and head toward Barkers, the site of a 5.6-hectare (14-acre) bird sanctuary that the restaurant looks out over. This tidal lagoon is home to numerous migrant birds, including ducks and white egrets. There are more birds to view in winter than in summer.

For your final look at West Bay, double back along Conch Point Road, heading west. When you reach the junction with Mount Pleasant Road, take Mount Pleasant Road south to the junction with Batabano Road. Turn left on Batabano Road and take it east to the settlement at:

⑦ Batabano

At Morgan's Harbour Marina, on the North Sound in the little backwater of Batabano, fishermen tie up with their catch of the day, much to the delight of photographers. You can often buy fresh lobster, fish, and even conch here. A large barrier reef protects the sound, which is surrounded on three sides and is a mecca for diving and sports fishing.

To head back to George Town or Seven Mile Beach, drive west along Batabano Road until you come to the junction with Willie Farrington Drive. Take this drive south to the junction with North West Bay Road and turn onto North West Bay Road. West Bay Road will carry you south along Seven Mile Beach and eventually back into George Town.

5 Organized Tours

Since getting around Grand Cayman can be difficult, even if you have a car, many visitors opt for an organized tour. These tours are especially helpful if you want to see more than just the standard sights.

Many visitors prefer a private taxi tour that includes such destinations as the turtle farm or botanical gardens. One to four people can create their own tour at a cost of $45 for one to three persons or $62.50 for four passengers. Call **Cayman Cab Team** at ⓒ **345/947-1173** or **Holiday Taxi** at ⓒ **345/945-4491.**

Reality Tours (ⓒ **345/947-7200**) offers half-day tours of West Bay, taking in such attractions as Cayman Turtle Farm. Reality Tours also goes to the East End, visiting such attractions as Stingray Brewery, Pedro St. James, and the blowholes. Tours in the east include either Queen Elizabeth II Botanic Park or Rum Point, with lunch at Champion House II Restaurant (lunch price not included). Tours of the whole island include the East Bay and West Bay attractions mentioned above. Half-day tours of the west cost CI$37 (US$46) for adults or CI$24 (US$30) for children 6 through12 (free for children under 6). Half-day tours of the east go for CI$56 (US$70) for adults or CI$36 (US$45) for children 6 through12 (free for children under 6). A full-day tour of the whole island is CI$69 (US$86) for adults or CI$45 (US$56) for children 6 through12 (free for children under 6).

Tropicana Tours (© 345/949-0944) is the original tour operator on Grand Cayman. Its best offering is a 6½-hour sightseeing tour of the island, costing US$53 for adults and US$22 for kids 12 and under, and visiting George Town, points along Seven Mile Beach, Pedro St. James, the East End, and the blowholes. If you'd like to spend less time touring, a 2½-hour sightseeing tour to the highlights of the island, including the Cayman Turtle Farm and George Town, is offered for a cost of US$31.

Janet and Geddes Hislop are the chief promoters of ecotourism on the island, operating **Silver Thatch Excursions** (© 345/945-6588). They provide the best tours of Mastic Trail, costing around $45 per person. Visitors are collected from Seven Mile Beach or George Town Monday to Saturday between 7:30 and 9:30am, returning between 12:30 and 1:30pm. Early-morning bird-watching trips can also be arranged.

7

Shopping on Grand Cayman

Shopping in the Cayman Islands has drastically improved recently, because of all the new business generated by cruise-ship arrivals. Though the Cayman Islands are not thought of as a shopping destination in the way that St. Thomas and Sint Maarten are, the Caymans now offer a vast array of merchandise, most of it imported. Since there's no sales tax, there is duty-free merchandise galore, ranging from jewelry to watches, from coral to rum cakes.

1 The Shopping Scene

You can get good deals on island-made art, crafts, and other products. Many local souvenirs tend to be a bit cheesy, and might be relegated to the basement when you find that they are at odds with the decor of your house. However, some handcrafts, such as those made of various types of coral, are artistic statements in their own right and have more lasting value. Jewelry fashioned from caymanite, a hard, marble-like stone harvested in the cliffs of Cayman Brac, is especially popular. In recent years, local art has made greater and greater strides, finding a ready market among the constantly arriving cruise-ship passengers and expat villa owners who want to brighten up their surroundings.

Many products, such as jewelry, are fashioned from black coral. Ecosensitive visitors urge other travelers not to purchase these products. Much of the black coral comes from Central American countries such as Honduras and Belize. The Cayman Islands themselves have strong marine laws to protect their reefs, but countries to the south often do not, and the coral reefs can be seriously harmed or damaged during the harvesting of this beautiful product of nature. Since black coral is known to grow at a rate of 7.6cm (3 in.) every decade, it qualifies as an endangered species.

Because the Cayman Islands are under the rule of Great Britain, you can sometimes get good deals on imports from Britain. You'll find an array of top-quality jewelry, some of it equal to jewelry in the stores of New York, London, and Paris.

Grand Cayman, especially around George Town, abounds with French and American perfumes; Spanish, French, and Swedish crystal; Swiss watches; premium liquor; Japanese cameras; and English china. However, the prices for some of these items are often on par with what you might find in your hometown. Know the average cost of a desired item before you head to the Caymans so that you'll be able to tell whether or not you're getting a bargain. Some of the best deals we discovered were on native crafts, watches, jewelry, designer sunglasses, rum, designer clothing, art, cameras, crystal, and cosmetics. Cuban products such as cigars are sold, but you can't bring them back into the United States. The carefully packaged Cayman rum cake is the most popular purchase.

Each U.S. citizen (including children) can return with up to $400 worth of goods duty-free. Since the amounts are collective, a family of three has a duty-free allowance of $1,200. No duty is imposed on handcrafts, art, food (including those famous Cayman rum cakes), and books.

Make sure you ascertain what dollar a merchant is quoting in, since the U.S. dollar is approximately 20% less than the Cayman dollar.

There is no local sales tax in the Cayman Islands.

Most stores keep regular business hours of Monday to Saturday from 9am to 5 or 6pm.

2 Shopping A to Z

ART GALLERIES

Art in very important on the Cayman Islands and there is an abundance of local artistic talent. As you visit the island's art galleries, the best of which are recommended in this chapter, you might want to remember the names of painters described below who define the Cayman Islands as their home and, often, as the source of their inspiration.

Canadian-born, silver-haired, and elegant, **Joanne Sibley** lived for 25 years in Jamaica, and at the time of this writing, has lived for more than 22 years in Grand Cayman. She's noted for her luminous portrayals of light on West Indian landscapes, creating canvases that seem to glow. Although her works are for sale at some of the galleries noted below, she welcomes interested visitors into her studio for private showings if they phone in advance. Contact her at © **345/947-7273** before heading out to see her at 1342 Bodden Town Rd., 3.2km (2 miles) east of Bodden Town, 21km (13 miles) east of George Town.

Charles Long is another well-known Caymanian painter, celebrated for his use of solid, bright colors in paintings that often depict Cayman flora and fauna. He is happy to give tours of his studio to art lovers who phone in advance. Contact him at © **345/ 947-6386.** His home is located at 114 West Lane, Pedro Castle Rd., in the hamlet of Savannah, about a 15-minute drive southeast of George Town.

Gladwyn Bush is a noted primitivist painter who's known to most of Grand Cayman by her affectionate nickname, **Miss Lassie.** There's never a retrospective of Caymanian art that doesn't prominently display some of her artfully naive paintings. Born in Grand Cayman in March 1914, 1 of 11 children, with no formal art training at all, she has left the Cayman Islands only once in her life: to attend an exhibition of her works in Curaçao. Widowed after a marriage that lasted 42 years, she paints the visions that come to her "in the state between sleeping and awakening." Most of her works are based on the religious insights that she has into the mysterious workings of God. Displayed in galleries as far away as Baltimore and Paris, her paintings depict, among other subjects, God talking with Elijah and Nicodemus chatting with Jesus. Many of her works sell in excess of CI$8,000 (US$10,000) each, although she's been known to donate works to the people, or to the families of the people, who have inspired their creation. Elderly and alert, Bush welcomes well-meaning visitors who appreciate art and who phone her in advance into her artfully painted home. Bush's house is separated from South Strand Road with a chain-link fence that's embellished with jagged glass and colorful ribbons. Inside the house, expect walls, doors, ceilings, even refrigerators, to be covered with her works of art, most of them expressions of her personal brand of religious ecstasy. You can reach Bush at © **345/945-1442.** You'll find her house very close to the intersection of South Sound Road and Walker's Road, 6.4km (4 miles) south of George Town.

Kennedy Gallery ⍟   This is the most important, visible, and influential art gallery in the Cayman Islands. Works by each of the recognized artists in the nation are showcased, including canvases from deeply entrenched local masters (Joanne Sibley and Charles Long, among others). Works by less widely recognized artists are also featured. Our favorite among these lesser-known artists is Petrina Wright, who teaches art in a high school on Cayman Brac, and whose canvasses seem to incorporate reggae, soca, Caymanian nationhood, racial pride, sexual liberation, and adolescent trauma, all at the same time. Among the offerings here, expect to find an excellent selection of seascapes and tropical landscapes, bronze castings of Caymanian sea turtles by artists in California, and absolutely brilliant sculptures by emerging artists in nearby Cuba. Works of art range from CI$8 to CI$50,000 (US$10–US$62,500). The members of the Hill family, who are extremely articulate spokespersons for the art scene on Grand Cayman, manage this fine gallery. West Shore Center, West Bay Rd., Seven Mile Beach (**C**) **345/949-8077.**

Kensington Lotte Fine Art Gallery   This is one of the two or three leading art galleries on Grand Cayman, located within about a 5-minute walk from the cruise-ship terminal. In a glossy showroom whose design might have been inspired by an upscale gallery in London or New York, you'll find a changing series of art, much of it by local artists, whose prices range from CI$10 (US$13) for a simple reproduction to as much as CI$25,000 (US$31,250) for an award-winning work. Harbour Place, George Town. (**C**) **345/946-9696.**

BEACH WARE
Brazilian Point   You'll be able to indulge fashion-plate tendencies at this stylish and whimsical shop where all the garments (for women only) are imported from Brazil. Each naughty, "minimalist" item seems permeated with the insouciance of a beachfront venue in Bahia. Bikinis average around CI$35 (US$44). There's also an inventory of belts, bags, shoes, and flesh-revealing "flirtware." In the Queen's Court Shopping Center, West Bay Rd., Seven Mile Beach (**C**) **345/945-5679.**

Latitude 19   Set close to the cruise-ship piers in downtown George Town, this shop sells everything you'll need for a sun-flooded day on the beach, including sunglasses, beach batiks, straw hats, sandals, sunblock, suntan lotion, and all kinds of beachwear. There's also a collection of undergarments with "Cayman Islands" emblazoned on the seat. N. Church St., George Town (**C**) **345/946-6178.**

BOOKS
The Book Nook   This is one of the largest bookstores on Grand Cayman, stocking novels, travel guides, cookbooks, diet books, and dictionaries. There's also a rambling, somewhat disorganized inventory of souvenirs, children's toys, porcelain, and gift items. There's a smaller branch of this outfit ((**C**) 345/949-7392) in the Anchorage Shopping Centre, on Harbour Street, directly opposite the cruise-ship terminal. A warehouse, also located in the Anchorage Shopping Centre, is jam-packed with additional inventories of books, gifts,

---

Tips Lighting Up a Stogie for Fidel

Although you can buy Cuban cigars in the Cayman Islands, it is still illegal to bring them back to the United States. If you want to enjoy one of these prized stogies, you'll have to smoke them in the islands.

---

and children's toys. In the Galleria Plaza Shopping Centre, West Bay Rd., Seven Mile Beach. ✆ 345/945-4686.

CAMERAS

Cayman Camera Ltd. This is the top outlet for all of your photographic needs and also the best shop at which to purchase duty-free cameras and binoculars. In addition to its regular cameras, compacts, and SLRs, the store also sells video cameras and does 1-hour processing. It can also make prints and enlargements from negatives, slides, prints, and digital sources, and it is the local distributor for Fuji and Hasselblad. On the waterfront (across from the Atlantis submarine), George Town. ✆ 345/949-8359.

CUBAN PRODUCTS

La Casa del Habano Tucked into an inner courtyard and accessible via a narrow alleyway from the busy sidewalk outside, this is a small-scale but charming emporium of Cuban cigars, Cuban coffees, and Cuban art objects. In the Cayside Building, Shedden Rd. at the corner of N. Church St., George Town. ✆ 345/946-4666.

DIVING/SNORKELING GEAR

Divers' World/Aqua-Fit/The Beach Boutique If you're even remotely interested in underwater or watersports, this trio of shops, each owned by the same entrepreneur and within the same shopping center, is a mother lode of virtually everything you'd need to play on or below the surface of the sea. The largest and most impressive of the stores is **Divers World** (✆ 345/949-8128), inventorying what's probably the Caribbean's largest collection of diving and snorkeling equipment. Expect an impressive inventory of underwater digital cameras, film, watches, scuba-tank regulators, swim masks and swim fins, wetsuits, weight belts, lighting devices, and scooters that propel scuba enthusiasts either above or beneath the surface of the water. If you're in the market for sports clothes, bathing suits, gift items, protective wading shoes, sunglasses, suntan oil, candles shaped like shells, and rash suits (a foam latex shirt that prevents you from being stung or scraping against a coral reef), head for either **Aqua-Fit** (✆ 345/949-8128) or **The Beach Boutique** (✆ 345/949-8128), both of which lie just a few storefronts away. In the Seven Mile Shopping Centre, West Bay Rd., George Town.

FASHION

Arabus Clothiers 🐾   Some of the mostly European clothing here costs less than the equivalent within the U.S., partly because of the duty-free status of natural fibers such as cashmere, silk, linen, and wool in the Cayman Islands. You may find some flamboyant items, such as a slinky, scarlet woman's evening dress, complementing merchandise that is for the most part restrained, subdued, and in very good taste. 8 Front St., George Town. ✆ 345/949-4620.

FOOD

Foster's Food Fair   This is the best food shop if you're renting a private condo or villa and want to do light cooking "at home." Just off Seven Mile Beach, it's a huge emporium of food products. Since nearly everything has to be imported, food is much more expensive in the Caymans than it is likely to be in your hometown. Expect to be shocked by the bill. Strand Shopping Centre, West Bay Rd., George Town. ✆ 345/945-4748.

GIFTS & SOUVENIRS

Also see the "Handcrafts" section and the "Jewelry" section, below, for other great gift and souvenir ideas.

Beyond the Horizon   An emporium that's loaded with good Asian handcrafts, this is the most exotic gift shop on Grand Cayman Island. Tara Parker operates the store and travels twice a year to Indonesia, India, and Southeast Asia to find the tables, armoires, Indian temple drawings, jewelry, and textiles that transform her shop into something akin to a bazaar. Expect kites from Bali shaped like Spanish galleons, wrought iron in a style known throughout India as the *jali* school, and furniture carved from Asian hardwoods. A small depiction of Buddha can sell for as little as CI$5 (US$6.25); a beautifully crafted chest of drawers can go for as much as CI$4,000 (US$5,000). In the Galleria Plaza Shopping Centre, West Bay Rd., Seven Mile Beach. ✆ 345/946-1498.

Bliss   Some philosophers define "bliss" as the state one achieves after a virtuous life and lots of meditation. This shop inventories the kinds of gifts and art objects from Thailand, India, Mexico, and China that might help you achieve that state. Items tend to be small-scale and intricately crafted, reflecting hours of human labor. Items include jewelry, housewares, handbags, silk scarves, and blouses crafted from raw Thai silk. In the Royal Plaza, at the corner of Edward St. and Shedden Rd., George Town. ℭ 345/945-8800.

Harley Davidson of Grand Cayman   This is an official outlet of the motorcycle and lifestyle purveyor. As such, expect commemorative T-shirts, gift items, and the kind of clothing that can protect you from windburn during your real or imagined roadfest with the Hell's Angels. In the Aqua World Mall, N. Church St., George Town. ℭ 345/949-4464.

Pure Art   This is the most creative, best-inventoried, and most imaginative gift shop in the Cayman Islands. Located within an unpretentious and low-slung wood-frame house about 2.4km (1½ miles) south of George Town proper, it has reached its present level of fascination under the stewardship of Debbie Chase, a U.S.-born artist. Chase's friendly relations with craftspersons throughout the Caymans has created a treasure trove of gift items that are a lot more interesting than what's available at many nearby competitors. Expect a densely packed environment loaded with paintings, artifacts, books, and clever handcrafted items from the Cayman Islands, Cuba, Jamaica, Key West, and Central America. The common denominator linking all the items is good taste, good humor, and an appreciation for detail-intensive labor. S. Church St. at Denham-Thompson Way, George Town. ℭ 345/949-9133.

Shellections   Few other shops on Grand Cayman sell seashells in as imaginative ways as Shellections does. Look for boxes covered with seashells, delicate shells accented with gold trim, shell-trimmed mirrors, and—best of all—some of the most artful Christmas decorations we've ever seen, including angels, cherubs, and infants in swaddling clothes, all of them crafted from fish bone, shells, gauze, scarlet, shiny gilt ribbons, and gilt paint. You'll also find T-shirts, black coral jewelry, and blown glass paperweights. N. Church St., George Town. ℭ 345/946-4590.

HANDCRAFTS

Also see Beyond the Horizon, Bliss, Pure Art, and Shellections under "Gifts & Souvenirs," above, and Black Coral Clinic, Coral, Mitzi's Fine Jewelry, and 24 K-Mon Jewelry, under "Jewelry" below, for more handcrafts.

Eileen's Native Crafts   You'll quickly get the sense that you've entered a private home when you step inside this handcrafts store. To get here, follow the signs along the coastal road near Sand Bluff.

Within a low-slung, peach-colored cement building, you'll find the handcrafts of Mrs. Eileen McLaughlin, a native Caymanian who has devoted most of her life to raising a family and mastering the time-honored Caymanian craft of weaving silver thatch into placemats, hats, baskets, handbags, and rope. The silver thatch products are cunningly intricate, especially the laundry baskets and tote bags. Virtually anything sold here can be folded away into your luggage without harming the integrity or the shape of the weaving. Most items, including the largest, sell for under CI$50 (US$63). 803 Austin Connoly Dr. Sand Bluff, near Gun Bay, East End. © 345/947-7438.

Horacio Esteban/The Esteban Gallery Here, you'll find the commercial headquarters of Grand Cayman's most celebrated crafts-man of Caymanite, the striated and very hard stone that's unique to the Cayman Islands. Caymanite ranges in color from pale pinkish-beige to deep russet, and here, it's crafted into letter openers with Caymanite handles, pendants and key chains, custom-designed company accessories and awards, and evocative and very unusual pieces of sculpture. Prices range from CI$10 (US$13) for a key chain to CI$3,200 (US$4,000) for a surreal and riveting depiction of an Arawak princess. You'll recognize the gallery because of the concrete statue, crafted by Esteban himself, of a giant turtle emerging from its shell. AALL Building, the Waterfront, George Town. © 345/946-2787.

JEWELRY

Black Coral Clinic *Finds* One of Grand Cayman's most eccentric coral jewelry designers operates a showroom from what was originally built as a sea-fronting garage on South Strand Road, in a mostly residential neighborhood about 4.8km (3 miles) south of George Town. Its owner is Carey Hurleston (Doctor Carey to his friends), a heavily tattooed, widely experienced biker who might drop an anecdote or two about his days with some of North America's more notorious motorcycle clubs. All the coral sold here comes from waters immediately off Grand Cayman. Hurleston removed the coral from deep waters some 2 decades ago, before the reef was protected, and his products are made from that long-ago supply. It's fashioned into earrings, pendants, and bracelets, with very few of the handcrafted items selling for more than CI$40 (US$50). 82 S. Sound Rd., near the junction of Walker Rd., South Sound. © 345/949-9569.

Brazilian Gems and Jewellry Unlike the high-style, high-security displays at Grand Switzerland (see listing below), this open and airy mini-boutique places all its wares out in the open, under bright lights, without any dividers between the gemstones and customers. The inventory is defined as "semiprecious," and consists of citrines, amethysts, garnets, blue topazes, peridots, and aquamarines, set into pendants, bracelets, earrings, and rings. Prices for jewelry here rarely exceed CI$300 (US$375). The venue is fun, whimsical, and funky. In the Anchorage Shopping Centre, the Harbour St., George Town. ⓒ 345/945-3122.

Cartier 🙌 This stores is targeted at the big spender and the connoisseur of such timeless pieces as the Trinity ring and the Tank ring, along with such classics as Cartier watches (including the Tank Francaise). The Nouvelle Vogue Jewelry Collection is stunning, bringing a touch of Paris's Place Vendôme to Grand Cayman. You can also visit the Cartier Boutique, selling fashionable leather goods, all highly stylized, along with elegant silk scarves and deluxe perfumes. Cardinal Ave., George Town. ⓒ 345/949-7477.

Colombian Emeralds International Splashy, elegant, and glittery, this is one of the largest jewelry stores on Grand Cayman, with a strategic position that's almost directly across the street from the cruise-ship terminal. As its name implies, there's a lot of emphasis here on colored stones, including emeralds. There's a wide selection of diamonds and timepieces as well. Harbour Drive, George Town. ⓒ 345/949-8808.

Coral This place is a bit more battered and a bit more dusty than some of the other stores that specialize in black coral jewelry, but if you're interested in the way jewelry is crafted, it might appeal to you. It's operated by two brothers (Carlo and Mauro Bertolino), who are very good at inserting shark's teeth into gold or silver settings, and polishing black coral into depictions of stingrays and Caymanian sea turtles. The brothers also design abstract patterns on black coral for pendants, bracelets, and key chains. You'll get the sense of being in a bona fide crafts studio, rather than just another sales outlet. In the West Shore Shopping Plaza, West Bay Rd., Seven Mile Beach. ⓒ 345/949-2743.

Grand Switzerland This cluster of stores, each opening onto the same enclosed shopping mall, is located just across the street from the cruise-ship terminal. You'll find separate departments devoted to Tiffany, John Hardy, and Michele watches. There are also racks of perfumes, cosmetics, and, within a high-security room, a boutique devoted only to the sale of diamonds. This store can craft individualized jewelry, placing the gemstones you select into the setting of your choice within just a few hours. In the Anchorage Shopping Centre, Harbour St., George Town. © 345/945-6868.

Links of London   This genuinely glamorous shop near the cruise-ship terminal specializes in silver accessories and silver gift items for men and women. This is the Cayman branch of a chain of upscale stores based in London. Designs are contemporary, slick, and sleek, with a daunting collection of cuff links priced from CI$80 to CI$1,300 (US$100–US$1,625) per pair, depending on their size and design. There are also business-card holders, charms for bracelets, jewelry, and perfume atomizers. There's also a collection of freshwater pearl jewelry for women. Harbour Place, S. Church St., George Town. © 345/946-9070.

Mitzi's Fine Jewelry   This plush, elegant jewelry store and art gallery was established by Mitzi Callan, the most famous and cele-brated craftsperson in the Cayman Islands, and winner of dozens of local and international art contests. Set about 450m (1,500 ft.) north of the Hyatt Hotel, on the opposite side of West Bay Road, it's a showcase for works that Ms. Callan imports, including Italian porce-lain and Carrera & Carrera sculptures, and for works that she designs herself from black coral, gold, platinum, and gemstones. Simple pieces of jewelry begin at around CI$25 (US$31), and can rise to as much as CI$50,000 (US$62,500) for artfully crafted black coral cru-cifixes. 5 Bay Harbour Centre, West Bay Rd., Seven Mile Beach. © 345/945-5014.

24K-Mon Jewelers   This is the main branch of one of the island's biggest jewelry emporiums, with rack after rack of gold, sil-ver, black coral, tanzanite, and mostly semiprecious stone jewelry (no watches). You'll find a wide and intriguing selection of gold and silver coins excavated from the underwater wrecks of 17th- and 18th-century galleons. Varying widely in size, design, and price, they're artfully set into pendants and bracelets. Fort St. at the corner of N. Church St., George Town. © 345/945-7000.

LEATHER

Der Bag Man   This is the best outlet in Grand Cayman for ele-gant, high-quality leather handbags and other leather accessories, including wallets and chic belts. The array of handbags ranges from informal to the latest, hottest fashion statements. Der Bag Man claims you can save significantly over U.S. prices because it imports its leather goods at "terrific savings," but it's always wise to know the latest prices on leather goods before making a choice. Galleria Plaza, West Bay Rd., George Town. © 345/945-5697.

LINGERIE

Ciara's Secret   The merchandise sold here is very similar to the sexy and erotic lingerie that's been successfully marketed in the U.S. by Victoria's Secret. Inside, you'll find the kind of "loungewear" that a consenting adult might wear to seduce the mailman, Mr. Right, or her husband, depending on the circumstances and her particular value system. Come here with a credit card (preferably your boyfriend's or husband's), a sense of humor, and a lot of imagination. In the Galleria Plaza, West Bay Rd. Seven Mile Beach. © 345/945-5571.

PERFUMES

La Perfumerie I and II   These stores, set directly across the street from one another on Cardinal Avenue, contain the largest selection of perfumes and cosmetics on the island. If you're especially interested in cosmetics and makeup, head for Perfumerie I, the branch on the north side of the street; if perfume is your weakness, head for Perfumerie II, on the avenue's south side. Cardinal Ave., George Town. © 345/949-7477.

RUM & LIQUEURS

Tortuga Rum Company   Founded in 1984, this company pioneered the first locally labeled rums in the Caymans, developing into the largest retail and duty-free liquor business in the little archipelago. Its most famous brands are Tortuga Gold, Rum Cream, Coffee Liqueur, Orange Rum Liqueur, and the 12-year-old Tortuga Gold Rum. Many people visit to purchase a carefully sealed rum cake, based on a century-old family recipe. The cake is the Cayman's number-one export and souvenir item. N. Sound Rd., George Town. © 345/949-7701.

TOYS

Hobbies & Books   This store sells toys "for all ages." The range of merchandise covers everything from the latest electronic toys to traditional board games. Special Saturday events are presented to amuse children. Piccadilly Centre, George Town. © 345/949-0707.

8

Grand Cayman After Dark

Until fairly recent times, a "rushed" day on Grand Cayman meant spending most of the time on Seven Mile Beach, perhaps doing a little shopping, and then sipping sunset drinks, followed by a long, leisurely dinner. To some extent that custom still prevails.

In recent years, however, the choice of after-dark diversions has slowly but steadily grown, although Grand Cayman hardly rivals Puerto Rico or Aruba for nightlife supremacy in the Caribbean. The party-till-dawn crowd should travel elsewhere for amusement, since most venues are shut tight by 1am, and licensing laws are strict in the Cayman Islands.

Often, some of the best bars on the island are attached to restaurants, so you can drink, dine, and party at the same place.

The live entertainment scene changes on a night-by-night basis. One club might be jumping with a live band one night, and then be calm, with no live entertainment, the following evening. The reception desk at your hotel can usually tell you what the hot spots are on any given evening. Or grab a copy of the *Cayman Compass,* which comes out every Friday and usually runs a complete list of entertainment possibilities for the evening. The *Cayman Compass* is available at most hotels.

If you're bored by drinking with a lot of fellow travelers and want to see where the Caymanians go, seek out and patronize some of our more offbeat recommendations, including Welly's Cool Spot.

There's no gambling on Cayman Island.

1 The Club Scene

The Jungle   Although The Jungle promotes itself as a disco and nightclub, most of the action in this place revolves around the bar, where you might find a hard-drinking but congenial crowd of middle-aged locals tossing back cocktails throughout the afternoon and early evening. The setting is a large, dimly illuminated room with a ceiling covered in jungle-camouflage netting and tree branches which in a way might remind you of guerrilla warfare in a place like

Vietnam. Be warned in advance that this is not the island's most popular or trendiest disco, and people usually only get up and dance on Friday or Saturday nights. But for an insight into the local way of life, and gossip from the regulars, it can be a lot of fun. You'll find this place on the (relatively obscure) side entrance of the same building that contains the much-more-visible restaurant Neptune's. The club is open Monday to Friday 1pm to 1am, Saturday and Sunday 1pm to midnight. Trafalgar Square, West Bay Rd. ⓒ 345/945-5383.

O Bar Set in a two-story shopping plaza off West Bay Road, this is the only disco and nightclub in the Caribbean that's open weeknights and closed on Saturday and Sunday. Located immediately adjacent to The Attic Billiard Lounge (a pool hall recommended later in the chapter), it's a large, glossy, terra-cotta-and-black space with an industrial-looking steel staircase that leads to a hideaway lounge upstairs. There's been a concerted effort here to appeal to the island's hip, urbanized, and trend-conscious yuppies, with DJs imported from faraway places like New York, and a focus on bringing in cutting-edge music. Look for lots of circle motifs in the decor (hence the name "O Bar"). Beer costs around CI$4 (US$5) a mug, and cocktails go for CI$6 (US$7.50) each. The club is open Monday and Wednesday 10pm to 3am, Tuesday 11pm to 3am, and Thursday and Friday 9pm to 3am. In the Queen's Court Plaza, West Bay Rd. ⓒ 345/943-6227. Cover CI$10–CI$15 (US$13–US$19).

Royal Palms Beach Club Opening onto Seven Mile Beach, this is one of the premier venues for both islanders and visitors, who come to listen and dance to live music. The bar, open to the trade winds, is a great place to dance the night away in the moonlight. There is an on-site restaurant, but many patrons dine elsewhere before coming here for the rest of the evening. Live bands play calypso and light reggae, among other music. The club caters to a wide age group, from those in their 20s and 30s to those beyond 50. The bar opens daily at 9am, but the action doesn't get under way until 8:30pm. The club closes at 1am. West Bay Rd. ⓒ 345/945-6358.

2 Bar/Restaurant Combos

Cecil's Restaurant/Kaibo Beach Bar & Grill This fun, relaxed, hip, counterculture venue—collectively called "the Kaibo Yacht Club"—contains both a bar and a special dining venue (see p. 84 for a review), and is perched on the island's distant corner, far from the madding crowd of tourists and touristic infrastructure closer to George Town. Cecil's, upstairs, is the more elegant of the two dining venues here, but the raffish beach-level bar is a major stop on the Grand Cayman nightlife circuit. Clients are fun and free-spirited. In many cases, customers are Canadian-born refugees from the snows of the frigid north who mingle gracefully with local Caymanians and boat owners. In the downstairs bar, you can enjoy a menu of sandwiches, burgers, salads, and savory cups of gumbo ya-ya, a New Orleans–inspired stew crafted from blackened chicken, andouille sausage, and Cajun seasoning. Drinks of choice, served in copious quantities throughout the day and evening, include Mudslides, Bloody Caesars, and Sex on the Beach, priced between CI$5.50 and CI$8.50 (US$6.90–US$11) each. The entire venue is fun, romantic, and appealingly permissive. The bar and grill are open daily from 11am to 11pm. In the Kaibo Yacht Club, North Side. ✆ **345/947-9975.**

The Havana Club Cigar Lounge   Previously recommended as a dining venue on p. 99, this bar and lounge is enormously appealing and fascinating to fans of the perhaps-mythical Cuba of the pre-Castro era. Cigars are celebrated here, either distributed from a walk-in humidor in back, or sold from a printed menu. Ninety-five percent of the stock derives from (guess where?) neighboring Cuba. Photographs on the wall, visible sometimes through clouds of smoke, include depictions of such celebs as James Gandolfini (Joey Soprano) and Frank Sinatra. The walk-in humidor stocks an all-Cubano inventory of already rolled cigars, but for something different, an employee named Jésus, who occupies a small work station near the entrance, will demonstrate the craft of cigar rolling as he produces his own brand of elegantly crafted, just-rolled stogies. Cigars cost from CI$5 to CI$25 (US$6.25–US$31) each, *mojitos* cost CI$6.50 (US$8.15), and if you want a really posh after-dinner drink, a shot of Cuban cognac—best in the house—goes for CI$40 (US$50). Open Monday to Friday 11:30am to 1am, Saturday and Sunday 11:30am to midnight. In the Regency Court Building, West Bay Rd. ✆ **345/945-5391.**

La Bodega   This is a cozy, friendly bar with a well-managed restaurant that is recommended on p. 99. You can come here to drink or dine, or both. There's an easy familiarity among the many attractive men and women who hang out here. The age range, for the most part, is 20s to 40s. The place really comes alive on Friday night with highly danceable salsa, retro, and Top 40 music. A local live band plays every Saturday night. In the West Shore Shopping Plaza, West Bay Rd. ✆ **345/946-8115.**

Welly's Cool Spot *(Finds)* Established by a Jamaican-born restaurateur more than 20 years ago and catering to a local clientele, this small but very hip bar and diner is famous throughout Grand Cayman. Every islander has been here at least once. The staff is accommodating and cooperative, and we always have fun (and sometimes a worthwhile dialogue or two) at Welly's. Set within a commercial neighborhood 1.6km (1 mile) northwest of George Town's center, and permeated with the sounds of recorded soca or reggae music, it's on the second floor of a big-windowed, breeze-filled building that has a bar against one wall, and a large area for clients to stand and flirt and gossip. In the garden at the building's base, which is illuminated by the glare of floodlights, you're likely to witness intense and aggressive (and often, curiously silent) games of dominoes. Come here for an insight into local culture and an ambience that's very different from the kind you'll find at the tourist-oriented venues of Seven Mile Beach. Red Stripe, the Jamaican national beer, costs CI$2.50 (US$3.15) per bottle. The various platters of island food change every day of the week, but they usually include, among others, oxtail and beans, steamed fish, curried goat, fried chicken, and stewed chicken with dumplings. Platters cost CI$7 to CI$11 (US$8.75–US$14). Welly's is open Monday to Friday 10am to 1am, Saturday and Sunday 10am to midnight. 110 N. Sound Rd. *(*) 345/949-2541.

3 Bars

Bamboo Lounge Few other bars in Grand Cayman have as aggressively (and successfully) tapped into a market of young, attractive, trend-conscious, and upwardly mobile singles as this one. Come here prepared to deal with local hipsters and/or hipster wannabes, and a strong dose of food and beverage marketing hype. Also expect to spend more than you would at an everyday pub. Set within the division of the Hyatt Hotel that's adjacent to the beach (not the main core of the Hyatt that's inland from the sea, on the opposite edge of West Bay Road), it features a bustling, intimate bar area on one side, a state-of-the-art sushi kitchen on the other side, and at the top of a short flight of steps, a stylishly minimalist lounge area with tables. If you opt to dine here, expect an ultramodern, Asian-influenced setting with full-grained wood detailing. There is a long list of light dishes, including sushi, sashimi, and artfully prepared appetizers, that can be artfully combined in a full meal. Live jazz is presented every Wednesday and Saturday night beginning at around 8pm. The ambience is fun, permissive, and flirtatious. Drinks run the gamut from the standard (beer and conventional martinis) to the "we're-students-on-spring-break-so-let's-get-bombed" variety. Examples of this latter category include the Wiki Waki Woo, which is made with an alarming blend of vodka, tequila, rum, three kinds of sweet liqueurs, and two kinds of fruit juice. According to the menu, this combination is guaranteed "to make you crazy." Another spring break style drink is the Samurai Sunset, made from raspberry-flavored sake, vodka, and peach schnapps. A list of martinis broadcasts headache inducing combinations of ingredients with names that you might find a bit corny (Foreplay and the Big O are two examples). Sushi, sashimi, and sushi rolls cost from CI$6.50 to CI$15 (US$8.15–US$19). The bar and restaurant are open Monday to Saturday 5pm to 1am, and Sunday 5pm to midnight. On the ground floor of the Hyatt Regency Hotel's Beach Suites, West Bay Rd. ✆ 345/947-8744.

Legendz   Legendz is a good lounge bar and restaurant that's rich with mahogany paneling, polished brass, stiff drinks, and lots of good-looking and available clients of both genders. On Tuesday nights a local band plays Top-40 pop hits, and on Sundays, excellent visiting stand-up comics (many from the U.S.) perform here. On other nights you'll find recorded music and a low-key atmosphere. Legendz shares interconnecting doors with two other eateries called Eats and Yoshi's Sushi. For more details, see the review of these restaurants on p. 106. West Bay Rd. ✆ 345/945-1950. Cover $10 on Sat night.

My Bar ✹ *Finds*   My Bar, located on the premises of the Sunset House hotel, is one of the most dramatically designed bars on Grand Cayman. It's set on a smooth cement platform near the coastline, about 1.2km (¾ of a mile) south of George Town. Because its two predecessors were swept away by hurricanes, its designers sank its foundations deep into the bedrock, and capped it with the highest and most elaborate Polynesian-style thatch roof (it contains an estimated 36,000 palm fronds) on Grand Cayman. Come here for a grandly proportioned and very relaxing indoor-outdoor venue that's focused around a large rectangular bar area. Many local residents have adopted this fun bar as their regular hangout, including lots of Caymanian lawyers, who engage in spirited games of dominoes that are followed by many of the bar's patrons. My Bar is especially busy on Friday nights, when there's live music and where the energy level is high. Open Monday to Thursday and

Saturday 9am to midnight, Friday 9am to 1am. At the Sunset House hotel, S. Church St., George Town. © 345/949-7111.

4 The Best Pubs

Fidel Murphy's ✦ This is the unofficial headquarters of Irishness on Grand Cayman, site of large gatherings of drinkers who avidly follow the pub's live broadcasts of Gaelic soccer, rugby, and hurling matches. The pub offers Irish wit, charm, and nostalgia with a Caribbean twist, as the owners tried to convey by adding "Fidel" to the name of the pub. The place originated in 1999 when the mostly Irish staff of a Cuban restaurant (La Habana) called in a team of architectural designers from the Guinness brewery in Ireland. Within a few months, the Guinness team had built and shipped, from Dublin, a dark-paneled, prefabricated, late-Victorian pub, complete with brass trim and ornate railings. The place is so authentic that after about an hour and a few drinks, even the Spanish-language speakers seem to develop a brogue. Expect a winning combination of bar space and dining space. Seven kinds of beer, plus cider, are on tap, and Irish breakfasts (bacon, sausage, tomato, black and white pudding, baked beans, and two fried eggs) are available at all hours. Other menu items include shepherd's pie, steak and Guinness pie, grilled lamb cutlets, shrimp and chips, and such island food as Fidel's chicken curry and Cuban-style pork tenderloin. An Irish breakfast costs CI$8.95 (US$11), with sandwiches and salads ranging from CI$6.95 to CI$8.95 (US$8.70–US$11). Main course platters range from CI$9.95 to CI$17 (US$12–US$21). The bar is open Monday to Friday from 10:30am to 1am, Saturday and Sunday from 10:30am to midnight. The kitchen closes at 11pm. In the Queens Court Shopping Plaza. © 345/949-5189.

Lone Star Bar & Grill You can enjoy juicy burgers in the dining room of this transplanted corner of the Texas Panhandle. Or head straight for the bar in back, where you can sip lime and strawberry margaritas beneath murals of Lone Star beauties. Several sports events are aired simultaneously on 15 different TV screens. Drink prices are reduced at happy hour, from 4 to 7pm Monday to Friday. Some nights are theme evenings such as fajita nights or all-you-can-eat affairs, the latter costing CI$13 (US$16). The bar and grill are open Monday to Saturday from 11am to 1am. West Bay Rd. © 345/945-5175.

P.D.'s Pub (The Pirate's Den) ✦ Dark-paneled, wood-filled, and appealingly battered in the way that only a genuinely popular pub can be, this is one of the most likable pubs on Grand Cayman. It's completely unpretentious, and although the door is always open to short-term visitors, the huge majority of its clientele are long-term residents who are very familiar with pub-side etiquette in the U.K. and/or sports bar etiquette in the U.S. High points in P.D.'s annual calendar include Super Bowl weekend (when it's mobbed), and important soccer and rugby games in Europe, when oversized TV screens blast out each game, play by play. Karaoke is presented about once a month. Four computer terminals offer Internet access for CI10¢ (US15¢) a minute. P.D.'s is the only venue on the island that offers NTN (National Trivia Network), a virtual, electronic trivia game that is popular at pubs throughout the world. For more on how this potentially addictive game works, refer to the box "Trivial Pursuit in Cyberspace" below.

Drinks include six kinds of beer on tap, priced at CI$3.50 (US$4.40) per glass, plus cocktails. The menu features burgers with a wide choice of toppings; beer-battered and deep-fried shrimp with blue cheese dressing; surf and turf; spiced pork tenderloin; grilled chicken wraps; and fish and chips. Burgers, salads, and platters cost from CI$6 to CI$15 (US$7.50–US$19). The pub is open Monday to Friday 7am to 1am, Saturday 7am to midnight, and Sunday 10am to midnight. In the Galleria Plaza, West Bay Rd. © 345/949-7144.

Rackham's Pub and Restaurant ⓖ Because of the hip, hospitable, and well-informed locals who congregate within its appealingly casual premises, Rackham's is the first pub we visit every time we come to Grand Cayman. The pub is set on an open-air pier jutting seaward, just south of the center of George Town, and is protected from the sun and rain by an overhanging roof. As you gaze seaward from your perch here, notice the schools of tarpon swimming beneath the pier. The pub was named after "Calico Jack" Rackham, an 18th-century pirate who seemed to delight in terrorizing the shipping lanes offshore. Come here for an insight into who's living and working on Grand Cayman these days. The friendly local crowd at Rackham's includes paralegals, financiers, and office workers from throughout Canada, Britain, and the U.S.; about half a dozen watersports professionals; and a healthy mixture of West Indian locals. Everyone—thanks partially to the party-colored cocktails served here—gets along swimmingly well. Shots of Jack Daniels cost CI$4 (US$5) each, and a head-spinning version of Cayman Islands lemonade (vodka, peach schnapps, triple sec, cranberry juice, and whiskey sour mix) goes for CI$6.50 (US$8.15).

Trivial Pursuit in Cyberspace: Playing NTN at P.D.'s Pub

Between rounds of drinks, ask the barman at P.D.'s for an NTN (National Trivia Network) device. The device will log you, via remote radio signal, onto an Internet server that will connect your box to equivalent boxes used by others in various pubs around the world.

A TV monitor will flash multiple-choice questions with five answer options. When you think you know the answer, press the corresponding button on your blue box. Since the questions and the possible answers are publicly displayed, you might get hints, or in some cases, false leads, from other clients. Nova Scotia–born Al Young, P.D.'s publican and manager, conducts NTN contests within the bar every Tuesday and Thursday night. The competition, while friendly, can become intense.

Questions derive from a grab bag of disciplines that include geography, history, entertainment, sports, and pop culture. Examples of some questions include:

• What kind of car did Tom Selleck drive in *Magnum, P.I.*? (A Ferrari)
• Who sang with the Blue Belles before breaking away for a solo career? (Patti LaBelle)

Games are free. NTN boxes are available every day at P.D.'s Pub (The Pirate's Den) from 11am till closing. The pub is located in the Galleria Plaza, on West Bay Rd. (✆ 345/949-7144.)

American and international fare is served here, including burgers, fries, conch salad, and such hot dishes as roast filet of beef with french fries and a salad. Salads and sandwiches cost CI$8.25 to CI$9.50 (US$10–US$12), with main courses priced from CI$13 to CI$28 (US$17–US$35). Open Monday to Saturday 9am to 11pm, Sunday 11am to 11pm. N. Church St. ✆ 345/945-3860.

5 Caymanian Pastime: The Pool Hall Bar

The Attic Billiard Lounge This bar and pool hall is located on the upper floor of a building in a shopping center off West Bay

Road. It attracts a higher percentage of off-islanders than the larger, noisier, more raucous, and, at least to bona fide pool players, more interesting Corner Pocket Pool Hall, which, frankly, we think is more fun. Here at The Attic, you'll pay a fee of CI$11.50 (US$14) per hour for use of any of the tables (a total of eight pool tables plus one snooker table) in the joint. Old Dutch beer (brewed locally and priced at CI$2.50/US$3.15) per pint) is the drink of choice for many of the players here, most of whom wouldn't dream of congregating until after 8 or 9pm. If you're hungry, burgers and sandwiches can be constructed in the tiny kitchen for CI$5 to CI$7 (US$6.25–US$8.75) each. The lounge is open Monday to Friday 5pm to 1am, Saturday noon to midnight. In the Queen's Court Plaza, West Bay Rd. (℅) **345/949-7665.**

Corner Pocket Pool Hall ✦   This is the most hip, crowded, and with-it pool hall on Grand Cayman, a haven where hundreds of locals drink, flirt, gossip, and in many cases, actually play some intense games of pool. It lies on the second floor of an industrial-looking, all-concrete building in a commercial zone about 2.4km (1½ miles) north of the center of George Town. If you can handle the transition from the glittery tourist-oriented world of West Bay Road to the dark, permissive, and distinctly insider-ish atmosphere here, this venue can be a whole lot of fun. The pool hall offers six pool tables. There is a very real possibility that you'll be invited to get involved in some off-the-record wagers (we don't advise this unless you really know what you're doing). You will pay CI$5 (US$6.25) per half-hour for a pool table, regardless of how many people are playing. There is often a waiting list for tables, so have a drink and relax while waiting. In addition to pool, you'll also find a steady diet of country-western or rap music, friendly dart competitions, and a genuinely welcoming group of patrons and staff. Open daily 4pm to 1am. 139 Allister Towers, N. Sound Rd., George Town. (℅) **345/946-8080.**

Shooters Bar and Billiard Hall   This is the smallest, but probably the most elaborate and (in terms of food and accessories) most ambitious, of the three pool halls on Grand Cayman. This place will interest anyone who wants an insight into local hobbies and diversions. Within four dark, clublike rooms, it boasts a half dozen computer terminals, a trio of pool tables, a small but elaborate bar area with a very large TV screen, and a small-scale restaurant (the Red Light Café) where tables are concealed within private, curtained compartments—a setup that's evocative of a Gaslight-era bordello. The food served at the restaurant is filling and straightforward, including choices such as steak with peppercorn sauce, roasted breast of chicken stuffed with layers of ham and cheese, and conch chowder. This is a real local dive. The clientele consists almost entirely of the rather irreverent and hip islanders. This place is an exception to the usually squeaky clean image of Grand Cayman, and a lone male is likely to find female companionship here if he so desires.

Use of a computer station costs CI$2 (US$2.50) for the first 10 minutes, and CI18¢ (US25¢) for each additional minute. Cocktails range from CI$4.25 to CI$8 (US$5.30–US$10). Main courses in the restaurant cost CI$14 to CI$21 (US$18–US$26) each and are served every day from 6:30 to 10:30pm. Use of the pool table costs around CI$5 (US$6.25) per half-hour, regardless of how many people are playing. In the Seven Mile Shopping Centre, West Bay Rd. ✆ 345/946-3496.

6 Other Diversions

Antica Gelateria   The variety of ice cream flavors sold here surpasses the selection at any other outlet in the Cayman Islands. Tucked away in a shopping center off West Bay Road, just behind the also-recommended Cimboco Caribbean Café, it was established in 2002 by the Casteldello family, an Italian family who presumably know a lot about gelato and how a *gelateria* should be run. You'll find about two dozen varieties of ice cream here, including all the flavors you might find on a street-fronting ice cream parlor in Rome or Palermo, as well as such Caribbean-influenced selections such as mango, pineapple, apricot, almond and rum, and chocolate and rum. Cups of ice cream cost from CI$3 to CI$5 (US$3.75–US$6.25), and ice-cream cones go for CI$3 (US$3.75) each. Take-away ice cream costs CI$6 (US$7.50) per pound. Open daily 2 to 11pm. In the Marquee Shopping Center, Harquail Bypass near West Bay Rd. ✆ 345/946-1400.

7 Theatrical Productions

The Harquail Theatre   Mrs. Helen Harquail donated this $4 million theater in memory of her late husband, F. J. Harquail. Musicals, dramas, and comedies featuring local performers are regularly produced on the Harquail stage. Seating 330, the theater is also the venue for classical concerts, opera, dance performances, art exhibitions, fashion shows, and other events. Before an event, the box office is open on Saturday from 10am to 1pm and for 1 hour before each performance. Tickets run between $5 and $30. Harquail Dr. (a bypass heading north from George Town). ✆ 345/949-5477.

9

Cayman Brac

The "middle" island of the Caymans was given the name *Brac* (Gaelic for "bluff") by the 17th-century Scottish fishermen who settled here. The Bluff for which the 19km-long (12-mile) island was named is a towering limestone plateau rising 42m (140 ft.) above the sea, covering the eastern half of Cayman Brac. Caymanians refer to the island simply as Brac, and its 1,400 inhabitants, a hospitable bunch of people, are called Brackers. Pirates occupied the Caymans in the early 18th century, and Edward Teach, the infamous Blackbeard, is supposed to have spent quite a bit of time around Cayman Brac. The island is about 143km (89 miles) east of Grand Cayman.

There are more than 170 caves honeycombing the limestone heights of the island. Some of the caves are at the Bluff's foot, while others can be reached only by climbing over jagged limestone rock. One of the biggest is Great Cave, which has a number of chambers. Harmless fruit bats cling to the roofs of the caverns.

You won't see many people on the south side of the Bluff, and the only sound is the sea crashing against the lavalike shore. You'll find the island's herons and wild green parrots here. Most of the Brackers live on the north side, in traditional wooden seaside cottages, some of which were built by the island's pioneers. Looking at the variety of flowers, shrubs, and fruit trees in many of the Brackers' yards, it's clear that many islanders have green thumbs. You'll see poinciana trees, bougainvillea, Cayman orchids, croton, hibiscus, aloe, sea grapes, cactus, and coconut and cabbage palms. Gardeners grow cassava, pumpkins, breadfruit, yams, and sweet potatoes.

There are no actual towns, only settlements, such as Stake Bay (the "capital"), Spot Bay, the Creek, Tibbitts Turn, the Bight, and West End, where the airport is located.

1 Essentials

VISITOR INFORMATION

Cayman Brac Tourist Office, West End Rd., North Side (© 345/948-1649), is open Monday to Friday 8:30am to noon and 1 to

5pm, dispensing information about the island. It's found to the east of the little airport.

GETTING THERE

Cayman Airways (© **800/422-9626** in the U.S. or 345/948-1210) offers four flights a week to and from Cayman Brac on Boeing 737s, which carry 122 passengers. The flights leave from Miami and make a short stop on Grand Cayman. With a 3-day advance purchase, fares begin at US$179 round-trip.

Island Airways (© **345/948-1656**) offers six flights a day to and from Grand Cayman, taking 40 minutes for direct flights or 60 minutes if a short stopover in Little Cayman is included. One-way flights cost US$91, with small reductions for round-trips.

Island Air (© **345/949-5252**) also flies daily between Cayman Brac and Little Cayman, costing US$35 (CI$28) one-way or US$56 (CI$45) round-trip. Flights from Cayman Brac leave at 8:35am and 5:25pm, with flights from Little Cayman to Cayman Brac leaving at 10:30am and 3:20pm.

GETTING AROUND

You have a choice of a taxi, bike, rental vehicle, or your trusty feet.

CAR RENTALS   Car-rental agencies will meet all incoming flights if you've made reservations in advance. There aren't many rental places here, so reserve as far in advance as possible during the winter season.

B&S Motorventures, 422 Channel Rd., South Side (© **345/948-1646**), is run by the helpful Steve and Nola Bodden, who will supply you with plenty of insider information about Cayman Brac. Cars cost US$40 per day, or US$35 per day after a 2-day rental. The best deal is their weekly rate, beginning at US$210 for 6 to 7 days. Jeeps can also be rented for US$40 to US$45 per day.

Brac Rent-a-Car, Tibbetts Square (© **345/948-1515**), rents Nissan Sentras for US$38 per day, Suzuki Jeeps for US$40 per day, and Ford vans for US$55 per day. **Four Ds Car Rental,** Kidco Building, South Side (© **345/948-1599**), offers car rentals for US$35 a day and up, and vans for US$45 a day. If you rent for 6 days, the 7th day is free.

TAXI   Service is slow and not very organized, but it's available. Be prepared, however, to wait. Taxis do not always meet incoming planes unless arrangements are made in advance. Most taxi companies will take you on a 2-hour tour for US$20 per person. All the taxis companies charge the same tariffs—for example, traveling from the airport to one of the resorts or villas on Stake Bay along the north side of the island costs about US$5 per person.

The leading taxis services are **D&M** (© **345/948-2307**), **Elo's Taxi** (© **345/948-0220**), and **Maple Edwards** (© **345/948-0395**).

BY BIKE & SCOOTER   You can explore almost all of Cayman Brac by bike or scooter, except for the area around the Bluff, which is too difficult. Most roads along the coast are flat and easy to traverse by bike. The main road across the west of Cayman Brac is also a relatively easy cycle route.

Many hotels either lend or rent bikes to guests. If yours doesn't, you can rent both scooters and bicycles from **B&S Motorventures** (© **345/948-1646**). Scooters cost US$30 per day or US$180 for 6 to 7 days. Bikes rent for US$10 per day. If you find that the bike your hotel lends or rents is too simple, you can get a bike with gears and good brakes from B&S. The company will deliver a bike or scooter to you at any location on the island.

 FAST FACTS: Cayman Brac

Banks The local branch of **Cayman National Bank** is at 14 West End, Cross Roads (© **345/948-1451**). It's open Monday to Thursday 9am to 2:30pm and Friday 9am to 4:30pm. It has the only ATM on island.

Emergencies Dial © **911**. The main safety issue here is climbers having accidents while attempting to scale the Bluff. In the event of an accident, the only rescue agency is the fire department. Call © **911**.

Hospitals & Clinics The government-run **Faith Hospital** is at Stake Bay (© **345/948-2225**). The hospital is open daily 24 hours. For a nonemergency consultation with a doctor, you can visit the hospital daily from 8:30am to 6pm. The **Cayman Brac Clinic** at Tibbetts Square, West End (© **345/948-1777**) is open Monday to Friday 8am to noon and 3 to 6pm, and Saturday 8am to noon. For clinic treatment outside opening hours, call © **345/948-2363**.

For dental service, call © **345/948-2618**.

Internet Access You can access the Internet at **Divi Tiara Beach Resort**, South Side (© **345/948-1553**), where computers in the lobby are available 24 hours a day, costing US$8 for 15 minutes, US$15 for 30 minutes or US$22 for 45 minutes.

Another choice is **Brac Reef Beach Resort,** South Side (© **345/ 948-1323**), which offers Internet access daily from 7am to 9pm, costing US30¢ per minute. Internet access is also available at the post office (see below), where use of computers costs CI$6 (US$7.50) per hour.

Language English is the official language of the island.

Pharmacies The hospital and clinic mentioned above under "Hospitals & Clinics" have small pharmacies.

Post Office The **Cayman Brac Post Office,** West End (© **345/ 948-1422**), is open Monday to Friday from 8:30am to 5pm. There are also branch post offices near Tibbetts Square in Stake Bay, at Watering Place, and at Spot Bay, each open Monday to Friday 9 to 11am and 1 to 3pm.

Water Drinking water is distilled seawater and is perfectly safe to drink.

2 Where to Stay

Important: Before you look through this chapter, see our "Tips on Accommodations" in chapter 2 for descriptions of various types of accommodations and tips on getting the very best deals. Also, be aware that all accommodation prices quoted in this chapter are in U.S. dollars.

THE MAJOR DIVE RESORTS

Brac Caribbean Beach Village ⟨⟨   The largest condo complex on the island offers 16 bright, spacious two-bedroom/two-bathroom or two-bedroom/three-bathroom condos on a white sandy beach, along with a pool and a scuba-diving program. Each unit has a fully equipped kitchen with a full-size refrigerator (with an ice-maker) and a microwave. A variety of items, including breakfast food, are stocked before your arrival. Twelve of the units open onto private balconies. The master bedroom is furnished with a queen-size bed and the guest bedrooms have twin beds. Bathrooms are medium in size, each with a shower/tub combination. Maid service costs an extra $35 per day. The units are rather simply furnished in a tropical Caribbean motif. The hotel offers some of the best dining on the island, at the Captain's Table (p. 173).

Stake Bay (P.O. Box 4), Cayman Brac, B.W.I. © **800/791-7911** in the U.S., or 345/ 948-2265. Fax 345/948-1111. www.866thebrac.com. 16 units. Year-round $185 apt for 2, $245 apt for 4; weekly rates $1,100 apt for 2 adults, $1,600 apt for 4 adults.

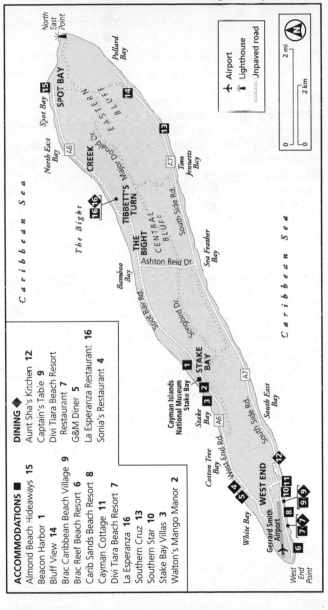

Accommodations & Dining on Cayman Brac

ACCOMMODATIONS ■

Almond Beach Hideaways **15**
Beacon Harbor **1**
Bluff View **14**
Brac Caribbean Beach Village **9**
Brac Reef Beach Resort **6**
Carib Sands Beach Resort **8**
Cayman Cottage **11**
Divi Tiara Beach Resort **7**
La Esperanza **16**
Southern Cruz **13**
Southern Star **10**
Stake Bay Villas **3**
Walton's Mango Manor **2**

DINING ◆

Aunt Sha's Kitchen **12**
Captain's Table **9**
Divi Tiara Beach Resort Restaurant **7**
G&M Diner **5**
La Esperanza Restaurant **16**
Sonia's Restaurant **4**

Scuba packages from $345 for 5 dives. AE, MC, V. **Amenities:** Restaurant; bar; watersports outfitter; coin-op washers and dryers. *In room:* A/C, TV, kitchen, coffeemaker.

Brac Reef Beach Resort ✿

On a sandy plot of land on the south shore, 3km (2 miles) east of the airport, this resort contains motel-style units comfortably furnished with carpeting, ceiling fans, air-conditioning, and shower/tub combination bathrooms. This is a durable resort, although frankly, you'll be more comfortably housed at Walton's Mango Manor or Brac Caribbean Beach Village. This location was once little more than a maze of sea grapes, a few of whose venerable trunks still rise amid the picnic tables, hammocks, and boardwalks. There are still lots of nature trails around the resort, which are good for bird-watching. On the premises are the rusted remains of a Russian lighthouse tower that was retrieved several years ago from a Cuban-made trawler. Some of the best snorkeling in the region is nearby.

Lunches are informal affairs, and dinners are served buffet style under the stars.

South Side (P.O. Box 56), Cayman Brac, B.W.I. ✆ **800/327-3835** in the U.S. and Canada, or 345/948-1323. www.bracreef.com. 40 units. Winter $321 double for 3 nights; off-season $225 double for 3 nights. Dive and meal packages available. AE, MC, V. **Amenities:** Restaurant; bar; outdoor pool; tennis court (lit for night play); fitness center; spa; Jacuzzi; watersports outfitter, game room; business center; babysitting; laundry service. *In room:* A/C, TV, hair dryer.

Divi Tiara Beach Resort ✿

Part of the Divi Divi hotel chain, the Tiara, about 3km (2 miles) east of the airport, offers a white-sand beachfront. It's an excellent choice for divers, with a well-regarded dive operation on-site (see p. 177 for a full description of the dive program). The landscaping, which incorporates croton, bougainvillea, and palms, is beautiful. All the rather basic accommodations are housed in motel-like outbuildings; 12 of the units are timeshares. Each timeshare has an ocean view, a Jacuzzi, and a king-size bed. Bathrooms in all accommodations, which feature combination tubs and showers, are well maintained.

At the bar, guests gaze out to sea while sipping their drinks before heading to the Poseidon dining room to enjoy good Caribbean and American cuisine. Most meals are buffet style.

South Side (P.O. Box 238), Cayman Brac, B.W.I. ✆ **800/367-3484** in the U.S. and Canada, or 345/948-1553. Fax 345/948-1316. www.divitiara.com. 71 units. Winter $140–$230 double; off-season $105–$188 double. Children under age 12 stay free in parent's room. MAP (breakfast and dinner) $46 per person extra. AE, MC, V. **Amenities:** Restaurant; bar; outdoor pool; tennis court (lit for night play); watersports outfitter; free bike loan; laundry. *In room:* A/C, TV, hair dryer, safe.

A GUESTHOUSE

Walton's Mango Manor 𝕉𝕉 (*Value* Unique on Cayman Brac, this is a personalized, intimate B&B that's more richly decorated, more elegant, and more appealing than you might have thought was possible in such a remote place. Originally the home of a sea captain, it was moved to a less exposed location and rebuilt from salvaged materials shortly after the disastrous hurricane of 1932. Set on 1 hectare (3 acres) on the island's north shore, within a lush garden, it contains intriguing touches such as a banister salvaged from the mast of a 19th-century schooner. The most desirable accommodations are on the upper floor, partly because these rooms boast narrow balconies that offer views of the sea. Each room has a small bathroom equipped with a shower stall. Your hosts are Brooklyn-born Lynne Walton and her husband, George, a former USAF major who retired to his native Cayman Brac.

Stake Bay (P.O. Box 56), Cayman Brac, B.W.I. 𝐂 and fax **345/948-0518**. www. waltonsmangomanor.com. 5 units. Winter $100–$110 double; off-season $90–$100 double. Rates include full breakfast. AE, MC, V. *In-room:* A/C, no phone

SELF-CATERING VILLAS & APARTMENTS

Almond Beach Hideaways 𝕉 (*Finds* Outside your door, the scene looks like a picture postcard, with a beachfront of white sand set against a backdrop of coconut palms. These free-standing, two-bedroom villas offer much tranquility and privacy. They are air-conditioned and boast their own sea-bordering patio, private bathrooms with a combination tub and shower, and a fully equipped kitchen including a large refrigerator. Think of these places as get-away-from-it-all hideaways. The master bedroom houses a queen-sized bed, the guest bedroom has two twins beds, and the living room includes a queen sofa bed. All bed and bath linens are supplied, and a member of the staff will meet you at the airport to transport you to your villa. In addition, there is maid service and a caretaker on call 24 hours a day. There are also hammocks, chaise lounges, a beach cabana, and a barbecue grill.

Spot Bay (P.O. Box 132), Cayman Brac, B.W.I. 𝐂 **866/222-8528**. Fax 503/472-6934. 2 villas. Year-round $215 double; $250 triple; $285 quad. Each additional person $30. Children 8 and under stay free in their parents' room. MC, V. **Amenities:** Babysitting. *In room:* A/C, TV, kitchen, coffeemaker, safe, self-service washer/dryer.

Beacon Harbour 𝕉 (*Finds* Built on piers, these luxury beachfront condos on the north side of the island were custom-made for scuba divers. They lie near Stake Bay, opposite a trio of excellent dive sites and near some spectacular offshore snorkeling. In the open area downstairs, which has room to park your vehicle, you'll find toilets, outside showers, and even wash-down facilities for scuba gear. Each of the upstairs accommodations can sleep six comfortably. The airy, comfortable rooms, each decorated with tile floors and tropical colors like seafoam green and peach, feature wicker furniture and vinyl cushions. Pictures of marine life off Cayman Brac decorate the walls. Each of the bedrooms comes with a queen-size bed and a large living room with a queen-size hide-a-bed. Guests often prepare their own meals in the fully equipped kitchen, and there's a grocery store just around the corner in Stake Bay. A separate washer-and-dryer room lies outside your front door, and sliding glass doors open onto a 92-sq.-m (500-sq.-ft.) attached deck. Maid service is included in the price.

Stake Bay, Cayman Brac, B.W.I. © **956/544-4396.** Fax 956/544-4396. www. beaconharbor.com. 2 2-bedroom condos. Year-round $190 double. Extra person $35. Children ages 3 and under stay free in their parents' room MC, V. **Amenities:** Babysitting; washer and dryer. *In room:* A/C, TV/VCR, kitchen, coffeemaker, hair dryer, iron.

Bluff View *(Value* Set against the backdrop of the Bluff, this rental unit opens onto a vista of coconut palms. Locals call it "the Climbers House" because it's owned by members of a hill-climbers group. On the south road toward the eastern end of the island, it lies just 45m (50 yards) from the sea. Constructed in 1993, the two rental units are housed in one wooden building, with each rental unit on one whole floor of the two-floor block. Each unit comes with one bedroom, a private bathroom with a tub and shower combo, and a fully equipped kitchen, along with simple and rather standard but comfortable furnishings. You're told to bring your own snorkeling and scuba gear, but everything else is provided except a TV. An outdoor shower and shed with a washer/dryer are shared among renters.

Southeast End, Cayman Brac, B.W.I. © **970/493-5801.** Fax 970/493-2283. www. tradgirl.com/caymans/house.htm. 2 1-bedroom units. Year-round $90 double; 3-night minimum stay. No credit cards. **Amenities:** Washer/dryer. *In room:* A/C, kitchen, coffeemaker.

Carib Sands Beach Resort *(Kids* Built in 1999, this is one of the island's most modern oceanfront condo resorts, with attractively furnished one-, two-, three-, or four-bedroom units that include fully furnished kitchens. The resort often attracts families. The first-class property opens onto one of the most idyllic strands of white sands on Cayman Brac and boasts an on-site dive center. The concrete condos are furnished with Navajo white wicker furniture, often set against dramatic tones of blue, burgundy, or sea green. All the bathrooms contain a tub-and-shower combo. Rooms open onto

either a garden view or a vista of the ocean. Rollaways can be provided for extra guests. There's a bar and restaurant about 90m (100 yards) from the resort. Maid service is included in the price.

Stake Bay (P.O. Box 4), Cayman Brac, B.W.I. © **866/THE-BRAC** or 345/948-1121. Fax 345/948-1122. www.866thebrac.com. 34 condos. Year-round $185 1-bedroom; $245 2-bedroom; $305 3-bedroom; $365 4-bedroom. Children 11 and under stay free in their parents' room. AE, MC, V. **Amenities:** Restaurant; bar; outdoor pool; exercise room; watersports outfitter; bike loan; babysitting; coin-operated washers/dryers. *In room:* A/C, TV, kitchen, iron.

Cayman Cottage ⊛ *(Finds*   If your dream is to retreat to a little West Indian cottage hideaway with a loved one, here's your chance for seclusion and privacy, lying just 23m (75 ft.) from a white sandy beach. The fully furnished cottage is located on the grounds of the owner's home on the West End/South Side of the island. The cottage offers 183 sq. m (600 sq. ft.) of living space, including a private bedroom, a large living and dining area, a bathroom with a tub-and-shower combo, a fully equipped kitchen, and a washer/dryer. Built in 1996, the cottage features ceramic tile floors and peach wicker furnishings.

South Side, Cayman Brac, B.W.I. © **800/898-6854** in the U.S. or 345/948-1617. Fax 345/948-1350. 1 guesthouse. Year-round $130 for 2–4 people. No credit cards. **Amenities:** Washer/dryer. *In room:* A/C, TV, kitchen, coffeemaker, hair dryer, no phone.

La Esperanza ⊛ *(Finds*   This modern complex consists of a series of apartment and cottage rentals on the north side, with easy access to a private beach on the south side (free transportation can often be arranged between the lodgings and the beach). The complex lies midway along the north shore. This place was launched in 1986 when it was a small gathering place for four friends and the only spot in the area for people to come to and relax in the "cool, cool, cool of the evening," as the popular '50s song went. The complex grew, but even today it's still relatively small and casual, and is better known for its restaurant and bar (p. 175) than it is for its accommodations.

The well-furnished and comfortable apartments, each decorated in a typical light, breezy West Indian style, consist of two bedrooms with one-and-a-half bathrooms (the full bathroom has a shower), a full kitchen, and a living/dining room. The cottage offers three bedrooms and two bathrooms with showers, plus a full kitchen, living room, dining room, and open-air deck. Under large shade trees or other open shelters on the grounds, you'll find a lot of extras, including washer and dryer facilities, an outside shower, gas grills, and hammocks. Sometimes the rare blue iguana will stroll onto the grounds looking for a tasty treat (they don't eat people, so don't worry).

Cars can also be rented here for $30 per day.

Stake Bay (P.O. Box 216), Cayman Brac, B.W.I. © 345/948-0531. Fax 345/948-0525. www.laesperanza.net. 11 units. Winter $100 double in apt, $125 double in cottage; off-season $60 double in apt, $75 double in cottage. Extra person $15. AE, MC, V. **Amenities:** Restaurant; bar; car-rental desk; babysitting. *In room:* A/C, TV, kitchen, coffeemaker.

Southern Cruz   Although the setting is a bit bleak—no lush landscaping except for a buffer grove of sea grapes—this is one of the most comfortable of the small-house rentals on the island. For many visitors, it would make an ideal "second home" in the Caribbean. Painted in pastels, it is a concrete structure with no particular architectural flourish. The interior is decorated in typical West Indian style, with pastels, whitewashed woods, and tiles. Each rental has a well-maintained medium-sized private bathroom with a shower. The sofa bed in the living room can be converted to receive additional guests. Each of the bedrooms offers a king-size bed and a walk-in closet. Double sliding glass doors open onto a view of the ocean. You can enjoy this view with a cup of coffee in the morning from your private patio, or a cocktail at night from the covered porch. Between the living and dining rooms is a four-stool bar. The kitchen is generously equipped with utensils and hardware. There's also a laundry room adjacent to the kitchen, and an outside shower to wash off the sand after a day at the beach. The oceanfront house accommodates up to six, and is ideal for honeymooners, families, or a small group of friends who will appreciate the casual, laid-back style. Hammocks are strung up on the covered porch for lazy enjoyment of the surroundings. Other features include a barbecue grill and covered parking.

South Side, Cayman Brac, B.W.I. © 877/229-6637 in the U.S. or 345/948-2308. www.mcginleyvacationcabins.com/caymanbrac.html. 2 units. Nov 15–May 15 $215 for up to 6; May 16–Nov 15 $200 for up to 6. MC, V. *In room:* A/C, TV, kitchen, washer/dryer.

Southern Star ⭐⭐   In the southwest, near such larger resorts as Brac Caribbean and Divi Tiara, this complex of five town houses is available for both short- or long-term rentals. Built and opened in 1999, each town house contains two bedrooms and two bathrooms with shower-and-tub combos. Furnishings are stylishly Caribbean, with lots of white wicker, and the space is generous. Each accommodation comes complete with a fully operating kitchen and a living room. Each unit can house at least four guests comfortably. Private porches, patios, and verandas add extra grace notes for easy living, as do hammocks and picnic areas with table and chairs. Ample closet and storage space are other highlights. Beach access is just a short walk across the street, where you'll find a reef-protected lagoon that's ideal for swimming and snorkeling, plus a 91m (300-ft.) private sandy beach with shade trees.

West End, near junction of South Side Road West and Cross Roads. ⓒ 345/948-1577. Fax 345/948-1578. www.thebrac.com/southernstar.html. 5 town houses. Winter $105 double; off-season $99 double. Extra person $10. MC, V. **Amenities:** Babysitting; washer/dryer. *In room:* A/C, TV/VCR, kitchen, coffeemaker, hair dryer, iron.

Stake Bay Villas   On the North Side of Cayman Brac, opening onto Stake Bay, this white wooden structure was constructed in 2001 in an idyllic location about 30m (100 ft.) from excellent snorkeling or swimming among rainbow-hued coral reefs. The house is an oceanside duplex near government offices, a bank, duty-free shops, a supermarket, and the local museum. Each unit has a single bedroom, an adequate closet, a bathroom with a tub/shower combo, a fully equipped kitchen, and a living room with a queen sofa sleeper. Furnishings are mainly rattan. Sunsets can be viewed from the screened-in porch. Maid service is included. You can have a cookout using the outdoor barbecue grill.

Stake Bay, Cayman Brac, B.W.I. ⓒ **345/948-1646.** Fax 345/948-1676. www.stake bayvillas.com. 2 1-bedroom villas. Year-round $120 for 2. Extra person $25. No credit cards. *In room:* A/C, kitchen, coffeemaker, hair dryer, washer/dryer.

3 Where to Dine

All prices are listed here in U.S. dollars.

MODERATE

Captain's Table 🌴 INTERNATIONAL/AMERICAN   Located at Brac Caribbean Beach Village (a previously recommended resort hotel), this is the most cosmopolitan restaurant and bar on Cayman Brac. The decor here is vaguely nautical, with oars over and around the bar and pieces of boats forming the restaurant's entryway. The restaurant offers both indoor air-conditioned seating and outdoor dining by the pool. Begin with the shrimp-and-lobster cocktail or perhaps a conch fritter, and then try one of the soups. Main dishes include everything from the catch of the day, often served pan-fried, to barbecue ribs. Some especially delightful dishes include blackened sea bass topped with sautéed onions, and a tasty pasta marinara studded with fresh fish, scallops, and shrimp. The most frequently ordered local favorite is the "cowboy cut" (16 or 18 oz.) of rib-eye dipped in blackened spices, pan seared, and topped with grilled onions. At lunch, you can order burgers and sandwiches.

In Brac Caribbean Beach Village, Stake Bay. ☎ **345/948-1418.** Reservations recommended. Lunch main courses $7.25–$11; dinner main courses $18–$31. AE, MC, V. Mon–Sat 11:30am–3pm and 6–10pm; Sun noon–3pm and 6–10pm.

Divi Tiara Beach Resort Restaurant *Kids* INTERNATIONAL/ BUFFET   Because of its generous and tasty buffets, this is the local choice for family dining. At lunch and dinner, everything is served buffet style, and on a good night at least 100 diners can be seated here. The food doesn't scale any culinary peaks, but it is very satisfying. The buffet selections are forever changing, but you can count on seeing a catch of the day—perhaps mahimahi, grouper, or snapper—which can be baked, grilled, or sautéed in butter. Other family favorites include zesty barbecue ribs and chicken with roasted potatoes, corn on the cob, and baked beans.

South Side. ☎ **345/948-3553.** Lunch buffets $17 for adults, $12 ages 11 and under; dinner buffets $37 adults, $18 ages 11 and under. AE, MC, V. Daily 12:30–2pm and 6:30–9:30pm.

INEXPENSIVE

Aunt Sha's Kitchen *Finds* CAYMANIAN/CHINESE   This bright pink building blinds you in the brilliant sunshine, luring you to its isolated location on the south side of Cayman Brac. While relaxing on the patio, you can often see sharks at high tide in the waters beyond. This restaurant is a local favorite, serving the type of food islanders have eaten for decades. You get such classic dishes here as turtle stew with rice and beans, homemade conch fritters, and Key lime pie. Other favorites include sweet-and-sour chicken with fried rice, and chicken or shrimp chop suey. We gravitate to the catch of the day, perhaps kingfish or mahimahi, which can be grilled or fried and topped with buttery onions and pepper. The prices are among the most affordable on the island. There's also a lively bar with a pool table (see "Cayman Brac After Dark").

South Side. ☎ **345/948-1581.** Main courses $10–$13. AE, MC, V. Daily 11:30am–11pm.

G&M Diner CAYMANIAN/SEAFOOD   This is one of the most authentic of the old island restaurants, popular with locals and drawing the occasional visitor. It's at its most festive on Sunday when church groups in their "Sunday-go-to-meeting" clothes pour in here for "a fill up." The restaurant is housed in a wooden structure decorated with ship carvings and pictures of Caymanian life. The cooks make the island's most savory kettle of turtle stew, served with rice, beans, potato salad, and cole slaw. You can also order such hearty fare as braised oxtail or roast beef in gravy with vegetables and rice. The choice selection is always the catch of the day—perhaps mahimahi, snapper, or kingfish—served fried or grilled.

West End. ✆ **345/948-1272.** Main courses $13–$14. No credit cards. Daily 11:30am–2:30pm and 6:30–8:30pm.

La Esperanza Restaurant ✿ *(Finds)* CAYMANIAN   Islanders, who flock here, call this place "Bussy's" in honor of its likable owner, Bussy Dilbert, who is the island's most popular and beloved innkeeper. (See p. 171 for details about making La Esperanza your vacation retreat.) For entertainment (see "Cayman Brac After Dark" later), a drink, a room, or a meal, many devotees of this place would go nowhere else. You're offered a choice of indoor or outdoor dining, and the restaurant is decorated with wood furnishings and pictures of nautical life and island memorabilia.

Bussy's jerk chicken is the best on island, and as zesty as any you'll find in Jamaica itself. Most dishes come with corn bread, rice, red beans, and fried plantains. Fresh and locally caught mahimahi, kingfish, or snapper appear frequently on the menu, and these catches of the day are served in a lemon sauce with sautéed vegetables. One of the island's best T-bones appears here with side dishes of your choice. Other delights include savory conch fritters; shrimp, lobster, or turtle dishes; and fish and chips. The Key lime pie is the eternal favorite.

Stake Bay. ✆ **345/984-0531.** Main courses $7.50–$21. AE, MC, V. Daily noon–2pm and 6–10pm.

Sonia's Restaurant *(Kids)* CAYMANIAN/SEAFOOD/CARIBBEAN   This is the island's most popular lunch stop, specializing in local cookery served the way it has been since before the Cayman Islands became a popular destination. This place is traditional looking, with dark-wood furnishings, although it's air-conditioned, a recent "novelty." A great family dining choice because of its children's menu, the restaurant has a nonsmoking section and provides for special diets if requested far enough in advance. There is a takeout service if you're planning a picnic on the beach. The all-time favorite meal is red-bean soup followed by roast beef with rice and beans. We're more drawn, however, to the steamed, freshly caught turbot with steamed vegetables, and the fried kingfish with rice and

beans. Chicken is another favorite dish here, and it comes baked, curried, or stewed.

West End. ℰ **345/948-1212.** Main courses $11–$14. No credit cards. Mon–Sat 11:30am–3pm.

4 Hitting the Beaches & Other Outdoor Pursuits

Come to Cayman Brac for spectacular outdoor offerings rather than man-made attractions. Scuba divers flock here in droves, and everybody, from singles to families, in all age ranges, loves the beaches here.

THE BEACHES Though Cayman Brac can hardly compete with Grand Cayman and its Seven Mile Beach, there are enough beaches on Brac to satisfy most tastes, even though they are on a smaller scale.

Most of the beaches lie in the southwest, the northeast, and the northwest. The East End, where the cliffs of the Bluff meet the sea, is definitely not beach country.

Most visitors use the small beaches along the southwest coast, since this is the site of such major resorts as Brac Reef and Divi Tiara. We've found that these beaches are better for sunning than snorkeling because of the huge outgrowth of turtle grass in the water.

Directly east of these resorts is the public beach, reached by heading east along South Side Road West. You'll find it to the immediate south of marshes/wetlands. With its gentle rollers, the beach itself is quite beautiful, though the wire enclosure enveloping the picnic area is pretty unappealing. There are public showers here, but we've never known them to be in order (plus the water in the bathrooms has an unpleasant odor), and the toilets are foul. You may want to do your showering elsewhere.

Many visitors opt to find their own small stretch of sand, particularly in the southwest area beyond Salt Water Pond. There is another stretch of coastline to the east at Hawkesbill Bay.

Along the northern tier, the only stretch of coastline with a reef is to the west of Spot Bay, though strong currents on both the eastern and western tips of the Cayman Brac make snorkeling a bit hazardous.

DIVING Since diving on Cayman Brac is rated among the best in the Caribbean, divers from all over the world, both experienced and beginner, are drawn here. Seas are usually calm and the best dive sites lie only a 5- to 20-minute boat ride offshore. All the dive outfitters recommended below also make visits to Little Cayman (see chapter 10), just 8km (5 miles) away, with most boat rides taking less than an hour.

Tips In Case of Inclement Weather: An Indoor Attraction

If it's raining outside (and even if it's not), history buffs might want to check out the **Cayman Brac Museum,** in the former Government Administration Building, Stake Bay (© **345/948-2622**), which has an interesting collection of Caymanian antiques, including pieces rescued from shipwrecks and objects from the 18th century. Hours are Monday to Friday from 9am to noon and 1 to 4pm, Saturday from 9am to noon, and Sunday from 1 to 4pm. Admission is free.

In all, there are about 50 prime dive sites, geared to all different levels of divers. The most dramatic is the wreck of the frigate MV *Captain Keith Tibbetts,* which was deliberately sunk in September 1996 after having been brought over from Cuba. This 99m (330-ft.) former Russian frigate, originally intended for the Cuban navy, lies 180m (200 yards) offshore in northwest Cayman Brac, its bow resting in 27m (90 ft.) of water, the stern just 12m (40 ft.) below the surface. Divers can swim through its trio of upper decks, keeping company with everything from the four-eyed butterfly fish to batfish.

After talking with you and finding out your interests, the dive operators recommended below will guide you to dozens of different sites.

Reef Divers, South Side (© **800/327-3835,** or 345/948-1642), is affiliated with the previously recommended Brac Reef Beach Resort. Divers' magazines consistently rate this outfitter as offering the best wall diving and wreck diving on the island. Reef Divers' fleet of dive boats, with a complete inventory of tanks and scuba gear, range from 13m to 14m (42 ft.–46 ft.). A one-tank dive costs US$45, a two-tank dive US$75, and a three-tank dive US$95. Snorkeling trips are also possible for US$25 and are available daily from 8:15am to 12:15pm and 1:45 to 3:30pm. Rentals of wetsuits, masks, fins, and snorkeling equipment, among other gear, are available.

Divi Tiara Dive School, at the Divi Tiara Beach Hotel, South Side (© **800/367-3484** or 345/948-1553), is run only for guests of the hotel, who, as might be predicted, are mostly divers or friends of divers. The resort offers five dive boats and is a five-star PADI center as well. A one-tank dive costs US$33 in the afternoon, with a two-tank dive going for US$60 and a three-tank dive for US$90. An open-water certification course is US$395.

Moments **Capturing Your Underwater Experiences on Film**

At **Photo Tiara,** found at the Divi Tiara Beach Resort, South Side (© 345/948-1553), underwater camera rentals are available, costing US$35 per half day or US$49 per full day. Underwater video cameras (Hi-8mm) go for US$75 per day. This full-service photo center also gives beginning underwater video and photo courses for US$85, and a comprehensive PADI underwater photo specialty course for US$199. Open daily 8:30am to 5pm.

Captain Shelby's, under "Fishing" below, also offers dives and snorkeling trips.

EXPLORING BY CAR   The Bluff ✦ is the island's most distinctive geographic feature. As mentioned before, the Bluff is a towering limestone plateau rising 42m (140 ft.) above the sea, covering much of the easternmost point of the island. To drive up the Bluff, take Ashton Reid Drive, the one paved road that leads to the summit. The panoramic view over the south side of the Bluff is well worth the journey up. If you suffer from vertigo, know that there is a sheer drop to the sea below. Many people choose to hike up the Bluff (see "Hiking" later in the chapter).

For those who want to meet the Brac version of Mother Nature, there is no better way than to take one of the **guided nature tours** run by T. J. Sevik, the government's tour guide. What he doesn't know about Cayman Brac isn't worth bothering with. He can, for example, name all 50 to 60 species of birds that, at least for part of the year, land on Cayman Brac. Tours, which last from 1 to 2 hours, are free. Mr. Sevik will join you in your car for the tour. Call © 345/948-2651 to establish a meeting time and place.

FISHING   Fishing is another reason that many visitors come to the island. The fishing here rivals that on Little Cayman. Bonefishing inside the reef along the coast to the southwest is especially rewarding. Catches around the island include wahoo, sailfish, marlin, tuna, grouper, and snapper.

Captain Shelby's, Watering Place (© 345/948-0535), offers everything from picnic trips to diving charters. Many visitors, however, book a vessel for a deep-sea fishing trip costing US$350 per half day or US$450 for a full day. Two to four fishermen are taken out at the same time. Bottom or reef fishing can also be arranged for US$300 per half day or US$400 for a full day. Snorkel trips are available for US$50 per person daily from 8:30am to 1pm, and picnic trips to a beach on Little Cayman costs US$70 per person and are offered daily from 8:30am to 4:30pm. Diving charters are only for those who have their own equipment. A one-tank dive costs US$70, a two-tank dive costs US$100, and a three-tank dive costs US$150.

Edmund Bodden, West End (© **345/948-1228**), is known for his bonefishing and bottom-fishing tours. Per person costs for bone-fishing are US$80 for a half day and US$150 for a full day. Per person costs for bottom fishing are US$90 for a half day or US$170 for a full day. Bodden has a small craft that fits three fishermen comfortably, and, of course, he knows all the best places to fish.

Gemini III, West End (© **345/948-2396**), is a 9m (30-ft.) cruiser that fits four to six passengers comfortably in the pursuit of deep-sea fish such as wahoo, marlin, tuna, and mahimahi. The cost of a charter is US$350 per half day or US$500 for a full day.

HIKING Hiking is becoming more and more popular on Cayman Brac, enough so that the **Cayman Brac Tourist Office** (p. 163) now offers free printed guides to the best hikes on the island, and the trails (though they are not always well maintained) are indicated by white "heritage markers." In all, there are some three dozen marked trails, some easy to reach and easy to hike, and others requiring more skills and experience. The hikes recommended below are moderately difficult.

Some of our favorite trails include **West End Point Overlook,** starting on South Side Road, west of the Brac Reef Beach Resort. At the far western point of Brac, this is an idyllic hike for bird-watching. Islanders also claim, and with good reason, that you have the best view of sunsets here. Locals watch for the "green flash" of light as the sun goes down.

Another good trail to follow is **Westerly Ponds,** South Side Road, across from the Brac Reef Beach Resort. The two ponds along this trail are the best spots for observing the life of wetland fowl. Boardwalks cut across the marshes, with small viewing sections.

The Lighthouse Trail ⚔, taking 3 hours, starts at Spot Bay in the far East End of the island. You'll approach the beginning of the trail by walking along Spot Bay Road. You can follow the trail up the northeast face of the Bluff. On your way, you'll pass the entrance to Peter's Cave, used in olden days as a hurricane shelter. As you continue hiking, you will come to a spot dubbed Peter's Outlook by locals, with a panoramic sweep across Spot Bay. There are two lighthouses in this area, one modern and the other from the 1930s.

The best nature trail on Brac is the **Parrot Reserve** ✿✿ in the center of the island, which is perfect for self-guided tours. The trail meanders for 1.6km (1 mile), taking hikers through the heart of the reserve, which is a visitor's best chance to see the endangered Cayman Brac parrot. Trails are always open and there's no fee to enter. You must, of course, bring your own provisions, including plenty of water. This preserve is reached along Major Donald Drive (sometimes called Lighthouse Road), a 9.7km (6-mile) dirt road leading to cliffs. From this vantage point on the Bluff, the best view of North East Point is spread before you. Many hikers come here to take in the most dramatic sunrise in the Cayman Islands.

SPELUNKING   Cayman Brac has a series of caves that are open for exploring. **Peter's Cave,** on the Lighthouse Trail in the East End, is mammoth, with tunnels leading off in several directions. **Rebecca's Cave** lies east of the Divi Tiara and is well marked. It's the best known of Brac's caves, and takes its name from a young child who died here during the disastrous hurricane of 1932 that destroyed the island. Rebecca's tomb can still be seen in the middle of the cave.

Bat Cave takes its name from its inhabitants, several species of which can be seen hanging from above if you shine your flashlight up to the roof of the cave. Most of the bats you'll see here are Jamaican fruit bats. The bats emerge in the evening to fly about, usually after 9pm. Bat Cave is on the south side of the island and is marked by signs.

A final cave, **Great Cave,** stands a mile or so from the lighthouse that designates the easternmost point of the island, at the top of the Bluff. Filled with stalagmites and stalactites, it is one of the most interesting caves to explore, although a bit eerie.

TENNIS   The best tennis court on the island is found at the previously recommended **Brac Reef Beach Resort,** South Side (✆ 345/948-1323). The court is open to nonguests at the cost of CI$4 (US$5) per day. The court is open daily from 7am to 9pm, and is lit for night play.

Another good court is found at the recommended **Divi Tiara Beach Resort,** South Side (✆ 345/948-1553). This court is available daily from 8am to 10pm (it's lit for night play), and is open to nonguests. It's best to call to reserve in advance. Admission to this court is free.

5 Shopping

There isn't much here in the way of shopping. The best shop for souvenirs (T-shirts and the like) is **Treasure Chest,** Tibbetts Square (© 345/948-1333), which is a relatively easy walk from the airport landing strip. Open Monday to Saturday 9am to 5pm.

If you're staying at one of the resorts along the north shore, the **Bayside Grocery,** at La Esperanza, Stake Bay (© 345/948-0531), is sure to come in handy, especially If you're in a self-catering villa. On-site is a grocery store plus a general merchandise mart, an electronics store, and a souvenir section.

Kirk Freeport, Kirk Freeport Plaza, Stake Bay (© 345/948-2612), is a small shop with a surprisingly wide range of merchandise, featuring everything from elegant coral items to china, jewelry, glassware, silver, and gold items, along with T-shirts and casual sports clothing. It's the best place for upmarket gifts on island. Open Monday to Saturday 10am to 6pm.

The best place on the island to purchase liquor is **Brac Freeport,** West End (© 345/948-1332), which is open Monday to Saturday 9am to 7pm.

Sharon's Hair Clinic, Tibbetts Square (© 345/948-1387), is the place to go for hair care. The salon is especially adept at braiding, and is open Monday to Saturday 10am to 7pm.

6 Cayman Brac After Dark

There isn't much nightlife here. Most visitors and islanders view hanging out at a bar and having dinner as an evening unto itself. Most travelers hit the sack early, preparing for their next day's adventure early in the morning.

Except on the slowest of evenings, there's usually one spot that's hotter than any other because it's featuring a DJ or live band that night. The venues vary, but your hotel staff will usually know where to direct you to find the evening's best entertainment.

We've already recommended that you check out **Aunt Sha's Kitchen,** South Side (© 345/948-1581), for its Caymanian and Chinese cuisine. On Friday and Saturday nights, Aunt Sha's becomes an island social center with music (mostly reggae and soca) supplied by a DJ. Islanders flock here to dance on the terrace. Live bands are rare here, mostly brought in on special occasions such as Valentine's Day. Happy hour is Wednesday, Thursday, and Saturday from 7 to 8pm, with reduced drink prices.

Live music is often featured here at the **Bar at Brac Reef Beach Resort,** South Side, (© 345/948-1323), which is one of the island's most popular bars, especially with visitors. Wednesday night is karaoke night, and nonguests are always welcome. Open 11am to 1am daily.

Coral Isle Club, South Side, east of Denis Point (© 345/948-1581), is the leading karaoke bar on the island, with a DJ playing the latest music on Wednesday, Thursday, Friday, and Saturday nights. The bartender's specialty is a Blue Lagoon, costing CI$5 (US$6.25) and made with tequila and vodka. The bar is open daily from 9am to 1am.

On Friday and Saturday nights the previously recommended hotel and restaurant **La Esperanza,** Stake Bay (© 345/948-0531), is the most jumping joint on island. Join the islanders filing into this place for a great time. Dig into mounds of barbecue or mountains of jerk chicken prepared by the owner himself, Bussy, and enjoy the island band that is often brought in on Friday and Saturday nights. On other nights a blaring jukebox is responsible for the music, which can range from top tunes of the 1940s to calypso. There's an inside lounge with a complete bar, TV, pool tables, and a seaside ambience. Open daily from noon to 2pm and 6 to 10pm (perhaps later on Friday and Saturday nights).

The **Tropical Storm Bar at Divi Tiara Beach Resort,** South Side (© 345/948-1553), often features live music at night. The bartender makes a wicked rum punch selling for CI$5 (US$6.25) and snacks are available at the bar. Open daily from 11:30am to 11pm.

10

Little Cayman

The smallest of the Cayman Islands, cigar-shaped Little Cayman has only about 125 permanent inhabitants, so nearly everybody you'll see will be a visitor, most often from the States. Little Cayman is 16km (10 miles) long and about 1.6km (a mile) across at its widest point. It didn't get electricity until 1990, or phones until 1991. It lies about 109km (68 miles) northeast of Grand Cayman and some 8km (5 miles) from Cayman Brac. The entire island is coral and sand. **Blossom Village,** the island's "capital," is on the southwest coast.

The Cayman Islands archipelago is made up of mountaintops of the long-submerged Sierra Maestra Range, which runs north into Cuba. Coral formed in layers over the underwater peaks, eventually creating the islands. Beneath Little Cayman's Bloody Bay is one of the mountain's walls—a stunning sight for snorkelers and scuba divers.

Little Cayman seems to have come into its own now that fishing and diving have taken center stage; the island is a near-perfect place for these pursuits. The late Jacques Cousteau hailed the waters around the little island as one of the three finest diving spots in the world. The flats on Little Cayman are said to offer the best bone-fishing in the world, and a brackish inland pool can be fished for tarpon. Even if you don't dive or fish, you can row 180m (200 yards) off Little Cayman to isolated and uninhabited Owen Island, where you can swim at the sandy beach and picnic by a blue lagoon.

There may still be pirate treasure buried on the island, but it's in the dense interior of what is now the largest bird sanctuary in the Caribbean. Little Cayman also has the largest population of rock iguanas in the entire Caribbean (you will surely spot them), and is home to one of the oldest species of reptiles in the New World—the tree-climbing *Anulis maynardi* (which is not known by any other name). This rare lizard is difficult to spot, because the females are green and the males are brown, and, as such, they blend into local vegetation. Keep your eyes open for them!

1 Essentials

VISITOR INFORMATION

Little Cayman is too small to have a tourist office. Before you go, you can visit the tourist office in George Town and pick up what limited information is available. See p. 14 for the location of the tourist office and other Cayman Islands information.

GETTING THERE

Most visitors fly from Grand Cayman to Little Cayman, arriving at the Edward Bodden Airport (really a grass airstrip). **Island Air** (© 345/949-5252 on Grand Cayman; www.islandaircayman.com) is a charter company that charges CI$77 (US$96) one-way or CI$123 (US$154) round-trip. Flights leave Grand Cayman four times daily at 7:45am, 9:45am, 2:35pm, and 4:35pm (you have to reserve for each flight). The return flights are scheduled daily at 8:55am, 10:30am, 3:20pm, and 5:45pm. Island Air also flies daily between Cayman Brac and Little Cayman, costing CI$28 (US$35) one-way or CI$47 (US$56) round-trip. Flights from Cayman Brac leave at 8:35am and 5:25pm with returns from Little Cayman to Cayman Brac at 10:30am and 3:20pm.

GETTING AROUND

There are four ways to get around this small island—you can use your own trusty feet, rent a Jeep, hire a bike, or go on an organized tour. Your hotel will often send a van to meet your plane if arrangements are made in advance.

JEEP RENTALS

The island's only car-rental outlet is **McLaughlin Enterprises,** Blossom Village (© 345/948-1000), whose office in a small shopping strip is clearly visible from the airstrip and within easy walking distance. You can also call the company through a courtesy phone at the airport and ask them to pick you up at the airport. Rates begin at CI$60 (US$75) per day, with a second driver costing another CI$12 (US$15). The insurance charge is CI$14 (US$18) daily.

Fun Fact   **Road Rules: Iguanas Have Right of Way**

One local rule to remember is that the prehistoric-looking gray iguana is the king of the road and always has the right of way should he want to make a leisurely crossing.

Since the jeeps are not four-wheel drive, you should avoid driving on soft sands. McLaughlin is open Monday to Saturday 8:30am to noon and 2:30 to 6pm, Sunday 8:30 to 10:30am and 4 to 6pm. The speed limit for the whole island is 40kmph (25 mph). The only places to get fuel are near McLaughlin and on the north of the island at Sam McCoy's.

BY BICYCLE

Little Cayman is too small to support a bike rental shop. The good news is that most of the hotels and little guesthouses will either lend you one (most often the case) or rent you one. There's little traffic, the land is flat, and it's relatively easy to cycle along the paved roads. The East End is to be avoided because the roads here aren't paved and it's a very bumpy ride. Drifting sand is also a menace.

 FAST FACTS: Little Cayman
_____

Banks Be warned that there are no ATMs on Little Cayman. The **Cayman National Bank,** Little Cayman Mall ((C) **345/948-1551**), is open Monday and Wednesday only from 9 to 11:30am and noon to 1:30pm.

Currency See "Money" in chapter 2, "Planning Your Trip to the Cayman Islands."

Customs See "Entry Requirements & Customs" in chapter 2, "Planning Your Trip to the Cayman Islands."

Documents See "Entry Requirements & Customs" in chapter 2, "Planning Your Trip to the Cayman Islands."

Emergency Dial **911.** There's only one police officer on island.

Hospitals or Clinics A nurse is based at the **Little Cayman Clinic,** Blossom Avenue on Guy Banks Road, in Blossom Village ((C) **345/948-0072**). Hours are Monday, Wednesday, and Friday 9am to 1pm, Tuesday and Thursday 1 to 5pm. In an emergency, the nurse can be contacted off-hours at (C) **345/948-1073.** The nearest hospital is the **Faith Hospital** on Cayman Brac ((C) **345/948-2225**), to which patients on Little Cayman are airlifted in an emergency. Should there be a scuba-diving accident, with a need for decompression, the patient is airlifted at once to Grand Cayman.

Internet Access Your hotel may have Internet access. If not, there are Internet and fax facilities at **McLaughlin Enterprises,**

Guy Banks Road, Blossom Village (© **345/948-1000**). The cost for using the Internet is CI$7 (US$8.75) for 15 minutes online.

Language English is the official language of the island.

Pharmacies There is a small pharmacy at Little Cayman Clinic (see "Hospital or Clinics" information above).

Post Office **The Little Cayman Post Office** (© **345/948-0016**) is easily spotted near the airfield on the southwest side of Little Cayman. Open Monday to Thursday 9 to 11:30am and 1 to 3pm, Friday 9 to 11:30am and 1 to 3:30pm.

Water If your hotel relies on rainwater collected in cisterns, it's best to drink bottled water. Ask about the water source when you reserve. Also, drink bottled water when dining out at restaurants.

2 Where to Stay

Important: Before you look through this chapter, see our "Tips on Accommodations" in chapter 2 for descriptions of various types of accommodations and tips on getting the very best deals. Also, be aware that all prices in this section are in U.S. dollars.

EXPENSIVE

The Club at Little Cayman 𝒜𝒜 Set on lushly landscaped grounds, this complex offers the most luxurious living on often bare-bones Little Cayman. It's a pocket of posh, boasting elegantly furnished luxury villas that you'd expect to spot along Florida's Gold Coast. The property opens onto one of the most magnificent beaches on the island. Villas, which are located in a setting of coconut trees and flowering plants, boast oversized balconies or porches. The pool is our favorite on island, custom designed with bench seating and waterfalls. The one-, two-, and three-bedroom rentals have glamorous architectural touches, including crown molding trim and elegant ceramic tiles. High-quality furnishings and luxury fabrics add to the allure. Each villa has a luxury bathroom with tub and shower combination. The on-site kitchens are the best on island, with such features as a glass-top range. If you tire of cooking inside, you can take advantage of the barbecue area outside. Guests at the club can use the amenities of the Little Cayman Beach Resort. Maid service is included in the price for all the villas.

Accommodations & Dining on Little Cayman

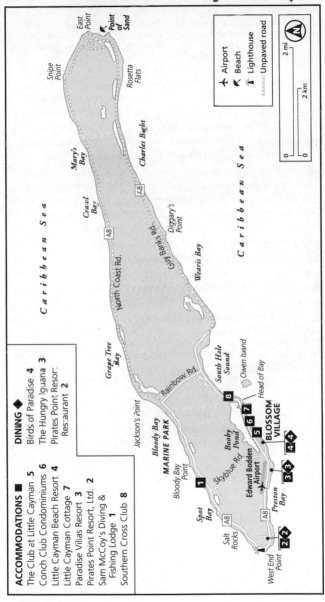

ACCOMMODATIONS ■

The Club at Little Cayman **5**
Conch Club Condominiums **6**
Little Cayman Beach Resort **4**
Little Cayman Cottage **7**
Paradise Villas Resort **3**
Pirates Point Resort, Ltd. **2**
Sam McCoy's Diving & Fishing Lodge **1**
Southern Cross Club **8**

DINING ◆

Birds of Paradise **4**
The Hungry Iguana **3**
Pirates Point Resort Restaurant **2**

Guy Banks Rd., Little Cayman, B.W.I. ℂ 345/948-1033. Fax 345/948-1040. www.
theclubatlittlecayman.com. 40 units. Winter $250 1-bedroom villa, $375 2-bedroom
villa, $500 3-bedroom villa; off-season $210 1-bedroom villa, $325 2-bedroom villa,
$450 3-bedroom villa. AE, MC, V. **Amenities:** Outdoor pool; putting green; sauna;
laundry service. *In room:* A/C, TV, kitchen.

Conch Club Condominiums *(Kids)*

One of the island's latest developments, and a great choice for families or small groups, this complex offers two- and three-bedroom self-catering condos opening onto secluded South Hole Sound, with its sandy white beaches. The condominiums are affiliated with Little Cayman Beach Resort, so guests here have use of all of the resort's facilities and amenities. All the attractively furnished, bright, and airy accommodations boast a patio and a seafront balcony. All rentals come with a fully equipped kitchen. Guests can check into a two-bedroom condo with two-and-a-half bathrooms, or a three-bedroom condo with three bathrooms. All of the bathrooms contain a shower and bathtub. Daily maid service is available for all condos.

Outside, you'll find two private freshwater pools with large outdoor deck areas. Rare for these sibling islands of Grand Cayman, there is a fully equipped fitness center and a health and beauty center on-site. The complex has an on-site dive operation.

Guy Banks Rd., Little Cayman, B.W.I. ℂ 800/327-3835 in the U.S. or 345/948-1026. Fax 345/948-1028. www.conchclub.com. 20 units. Winter $375 for 4 adults in a 2-bedroom unit; off-season $300 for 4 adults in a 2-bedroom unit, winter and off-season $400 for 6 adults in a 3-bedroom unit. Extra person $25. MC, V. **Amenities:** Restaurant; bar; 2 pools; tennis court (lit for night play); fitness center; spa; Jacuzzi; watersports outfitter; free bike loan. *In room:* A/C, TV, coffeemaker, iron, washer/dryer.

Little Cayman Beach Resort *(★★)*

Located on the south coast, this resort is close to many of the island's diving and sporting attractions, including bonefishing in the South Hole Sound Lagoon. It's popular with anglers, divers, bird-watchers, and adventurous types. The hotel, owned by Dan Tibbetts, lies only 1.2km (¾ mile) from the Edward Bodden Airport. The resort fronts a white-sand beach fringing a shallow, reef-protected bay. Rooms are found in two pastel, two-story coral buildings with gingerbread trim. The most desirable units are the four luxurious oceanfront rooms with superior views. Rooms have one king-size or two double beds, plus a combination bathroom (tub and shower). Ceiling fans and tropical colors make for an inviting, airy atmosphere. Nonsmoking rooms are available. Units can only be rented for 3 or more nights.

Guy Banks Rd., Blossom Village, Little Cayman, B.W.I. © 800/327-3835 in the U.S. and Canada, or 345/948-1033. Fax 345/948-1040. www.littlecayman.com. 40 units. Winter $663–$797 per person double (diver), $483–$617 per person double (nondiver); off-season $596–$730 per person double (diver), $416–$550 per person double (nondiver). Rates are for 3 nights and include MAP (breakfast and dinner). Longer-term packages are available. AE, DC, MC, V. **Amenities:** Restaurant; bar; outdoor pool; tennis court (lit for night play); fitness center; Jacuzzi; watersports outfitter; bike rental; game room; babysitting; laundry service; dry cleaning. *In room:* A/C, TV, fridge (in oceanfront rooms), coffeemaker (in oceanfront rooms), hair dryer, no phone.

Little Cayman Cottage 🐠 *(Finds)* This cottage, located about 1.6km (a mile) from the airport, is the type of place where you could hide away and write the great American novel. The cottage is set among sea grape and swaying palm trees, with a view of a white sandy beach—a cliché of Caribbean charm and style. You can spend the entire day lying in the hammock or you can actively pursue various watersports. Six people are accommodated comfortably in the single one-floor villa, which features tiled floors and rattan furnishings. The two midsize bedroom areas are furnished in a light, breezy style. Bedroom areas feature two twin beds, a king-sized bed, and a convertible queen-size couch. There is one bathroom, which has a shower. The cottage also features a living and dining area and a fully equipped kitchen with a screened porch, plus a grill for barbecuing and two bicycles.

117 Airport Rd., Little Cayman, B.W.I. © 345/945-4144. Fax 345/949-7471. www. caymanvillas.com. 1 2-bedroom cottage. Winter $380 for 6 people; off-season $215–$285 for 6. AE, DISC, MC, V. **Amenities:** Babysitting. *In room:* A/C, TV/VCR, kitchen, coffeemaker, washer/dryer, no phone.

Pirates Point Resort, Ltd. 🐠 *(Kids)* Great for watersports or just relaxing, this resort is located near West End Point, just minutes from the airport, and offers a family environment and gourmet cuisine. Although it's a notch down from Little Cayman Beach Resort, the newly remodeled accommodations are attractively and simply furnished, and some of them open onto views of the water. Our favorite is no. 5 because of its great comfort and scenic vistas. In addition to the regular rooms, the resort offers a non-air-conditioned family cottage with two large rooms, each suitable for three or four people. The resort also has four recently built seaside cottages, with balconies overlooking Preston Bay. All cottages are rented by the room. Bathrooms in all accommodations are well maintained, with shower stalls. A family atmosphere prevails, although many rooms are booked by retirees who visit the island annually.

The resort's packages include a room, three excellent meals per day with all alcoholic beverages included, and two-tank boat dives daily, featuring tours of the Bloody Bay Wall, the Cayman Trench, and Jackson Reef. Other activities include snorkeling, bird-watching, bonefishing, tarpon fishing, and exploring.

The resort often has the atmosphere of a house party, especially when guests gather in the wood-paneled bar to discuss the adventures of the day, often relating their recent underwater experiences. The most popular nights here are Thursday and Saturday, when the resort offers a barbecue and a convivial crowd pours into the place.

Guy Banks Rd., Little Cayman, B.W.I. © 345/948-1010. Fax 345/948-1010. www. piratespointresort.com. 11 units. Winter $260 per person double (diver), $205 per person double (nondiver); off-season $240 per person double (diver), $180 per person double (nondiver). Rates are all-inclusive (nondiver rates do not include bar tab); triple rates are slightly lower. MC, V. No children under age 5. **Amenities:** Restaurant; pool; Jacuzzi; watersports outfitter. *In room:* A/C, no phone.

MODERATE

Paradise Villas Resort 🐾 (Kids)   On high-priced Little Cayman, this resort on the beach is the best deal. It's also the best choice if you're traveling with family (babysitting can be arranged). The style is typically Caymanian, with gingerbread decoration, metal roofs, and porches in the front and back. Guests prepare their own meals in a kitchenette. The resort consists of six duplex cottages that border the sea; each cottage is divided into two one-bedroom units. Pullout couches in the living room easily accommodate extra guests. Rooms are small but comfortable. The compact bathrooms contain shower stalls. The resort is on the island's south side, near the little airport, and pickup is provided free. A grocery store, boutique, and a liquor store are all within walking distance, and the resort offers free bikes. The resort also rents cars to guests. On the premises is the best affordable restaurant on the island, The Hungry Iguana (see "Dining," below). Diving is arranged through Paradise Divers.

At Edward Bodden Airport, P.O. Box 48, Little Cayman, B.W.I. © **877-3CAYMAN** or 345/948-0001. Fax 345/948-0002. www.paradisevillas.com. 12 units. Winter $185 double, $207 triple; off-season $168 double, $190 triple. Children 11 and under stay free in parent's room. Dive packages available. AE, MC, V. **Amenities:** Restaurant; bike loan; airport shuttle. *In room:* A/C, TV.

Sam McCoy's Diving & Fishing Lodge 🐾 (Finds)   Set on the island's northwestern shore, this all-inclusive hotel, founded in 1983, reflects the personalities of Sam McCoy and his family, who include their guests in many aspects of their day-to-day lives. There's not really a bar or restaurant in the traditional sense; rather, you'll pour

your own drinks (usually from your own bottle) or drink at a beach bar that rises from the sands of Bloody Bay, a short walk from the hotel. Light snacks and simple platters are offered at outdoor tables near the main lodge with Sam and his gang, many of whom are associated in one way or another with diving operations on the reefs offshore. The bedrooms are ultrasimple, with few adornments other than beds with a firm mattress, a table and a chair, and a ceiling fan. Bathrooms are small with dated plumbing and a shower stall. Maid service is included in the price. There's a pool on the premises, but most visitors opt for dips in the wide blue sea instead, usually taking part in any of the wide choice of scuba explorations offered by Sam and his staff. Picnics can be arranged on the offshore sands of Owens Cay. This is a place built by divers, and intended for divers, even those with children in tow.

643 North Coast Rd., P.O. Box 12, Little Cayman, B.W.I. © 800/626-0496 in the U.S. and Canada, or 345/948-0026. Fax 345/949-0057. www.mccoyslodge.com.ky. 8 units. Winter $180 double; off-season $160 double. 75% discount for children ages 3–12. Rates include all meals and all dives. AE, DISC, MC, V. **Amenities:** Bar; outdoor pool; watersports outfitter; babysitting. *In room:* A/C, coffeemaker.

Southern Cross Club 🦀 Opened in 1959, this was the first resort ever on Little Cayman. The inn, which attracts many divers and fishermen, must be doing something right, as two-thirds of its patrons are repeat business—this is the highest such rate anywhere in the Cayman Islands. The rooms open onto 240m (800 ft.) of golden sands. The Southern Cross is named after the constellation, which can be seen here on a clear winter's night. On the southern side of Little Cayman, the resort lies to the southeast of Booby Pond, opening onto Head O' Bay, with the offshore Owen Island clearly visible.

Accommodations are in comfortably furnished one-bedroom cottages, with one unit containing two bedrooms. Bedrooms are decorated in a simple Caribbean style, and each has a sitting room and a small bathroom with shower. Hotel guests, islanders, and nonguest visitors heavily patronize the restaurant and bar. This resort is among the very best for fishing, offering two boats—one deep sea, one flat. No more than 12 divers go out at one time in the resort's dive boat. Bikes and kayaks are provided free.

South Hole Sound, P.O. Box 44, Little Cayman, B.W.I. © 800/899-2582 in the U.S., or 345/948-1099. Fax 345/948-1098. www.southerncrossclub.com. 10 units. Winter $180 1-bedroom cottage for 2, $185 2-bedroom cottage for 4; off-season $154 1-bedroom cottage for 2; $160 2-bedroom cottage for 4. Extra person $80–$100. AE, DISC, MC, V. No children under 5 allowed. Rates include all meals. **Amenities:** Restaurant; bar; outdoor pool; watersports outfitter; bike rental. *In room:* A/C, coffeemaker, no phone.

3 Where to Dine

Birds of Paradise AMERICAN/CONTINENTAL This spot ends up catering primarily to Little Cayman Beach Resort guests, though it welcomes anyone. The specialty is buffet-style dinners— the kind that people enjoyed back in the 1950s or 1960s. Saturday night features the island's most generous barbecue spread—all the ribs, fish, and Jamaican-style jerk chicken you'd want. On other nights, try the prime rib, fresh fish Caribbean style (your best bet), or chicken either Russian style (Kiev) or French style (cordon bleu). There's a salad bar with fresh fixings, and homemade desserts are yummy, especially the Key lime pie. At night, opt for an outdoor table under the stars.

Breakfast here is of the American ilk, with egg omelets, bacon, hash browns, sausages, and other simple classics on the menu.

At Little Cayman Beach Resort, Guy Banks Rd., Blossom Village. ℂ 345/948-1033. Reservations recommended for dinner. Dinner US$32, lunch US$19, breakfast US$19. AE, MC, V. Daily 7–8:30am, 12:30–1:30pm, and 6:30–8pm.

The Hungry Iguana AMERICAN/CARIBBEAN You'll spot this place immediately with its mammoth iguana mural. Some of the island's tastiest dishes are served here, a winning combination of standard American fare spiced up with zesty flavors from the islands south of the Caymans. It's the rowdiest place on the island, especially in the sports bar with its satellite TV in the corner, where a sort of T.G.I. Friday's atmosphere pervades. Lunch is the usual burgers and fries, along with some well-stuffed sandwiches. We are always pleased with the grilled chicken salad. Dinner gets a little more elaborate—there's usually a special meat dish of the day, depending on the market (supplies are shipped in once a week by barge). The chef is always willing to prepare a steak as you like it. Marinated shrimp with rémoulade is a tasty choice, or try one of the seafood platters.

Paradise Villas Resort, Edward Bodden Airport. ℂ 345/948-0007. Reservations recommended. Dinner CI$14–CI$38 (US$18–US$48); lunch CI$5–CI$13 (US$6.25–US$16). AE, MC, V. Daily noon–2:30pm and 5:30–9pm. Bar open Mon–Fri noon–1am, Sat–Sun noon–midnight. Closed Sept 15–Oct 20.

Pirates Point Resort Restaurant ⍟ INTERNATIONAL The cuisine here is the island's best, as the owner and manager, Gladys Howard, is a graduate of Cordon Bleu in Paris and has studied with such culinary stars as Julia Child and the late James Beard. Howard has written several cookbooks of her own. She uses fresh fruits and locally grown vegetables, as well as seafood caught in local waters, and she imports as little as she has to. The menu changes, but some of its most memorable dishes include a zesty conch ceviche and a saffron scallop couscous. Ever had a smoked salmon cheesecake with a green-onion coulis? Try it. We think you'll like it. Two of the best dishes we've sampled here are the macadamia-crusted mahimahi in a lemon dill sauce, and the herb-roasted leg of lamb with a Burgundy demi-glace. Desserts are luscious, including a four-layer chocolate cake and a white-chocolate tropical torte.

Pirates Point Resort, Guy Banks Rd. (**©** 345/948-1010. Reservations needed 24 hours in advance for nonguests of hotel. 2-course fixed price lunch menu US$20/dinner menu US$40, including wine and pickup and return from your hotel. MC, V. Daily 1:45–2:30pm and 7:30pm (1 seating).

4 Diving & Other Outdoor Pursuits

Visit Little Cayman for the diving, the fishing, and the beaches, not for the sightseeing attractions, although there are some (see the following section for recommendations).

The island has long been popular with birders and anglers, but it is scuba diving that is its main allure. Some 57 dive sites—marked with moorings—are found along the island's 16km (10-mile) length. The most celebrated site is Bloody Bay Wall on the northern tier of the island.

SCUBA DIVING & SNORKELING

One of the most spectacular and most varied dive locations in the world is **Bloody Bay Marine Park** 𝕽𝕽𝕽, reached along the North Coast Road and lying between Sam McCoy's Diving & Fishing Lodge in the west and Jackson Point to the northeast. To the east is Jackson Wall, with the Bloody Bay Wall lying to the west. A total of 22 listed dive sites are found in this park alone.

The drop at Bloody Bay begins at only 6m (20 ft.), but soon plunges to more than 360m (1,200 ft.). At one point, the reefs plummet to 1,800m (6,000 ft.).

Of course, it's best to explore the dive sights with one of the experienced dive operators recommended below.

Conch Club Divers is based at the previously recommended Conch Club Condominiums, Guy Banks Road (**©** 800/327-3835 or 345/948-1026; www.conchclub.com). These experts offer everything from relaxing snorkel tours to advance diving courses. The outfitter's 42-foot boat, *Sea-esta,* features customized dive excursions to the area's major dive sites, including Bloody Bay Wall. A one-tank dive costs US$45, a two-tank dive is US$88, and a three-tank dive goes for US$95. Snorkeling gear costs US$10 for a day's rental.

Paradise Divers is installed at another previously recommended resort, Paradise Villas Resort, at Edward Bodden Airport (© 345/948-0001). Like all the other dive outfitters, it offers PADI and NAUI certification courses, plus advanced courses for US$350 (which is more or less the standard price islandwide). A single dive costs US$45, a two-tank dive costs US$80, and a three-tank dive is $110, with night dives costing US$55 and snorkeling trips going for $25.

Reef Divers at Little Cayman Beach Resort (also previously recommended as lodging) on Guy Banks Road in Blossom Village (© 800/327-3835, or 345/948-0133; www.littlecayman.com), was established in 1993. It offers a trio of 13m (42-ft.) boats and all the latest equipment. On-site is a dive shop, and the staff here offers PADI courses. Certified divers are charged US$90 per tank dive. Kayak rentals are also available here.

Southern Cross Club, South Hole Sound (© 345/948-1099), is another one of the island's leading dive outfitters, offering an intimate dive with no more than a dozen divers per boat at one time. This outfitter has all the latest equipment and is very experienced at directing divers to some of the most dramatic offshore dive sites. A one-tank dive goes for US$50, with a two-tank dive costing US$80, a three-tank dive US$130, and night dives US$60. Snorkeling trips cost US$10.

FISHING

Little Cayman is recognized as the best island to fish year-round for tarpon, bonefish, and permit (a type of pompano fish).

Anglers can catch bonefish averaging 3 to 6 pounds in the shallow areas of South Hole Sound near Owen Island. Bonefish can be spotted in areas known as "muds," or patches of water where the sea looks milky because of fish churning up the bottom while feeding. Muds are especially visible from the air on approach to the island.

Many guides use fry (young fish) rather than flies for bonefish. Anglers who want to try fly-fishing should bring their own tackle (although Sam McCoy's Diving & Fishing Lodge may be able to set you up with fly-fishing gear). South Hole Sound provides the best action. Although these fish bite all day, local guides agree that finding bonefish depends on tides and weather conditions. They often prefer to fish from the beach rather than stalk fish in the mud of the lagoon.

Tarpon are plentiful in Tarpon Lake, the landlocked, brackish natural pond that offers excellent action for fly fishermen. These fish once grew no larger than 4 to 8 pounds, but larger specimens (up to 20 lb.) are now caught frequently, especially in the early morning and late afternoon.

Permit of 15 to 35 pounds frequent Little Cayman waters—maybe the Cayman Islands' best-kept secret. Schools are especially abundant on the Cayman Islands' southeast end and in the flats of the northwest coast.

Although Little Cayman offers good deep-sea fishing, its main attraction is light tackle and fly-fishing, and the island is best prepared to accommodate anglers. McCoy's Lodge and the Southern Cross Club cater to both divers and light-tackle fishing enthusiasts. Anglers can also be accommodated on day trips with advance reservations. Light tackle gear is available, but anglers must bring their own fly-fishing equipment. Visitors should contact **Sam McCoy's Diving & Fishing Lodge** (📞 **800/626-0496,** or in the Cayman Islands 📞 345/948-0026), or **Southern Cross Club** (📞 **800/899-2582,** or in the Cayman Islands 📞 345/948-1099), to arrange fishing excursions and to confirm the availability of experienced local guides for the duration of the visit.

In addition to these previously recommended outfitters, we also recommend **Captain Castro's Fishing Excursions,** Village Square (📞 **345/917-1434**). Fidel Castro Christian was born on Cayman Brac, but moved long ago to Little Cayman, where he is known for running some of the island's best fishing charters. He takes fishermen out in his 5m (17-ft.) boat for bonefishing, deep-sea fishing, and night-fishing jaunts. Shark and grouper are the main catches. The cost for up to two people is US$200 total for a half day of bonefishing or US$400 total for a half day of deep-sea fishing. Night fishing is US$150 total for up to two people. Christian will also take you on snorkeling trips for US$50 total per hour, for up to three passengers.

BEACHES

Point of Sand 🏖 is our favorite beach on the island, lying at the very southeastern tip of Little Cayman and accessible from Blossom Village by heading east along Guy Banks Road. Point of Sand is not only one of the island's finest beaches, it's also great for snorkeling. The sand here is luminescent pink. On most weekdays you'll have the beach to yourself, although many visitors come over on Saturday and Sunday from Cayman Brac. Plan to take a picnic lunch with you and enjoy it at a covered picnic table. There are bathrooms and changing facilities here. It's dangerous to attempt to take a Jeep down to the beach because you might get stuck in the deep sands.

Owen Island ✍ lies off the southwestern coast, east of Blossom Village and South Town, in South Hole Sound, which is between Booby Pond and Tarpon Lake. The island is an easy 180m (200-yard) rowboat ride off the coast. Once on the island, you can enjoy a beautiful sandy beach. Plan to pack a picnic lunch and make a day of it. Owen Island—locals call it "the Cay"—is the fourth largest island in the Cayman archipelago, yet it consists of only 4.4 hectares (11 acres). It's an idyllic spot with trees and plenty of sands, plus gulls and migrant waders in its shallow waters and flats. Many resorts on Little Cayman schedule picnic trips to this secluded island, and perhaps will do so at the time of your visit. The snorkeling is especially good on the south side. Many visitors rent a kayak at Little Cayman Beach Resort (see below) and spend a day here, which could be as close as you'll get to living a Robinson Crusoe existence.

KAYAKS

Several resorts rent kayaks, which are especially useful in getting to Owen Island (see above), notably **Little Cayman Beach Resort,** Blossom Village, Guy Banks Road. (② **345/948-0133**). Nonguests can hire kayaks here at a cost of US$20 per half day for a single or US$30 per half day for a two-person kayak.

TENNIS

The best court, at **Little Cayman Beach Resort,** Blossom Village, Guy Banks Road (② **345/948-0133**), is open to nonguests. The charge is US$5 per game. The sun is often fierce for most of the year, so the best times for games are in the early morning or after 4pm. The court is lit so that you can play after dark.

5 Exploring the Island

Birders flock to the **Booby Pond Visitors Centre** (② **345/948-1010**), which is operated by the National Trust. The Visitors Centre is located in an 83-hectare (206-acre) nature reserve, and features exhibits on Little Cayman's indigenous species, including the common crab and the seed shrimp. There are two telescopes on the Visitors Centre porch, which you can look through for a closer view of the bird life. A gift shop sells locally made crafts and island art.

Admission is free and the center is open Monday to Friday from 3 to 5pm.

Booby Pond ✸✸ itself is a 1.9km-long (1.2-miles) brackish mangrove pond, home to a breeding colony of splendid frigate birds. The red-footed boobies who live at this pond are the Caribbean's largest booby breeding colony. It's estimated that some 7,000 feathered creatures of different types call this pond home, including the black-necked stilt, the West Indian whistling duck, the graceful egret, the heron, and, of course, the booby.

Of minor interest is **Little Cayman Museum,** Guy Banks Road (© **345/948-1033**), open Monday to Friday 3 to 5pm. It's free, although the staff will request a donation. In a green-and-white building with a wood veranda, the museum contains relics from Little Cayman's past. Some of the memorabilia dates back a century and a half. The collection stemmed from the private treasures of Linton Tibbetts, an islander who sailed to the United States with $50 in his pocket and returned to Little Cayman a multimillionaire. Everything from the attics of Little Cayman is here, including Grandmother's old sewing machine.

Since getting around Little Cayman might be difficult, you may want to take an organized tour. **LCB Tours,** Blossom Village (© **800/327-3835** in the U.S., or 345/948-1033), offers a guided tour that visits all of the island highlights for US$25 per person, with lunch costing an extra US$20 if you want it. Snorkeling gear can be rented from the company, as can kayaks, sailboats, pedal boats, and surf bikes (which are basically floating bicycles).

The previously recommended **Little Cayman Beach Resort** (© **345/948-0133**) offers snorkeling and bus tours of the island for US$25 per person. The best tours, however, are the guided nature hikes conducted by Gladys Howard, owner of **Pirates Point Resort** (© **345/948-1010**). These tours are sponsored by the National Trust, and only a CI$1 (US$1.25) donation is asked. These tours can only be arranged by appointment.

6 Shopping

There isn't much here for shopaholics. At some point, all visitors seem to stop in at **Village Square** (© **345/948-1069**), which sells a little bit of everything. Villa owners come here for supplies, groceries, and hardware. You can purchase fishing gear, household goods, film, newspapers, and magazines. You can even rent a video.

Prices are high because everything has to be shipped in by boat. Open Monday to Saturday 8:30am to 6pm.

Nature Spa Health & Beauty, at the Little Cayman Beach Resort, Blossom Village, Guy Banks Road (© **345/948-0058**), offers a full range of services, including massage, pedicure, facials, manicure, and hairdressing, plus beauty supplies. The spa is open daily 11am to 6pm, and requires an appointment.

Reef Photo & Video Centre, at the Little Cayman Beach Resort, Blossom Village, Guy Banks Road (© **345/948-1063**), offers daily film processing, and underwater video and camera rentals for US$12 per half day. Open daily 7:30am to 5pm.

7 Little Cayman After Dark

Nightlife in Little Cayman usually means hanging out in a bar and ordering dinner. We like to go to **Sam McCoy's Diving & Fishing Lodge,** 643 North Coast Rd. (© **345/948-0026**), which is discussed in detail on p. 190. The most popular time to go is Saturday night at 7pm for the barbecue, which costs US$15 per person.

Friday night at 7pm is the best time to hit the **Southern Cross Club,** South Hole Sound (© **345/948-1099;** see p. 191), as it too stages barbecues, held at the poolside deck near the beach and costing US$15 per person. There's no live entertainment, but locals, expats, and visitors gather at the bar here daily from 11am to midnight.

Index

FROMMER'S® COMPLETE TRAVEL GUIDES

Alaska
Alaska Cruises & Ports of Call
Amsterdam
Argentina & Chile
Arizona
Atlanta
Australia
Austria
Bahamas
Barcelona, Madrid & Seville
Beijing
Belgium, Holland & Luxembourg
Bermuda
Boston
Brazil
British Columbia & the Canadian Rockies
Brussels & Bruges
Budapest & the Best of Hungary
California
Canada
Cancún, Cozumel & the Yucatán
Cape Cod, Nantucket & Martha's Vineyard
Caribbean
Caribbean Cruises & Ports of Call
Caribbean Ports of Call
Carolinas & Georgia
Chicago
China
Colorado
Costa Rica
Cuba
Denmark
Denver, Boulder & Colorado Springs
England
Europe
European Cruises & Ports of Call

Florida
France
Germany
Great Britain
Greece
Greek Islands
Hawaii
Hong Kong
Honolulu, Waikiki & Oahu
Ireland
Israel
Italy
Jamaica
Japan
Las Vegas
London
Los Angeles
Maryland & Delaware
Maui
Mexico
Montana & Wyoming
Montréal & Québec City
Munich & the Bavarian Alps
Nashville & Memphis
New England
New Mexico
New Orleans
New York City
New Zealand
Northern Italy
Norway
Nova Scotia, New Brunswick & Prince Edward Island
Oregon
Paris
Peru
Philadelphia & the Amish Country
Portugal

Prague & the Best of the Czech Republic
Provence & the Riviera
Puerto Rico
Rome
San Antonio & Austin
San Diego
San Francisco
Santa Fe, Taos & Albuquerque
Scandinavia
Scotland
Seattle & Portland
Shanghai
Sicily
Singapore & Malaysia
South Africa
South America
South Florida
South Pacific
Southeast Asia
Spain
Sweden
Switzerland
Texas
Thailand
Tokyo
Toronto
Tuscany & Umbria
USA
Utah
Vancouver & Victoria
Vermont, New Hampshire & Maine
Vienna & the Danube Valley
Virgin Islands
Virginia
Walt Disney World® & Orlando
Washington, D.C.
Washington State

FROMMER'S® DOLLAR-A-DAY GUIDES

Australia from $50 a Day
California from $70 a Day
England from $75 a Day
Europe from $70 a Day
Florida from $70 a Day
Hawaii from $80 a Day

Ireland from $60 a Day
Italy from $70 a Day
London from $85 a Day
New York from $90 a Day
Paris from $80 a Day

San Francisco from $70 a Day
Washington, D.C. from $80 a Day
Portable London from $85 a Day
Portable New York City from $90 a Day

FROMMER'S® PORTABLE GUIDES

Acapulco, Ixtapa & Zihuatanejo
Amsterdam
Aruba
Australia's Great Barrier Reef
Bahamas
Berlin
Big Island of Hawaii
Boston
California Wine Country
Cancún
Cayman Islands
Charleston
Chicago
Disneyland®
Dublin
Florence

Frankfurt
Hong Kong
Houston
Las Vegas
Las Vegas for Non-Gamblers
London
Los Angeles
Los Cabos & Baja
Maine Coast
Maui
Miami
Nantucket & Martha's Vineyard
New Orleans
New York City
Paris
Phoenix & Scottsdale

Portland
Puerto Rico
Puerto Vallarta, Manzanillo & Guadalajara
Rio de Janeiro
San Diego
San Francisco
Savannah
Seattle
Sydney
Tampa & St. Petersburg
Vancouver
Venice
Virgin Islands
Washington, D.C.

FROMMER'S® NATIONAL PARK GUIDES

Banff & Jasper
Family Vacations in the National Parks

Grand Canyon
National Parks of the American West
Rocky Mountain

Yellowstone & Grand Teton
Yosemite & Sequoia/Kings Canyon
Zion & Bryce Canyon

Frommer's® Memorable Walks

Chicago
London
New York
Paris
San Francisco

Frommer's® With Kids Guides

Chicago
Las Vegas
New York City
Ottawa
San Francisco
Toronto
Vancouver
Washington, D.C.

Suzy Gershman's Born to Shop Guides

Born to Shop: France
Born to Shop: Hong Kong,
  Shanghai & Beijing
Born to Shop: Italy
Born to Shop: London
Born to Shop: New York
Born to Shop: Paris

Frommer's® Irreverent Guides

Amsterdam
Boston
Chicago
Las Vegas
London
Los Angeles
Manhattan
New Orleans
Paris
Rome
San Francisco
Seattle & Portland
Vancouver
Walt Disney World®
Washington, D.C.

Frommer's® Best-Loved Driving Tours

Britain
California
Florida
France
Germany
Ireland
Italy
New England
Northern Italy
Scotland
Spain
Tuscany & Umbria

Hanging Out™ Guides

Hanging Out in England
Hanging Out in Europe
Hanging Out in France
Hanging Out in Ireland
Hanging Out in Italy
Hanging Out in Spain

The Unofficial Guides®

Bed & Breakfasts and Country
  Inns in:
  California
  Great Lakes States
  Mid-Atlantic
  New England
  Northwest
  Rockies
  Southeast
  Southwest
Best RV & Tent Campgrounds in:
  California & the West
  Florida & the Southeast
  Great Lakes States
  Mid-Atlantic
  Northeast
  Northwest & Central Plains
Southwest & South Central
  Plains
  U.S.A.
Beyond Disney
Branson, Missouri
California with Kids
Central Italy
Chicago
Cruises
Disneyland®
Florida with Kids
Golf Vacations in the Eastern U.S.
Great Smoky & Blue Ridge Region
Inside Disney
Hawaii
Las Vegas
London
Maui
Mexio's Best Beach Resorts
Mid-Atlantic with Kids
Mini Las Vegas
Mini-Mickey
New England & New York with
  Kids
New Orleans
New York City
Paris
San Francisco
Skiing & Snowboarding in the West
Southeast with Kids
Walt Disney World®
Walt Disney World® for
  Grown-ups
Walt Disney World® with Kids
Washington, D.C.
World's Best Diving Vacations

Special-Interest Titles

Frommer's Adventure Guide to Australia &
  New Zealand
Frommer's Adventure Guide to Central America
Frommer's Adventure Guide to India & Pakistan
Frommer's Adventure Guide to South America
Frommer's Adventure Guide to Southeast Asia
Frommer's Adventure Guide to Southern Africa
Frommer's Britain's Best Bed & Breakfasts and
  Country Inns
Frommer's Caribbean Hideaways
Frommer's Exploring America by RV
Frommer's Fly Safe, Fly Smart
Frommer's France's Best Bed & Breakfasts and
  Country Inns
Frommer's Gay & Lesbian Europe
Frommer's Italy's Best Bed & Breakfasts and
  Country Inns
Frommer's Road Atlas Britain
Frommer's Road Atlas Europe
Frommer's Road Atlas France
The New York Times' Guide to Unforgettable
  Weekends
Places Rated Almanac
Retirement Places Rated
Rome Past & Present

AOL Keyword: Travel

Booked aisle seat.

Reserved room with a view.

With a queen - no, make that a king-size bed.

With Travelocity, you can book your flights and hotels together, so you can get even better deals than if you booked them separately. You'll save time and money without compromising the quality of your trip. Choose your airline seat, search for alternate airports, pick your hotel room type, even choose the neighborhood you'd like to stay in

Travelocity
Visit www.travelocity.com
or call 1-888-TRAVELOCITY

Fly.
Sleep.
Save.

Now you can book your flights and
hotels together, so you can get even better deals
than if you booked them separately.

Travelocity
Visit www.travelocity.com
or call 1-888-TRAVELOCITY